Exam Practice Workbook Contents

Understanding and producing non-fiction texts

References

For more details on Section A and Section B of the exam, see:

pages 6–7
for Section A

pages 54–55
for Section B

Exam paper

- Your examination is worth 40% of your overall GCSE grade.

- The exam is two hours long and has two sections: **Section A: Understanding non-fiction texts** and **Section B: Producing non-fiction texts**. Each of these sections is worth an equal 20% of your overall GCSE grade.

- Section A tests your **Reading** skills

- Section B tests your **Writing** skills

- You have to answer **all the questions** on the exam paper.

The remaining 60% of the GCSE is split between Controlled Assessment tasks in Speaking and Listening, Reading and Writing.

The skills you are assessed on

When the examiners mark your answers, they are looking for certain skills. These are summarised in the four **Assessment Objectives**. This book supports all the assessment objectives for Reading and Writing.

The reading skills you are assessed on

In **Section A** of the exam, you need to show that you can:

- **demonstrate an understanding of the texts' purpose and audience.**

  This means explaining the content, audience and the purpose of the text: what a writer says and is suggesting.

- **select evidence from the texts to use in your answers.**

  This means picking appropriate quotations to use to support the points you make.

- **make comparisons between the texts.**

  This means explaining the ways in which a text is similar to, or different from, another text. You need to refer to examples when you compare.

- **evaluate how effective the text is.**

  This means explaining how well you think the text does its job – how well it appeals to the audience it is intended for, and the purpose it is intended for.

- **understand the techniques that writers use.**

  This means writing about the language and the ways the words and presentational features have been used.

- **understand the ways in which the texts are organised and presented on the page.**

  This means writing about the position and appearance of pictures and text elements on the page and how they relate.

The writing skills you are assessed on

In **Section B** of the exam, you need to show that you can:

- **communicate clearly, effectively and imaginatively.**

  This means writing so that the reader understands what you are saying and is interested in it.

Collins **Revision**

GCSE

English

✔ For GCSE English from 2010

Higher

Written by Sarah Darragh

Series Edited by Keith Brindle

Revision Guide Contents

- **demonstrate a clear idea of the purpose and audience.**

  This means being able to write in a particular form (e.g. a letter or a newspaper article) and for a particular audience (e.g. for older people).

- **organise your writing.**

  This means using sentences and paragraphs, and giving your writing structure.

- **use a range of interesting words and sentence structures.**

  This means using varied vocabulary, techniques such as repetition and contrast, and different types of sentence for different effects.

- **punctuate and spell accurately.**

  This means using a range of punctuation, such as question marks and semi-colons as well as full stops and commas, and showing that you can spell accurately.

GCSE English and English Language at a glance

GCSE English/English Language

Examination paper		40% of total marks
2 hours		
• Section A: Understanding non-fiction texts	20%	
• Section B: Producing non-fiction texts	20%	

Speaking and Listening	20% of total marks
3 assessments	
Presentation	
Discussing and listening	
Adopting a role	

English Controlled Assessments	English Language Controlled Assessments
2 assessments	3 assessments
Literary Reading	Extended Reading
20% of final marks	15% of final marks
Producing Creative Texts	Creative Writing
20% of final marks	15% of final marks
	Spoken Language Study
	10% of final marks

Understanding non-fiction texts

Section A: Understanding non-fiction texts

Examiner's tip

In Section A, you are being assessed on your Reading skills, so no marks are awarded for spelling, punctuation or grammar. The examiners are looking for how well you **understand** the texts. Focus on your Reading skills, not your Writing skills, in this section.

- **Section A** of your English exam will assess your **Reading skills**.

- You will be given **three media/non-fiction texts** to read. You will be asked **four** questions. There will be *one* question on *each* of the three texts, and the fourth question will ask you to **compare** language in two of the texts.

- You will have an hour to complete this section, and must answer **all** the questions.

The texts

- The texts you will be given will be media and non-fiction texts. This means any type of text which has been written for a **non-literary purpose**: leaflets, articles, reports, biography and travel writing are all examples of this type of text.

- Each text will have a clear **form**, **purpose** and **audience**.

- There might also be a connection between the texts: possibly a thematic similarity such as 'healthy eating' or 'transport'.

- However, there will be clear differences between the texts in terms of the form, audience and purpose, allowing you to make comparisons between them.

The exam paper – Section A

Higher Tier

Section A: Reading

Answer all questions in this section.

You are advised to spend about one hour on this section.

Read **Source 1**, the newspaper article headed *Can this be true?* by Steven Gale.

1 What do you learn from Steven Gale's newspaper article about the strange sightings over Kennilworth?

(8 marks)

Now read **Source 2**, the letter and picture that goes with it called *What I saw – and it's not fiction!* by Ailsa McMurray.

2 How do the headline and picture add to the effectiveness of the text?

(8 marks)

Now read **Source 3**, *My other life*, which is an extract from an autobiography.

3 What thoughts and feelings does Zac have during his adventure?

(8 marks)

Now you need to refer to **Source 3**, *My other life* and either **Source 1** or **Source 2**. You are going to compare two texts, one of which you have chosen.

4 Compare the ways in which language is used for effect in the two texts. Give examples and explain what effects they have.

(16 marks)

The skills you will be assessed on in Section A

The questions that you will be asked in Section A are based on Assessment Objectives. Some questions will test more than one objective, but within the Section as a whole you will be assessed on your ability to achieve the following:

Assessment Objective	What this means in detail
Read and understand texts	You will be expected to understand the **literal meaning** of the texts, so that you can explain the content and recognise the **form**. However, you will also be expected to understand the **purpose** of the text and recognise the **target audience**. You will also be assessed on how well you can write about whether the **aims** of the text are achieved.
pages 10–37	
Select material appropriate to purpose	You will be expected to provide supporting **textual references** in the form of **quotations**, using these as a basis for your comments.
pages 12–13	
Collate material from different sources, making comparisons and cross-references as appropriate	You will have to refer appropriately to the texts, gathering evidence to provide to support your points. One of the questions will ask you to **compare** elements of two of the texts. This will mean identifying and clearly comparing how writers use language to achieve their effects.
pages 46–49	
Explain and evaluate how writers use linguistic, grammatical, structural and presentational features to achieve effects and engage and influence the reader, supporting comments with detailed textual references	You will be asked about **language**, and how it is used to create effects and help the writer to achieve their **purpose**. You will be writing about the ways in which the language has been deliberately used for a particular **audience** and **purpose**. You will also be asked to write about the use of **presentational features**, **structure** and **layout** of a text. Again, you will be expected to use **evidence** from the texts you are writing about to support your ideas.
pages 38–53	

Kinds of non-fiction texts

Key points

- Section A of your examination will ask you to read **three non-fiction texts** that you will not have seen before.

- You will complete **four questions** on these three texts.

The skills tested

- There will be one question based on each text and then the fourth question will ask you to compare two of the texts. This fourth question is worth more marks.

- The four questions you will be asked will test your ability to:
  - find information (this is **information retrieval**) (8 marks)
  - write about **presentational features** (8 marks)
  - analyse what is being **suggested** or **inferred** (8 marks)
  - **compare** how **language** is used in two texts (16 marks)

- All four of the Assessment Objectives are tested through this part of the exam.

What to expect from the texts

- This exam is assessing your ability to read and understand non-fiction. In its broadest sense, a non-fiction text is anything that has **not** been 'made up' for the purpose of entertaining or describing.

- So, for example, an extract from a novel, a short story or a poem would **not** come up on this examination paper. A **non-fiction text** is based on **facts, events, reality** and **point of view**.

What is a non-fiction text?

- Non-fiction falls into two broad areas: media texts and general non-fiction.

- Types of **media text** include: newspaper and magazine articles, advertisements, reviews, editorials, web pages, obituaries, advice sheets or leaflets. A media text will come from a **media source** – for example, a newspaper, a magazine or a web page.

- A **general non-fiction text** might not be from a media source but will still be based **on fact rather than fiction** – for example, extracts from biographies or autobiographies, letters, sections from an instructional book, or report writing.

REMEMBER

The word **media** means 'means of communication'. If you think about the purpose of newspapers, web pages, leaflets, magazines, their primary purpose is to **communicate with an audience**.

Analysing text types

- There are a number of different text types within media and non-fiction. Each is targeted at a particular audience and is written for a particular purpose.

- Each text type uses particular devices – language, layout and presentational features – to achieve its purpose and to reach its target audience effectively.

Examiner's tip

The key thing to focus on when answering questions is **how** the writer has used language or layout and/or presentational features to achieve their purpose. It is never enough to just identify the features themselves.

The 'what', 'why' and 'how' of the text

- To be successful in your exam, you need to focus clearly on what the writer wants to achieve and the methods used. In other words, the What, Why and How of the text.
  - **What** is the text saying?
  - **Why** has it been written? What is its purpose?
  - **How** has the writer used language and presentation to achieve their purpose?

- Each examination question will tell you the **form** of each non-fiction text. A typical instruction might look like this:

'Read **Source 1**, *Meeting the Locals*, which is an extract from a travel book.'

Read texts efficiently

- The first time you read the exam texts, you will probably be 'skimming and scanning' – in other words, getting a general sense of what the text is about.

- When you are preparing to answer the question, however, you need to read in a more careful, efficient way. You will achieve better marks if you comment on/analyse the use of precise parts of the text – words and phrases – with clear supporting evidence. It is really important to *be specific* rather than make generalised statements.

- One of the four exam questions will ask you to find particular pieces of information (**information retrieval**). This is designed specifically to assess your ability to *read and understand the text and select appropriate evidence*. This type of question might ask you to 'find 3 examples' or 'say what you learn/discover about' a particular subject from the text. However, don't forget, **all** of the exam questions require you to show your ability to select relevant information and to support your comments with close reference to the text.

Allocating the exam time

- Questions 1, 2 and 3 are all worth an equal number of marks. However, Question 4, which asks you to compare two texts, is worth twice the marks.

- If you spend the first 5–10 minutes reading through the questions and the three texts, you can then divide up the rest of the time according to how many marks each question is worth. It works out at 10 minutes each for Questions 1–3 and 20 minutes for Question 4. Those first ten minutes will be invaluable preparation time. Remember, this exam is testing your **reading ability** so devoting some time to reading the texts is extremely important.

- It is also a good idea to leave **five** minutes at the end of your hour to check through your work.

REMEMBER

Allow yourself more time to answer Question 4 which asks you to compare two texts. It is worth double the marks of each of the other questions. So spend around 20 minutes on it.

Purpose and audience

- Every single text you read has a **purpose** and an **audience**. It is difficult to write an effective text without an audience and purpose in mind.

- In the exam you will be provided with a range of different text types or forms. The purpose and audience are key considerations for your understanding of these texts.

Examiner's tip

As you first read a text, explore whether it might have more than one purpose. For example, the purpose of a leaflet for a local attraction is to persuade visitors to visit but it will also offer lots of information.

REMEMBER

Form is often linked to **purpose**: for example, a newspaper report is more likely to be informative and explanatory.

Purpose

Here are some general, common purposes for writing, with which you are probably familiar:

Inform	Explain	Entertain	Advise
Describe	Argue	Persuade	Review

When you first read the text, try to identify the purpose and the audience. Bearing these in mind as you respond will help you understand why certain language or presentational features have been used. This following response to a preview of a talent contest from a TV listings magazine demonstrates this:

> The writer's purpose is mainly to persuade viewers to watch the programme. The facts about the appearance of the, 'long-awaited return to our screens of Robbie Williams', are surrounded by language designed to attract a large audience, for example 'eagerly-anticipated final', 'the nation on the edge of its seat'.

> Makes early reference to the purpose and audience of the text

> Understanding the purpose and audience also helps to identify why key language features of this text are used by the writer.

> Use of direct evidence as support for points made

Audience

When you are considering audience, think carefully about:

- Who is the intended **target audience**? A particular age-group, interest group, group in society?

- What is the intended effect of the text on the target audience?

These key aspects of the text will have been chosen to appeal to the target audience:

- The **presentation** of the text – the use of colour, pictures, diagrams, font style/size

- The **language** used – level of difficulty and variety of vocabulary and sentence structure

- The **content** and **style** of the text.

Writing about purpose and audience

Read the article opposite from a national newspaper and the student's response to these questions below:

- Who is the audience and what is the purpose of this text?

- How is the language chosen appropriate for the purpose and audience?

School Puts Slang on Curriculum!!

'Slang is sabotaging the way we speak' say critics. Some people want it banned altogether. However, a London school has recently added to the furore over the way slang is being increasingly used in daily life, by offering a course on slang to its A-Level students. In addition to studying Chaucer, Beowolf and Shakespeare, students will be learning about street-talk and studying 'wigging'.

'Slang has always been part of the way we speak', says a spokesperson from the school. 'It is fascinating for students to learn about the history and heritage of slang – it enables them to use language in a much more powerful, manipulative way'. However, another school is so concerned about the ways in which their students speak that it has banned 'street talk' from the corridors and classrooms. 'Young people need to learn about appropriateness and register in their

"studying 'wigging'!"

communication with others – to allow the sloppy, often disrespectful forms of non-standard English to develop is having a direct negative influence on their ability to communicate in a range of situations.'

Here are one student's notes in response to the questions on page 10.

Notes

Audience: general adult – 'sabotaging' and 'appropriateness' are quite high-level vocabulary choices.

Language: impersonal style – no direct opinions from the writer, but two opposing opinions are presented and expressed in strong terms: against slang – 'sloppy/disrespectful'; for slang – 'powerful/manipulative'.

Purpose: on the surface informative, although the use of exclamation marks in the headline and pull quote suggests that the writer assumes the reader will not approve of the decision to teach slang. Could this be a right-wing newspaper?

Examiner's tip

Inferring meaning, or 'reading between the lines', is an important reading skill. One of the questions in your reading paper will ask you to infer meaning from the texts. For example, these notes show that you can infer from the exclamation marks in the headline that the writer thinks the idea is ridiculous.

(See pages 40–41 for more on Inference.)

Analysing a range of features

Effective reading involves more than simply the words on the page. Reading simply means 'de-coding' but effective readers de-code meaning from everything on the page, not just the main text itself, including:

- The use of colour, fonts, images

- The position or layout of particular features or information

- Headlines, sub-headings, pull quotes.

Task

Develop the student's notes above into a response about the newspaper report. How does the report appeal to its target audience and fulfil its purpose?
Write about how language is used.

Selecting and using information

Key points

■ Section A of your examination will ask you to read and answer questions on some **unseen non-fiction** texts. You are assessed on your ability to read and understand the text.

■ It is essential to read each question carefully to see exactly what it requires and then to select relevant information from the text to use in your answer.

Examiner's tip

Reading the question before reading the text can save time, as then you will be reading it with real **purpose**.

Examiner's tip

Don't just copy text – use your own words to maximise your marks.

Examiner's tip

In the exam, it helps to underline the important information.

Selecting information

- Find key words or phrases in the question that indicate what to look for in the text and where to look for it. For example:

    - From the *opening paragraph*, what do you discover about...

    - Find *three pieces of evidence* to support the writer's view that...

    - What *four reasons* does the writer give to explain why they feel...

Read the following question and then the text which is from a biographical article about Cheryl Cole (Tweedy). Select five key facts that would help you to answer the question.

What do you learn about Cheryl Cole's early career from this article?

Cheryl Ann Tweedy has spent nearly her entire life in the limelight. Born June 30, 1983, in Newcastle upon Tyne, England, Cheryl began her modeling career at the tender age of 6 when she won the prestigious World Star of Future Modeling competition. And she didn't stop there. In the years that followed, she was named 'Best Looking Girl of Newcastle,' 'Most Attractive Girl' at the Metro Square, and she starred in a string of popular commercials seen throughout the British Isles.

'Chezza,' as she's known in the media, won another competition of sorts, at the age of 16, when she beat out thousands of other young women to earn a place at the Royal Ballet Summer School in London. Despite her success as a dancer, Cheryl's true love was singing and she longed for the opportunity to show off her dazzling vocal prowess.

Try writing up your facts as a paragraph to answer the question above.

Compare your five facts and your answer with the ones on page 96.

Using textual references

- To support the points you make in your answers, you need to **refer directly to the text**.

- By making a textual reference you demonstrate that you have **read the text carefully** and that any ideas you are putting forward come from the text itself. In other words, you are interpreting meaning from the text and not just offering random thoughts and opinions.

- However, using textual reference does not mean 'copying out chunks of text'. You do not have much time to respond to each question, so your choice and use of evidence needs to be **short, snappy** and **purposeful**. Avoid long quotes.

How to quote

- Quotations which are fluently 'embedded' into your sentences make your writing more stylish and sophisticated.

- If you are using a longer quotation, place a colon at the end of your comment. Then start a new line and indent the quotation.

Read this extract from a tourist guide and then have a look at how this Grade A student has used evidence in their analysis. They have been asked to comment on how the writer uses language to make the area seem attractive to tourists.

Notice how both ways of using quotations are included in the response.

Wicken Fen

Discover a lost landscape, as you explore this remnant of ancient fenland, with its amazing abundance of wildlife. Imagine yourself in the past, where only the sound of the wind in the reeds and the songs and call of warblers and wildfowl mingle with the buzz of insects.

Our lush grass droves and raised boardwalk allow you to get close to the wetland flowering meadows, sedge and reedbeds, and possibly encounter rarities such as water voles, otters, hen harriers and bitterns. Or for a different view of the fen, why not take a trip in our traditional fen lighter boat.

The writer makes the area seem exciting and full of things to see. The extract begins with the word 'Discover', which makes it all seem adventurous and new; then it all sounds special because it is just a 'remnant' – something left behind, surviving – of 'ancient fenland'. We have visions of warrior chiefs, from times gone by, striding through this landscape. Obviously, everything is still alive, though. The writer mentions the 'amazing abundance' of wildlife, and the alliteration makes it sound huge and rich – even the word 'abundance' seems big and impressive. Meanwhile, the writer is giving us instructions ('Discover', 'Imagine') as if we need to be told how to cope with such an 'amazing' experience.

> The alliteration of 'warblers and wildfowl' creates sounds that are vibrating to us, and the noises are intermingled:
>
> 'the call of warblers and wildfowl mingle with the buzz of insects'.
>
> The onomatopoeia of 'buzz' suggests a heavy, hot atmosphere packed with a host of midges and flies. It makes us imagine a hot summer day where everything is buzzing with life...

Effects identified

Technical terms, with analysis of how they affect the reader

Ideas extended and developed

A*

Examiner's tip

Every piece of evidence you select needs support. A barrister would never simply present a piece of evidence to a jury (for example, CCTV footage). They would explain why this piece of evidence proved their client's innocence beyond a shadow of a doubt!

Good points

- The response focuses sharply on how the language has been used.
- Not only is language usage explained, there is also regular comment on the effect it is having on the reader.

REMEMBER

- Examiners always reward the development of ideas so explain what the material is saying – why and how.
- Link any specific reference to the rest of the text and analyse its significance.

Task

Complete the analysis of how language is used in the text to make the area seem attractive to tourists.

Perspective and point of view

- Demonstrating clear understanding through your reading involves your ability to recognise and comment on the **perspective** of the text.

- This means more than simply paraphrasing (putting into your own words) what the writer has already said. Careful consideration of the writer's **point of view** is part of skilful reading and is likely to be necessary when dealing with inference in the exam.

- Writing about perspective often involves analysing and commenting upon the **structure** and **language techniques** used to construct the text.

Writer's perspective

- **Perspective** means 'attitude' or 'standpoint'. If you are being asked to comment on the writer's perspective, first identify what this perspective is and then show how aspects of language and structure in the text make this point of view clear.

Read the following article from the BBC's *Panorama* website about the rise in youth crime. Consider this question and refer to the annotations:

What do you learn about the writer's feelings about this place from the way they write?

Strong statement in first sentence, makes perspective clear	Aberfeldy, a small rural town in Perthshire, in the Central Highlands of Scotland, could not have a more beautiful geographical setting but the attraction of the town ends there. The central square is the focal point of gatherings of underage 'neds' drinking Buckfast [alcohol] every night. Drugs are rife and this is one of the nastiest, most violent little communities I have ever come across. The town has one policeman – the local 'Community Liaison Officer'. There are beatings and acts of violence on a daily basis and at weekends the streets are more dangerous than many large cities, even Glasgow. You are at serious risk after the pubs kick out on a Friday or Saturday night of being set upon by drunken louts, many of whom are under-age and high on an alcohol speed combination. There have been many serious assaults over the past year yet, although the police have been involved, there have been no prosecutions. This is a town with serious anti-social behaviour problems which are being ignored by the authorities. The main offenders are well known to the police but there is no effort to impose ASBOs or address these issues. One police officer says he counted 92 young people in the square at 2am one Sunday morning. Is counting yobs a policing method? Maybe it's a new way to sleep off your responsibilities. The town is a disgrace.

Annotations:
- **Strong statement in first sentence, makes perspective clear**
- **Use of emotive language**
- **Use of personal pronoun to make the problem more immediate**
- **Short, summative sentence to reinforce the points made**
- **Point of view obvious**
- **The use of inverted commas suggests irony here.**
- **Appears to be about the lack of police support**
- **Clear criticism of police methods**
- **Sarcasm, poking fun at police**

Here is the beginning of one student response to the question:

The article begins positively, describing the town as having a 'beautiful geographical setting', but says 'the attraction of the town ends there', and the writer switches to a much more negative viewpoint. The mention of 'underage 'neds' drinking Buckfast' gives an image of violent young people and a dangerous environment; indeed, he labels it 'one of the nastiest, most violent little communities I have ever come across'. This statement is very absolute and sums up

- **Sensible use of quotations to support points**
- **Ideas extended**

the writer's viewpoint. He also mentions, specifically, 'beatings and acts of violence', which are hardly surprising when the town only has one 'Community Liaison Officer': the inverted commas are to make the position seem ineffectual. The writer is being sarcastic about any idea of liaison taking place...

> Keeps question in mind

> Intelligent analysis of language effects

Identifying perspective in an argument

- One simple way of identifying a well-written text and establishing its perspective is by reading the first and last paragraphs and the topic sentence of each paragraph in between. If the writer is skilful, they will **guide** the reader through their argument by the careful **structure** of their writing.

Read the article below. Consider how the writer has structured the article, by focusing on the topic sentences and by reading the annotations.

A clear and present failure

> Sets out writer's viewpoint: society has failed young people in deprived areas

> First pull quote and image imply that the article will be a negative portrayal

> Presents alternative viewpoint

> Mocks the alternative viewpoint

Why is it that groups of young people hang about tenement blocks with resignation written on their dulled expressions? Their eyes have lost their lustre and their thin young bodies are wasted due to lack of proper nutrition. There is nothing for them to aim for and nothing for them to do. Most of them sleep in their dirty bed sheets or sleeping bags until midday, while their mothers gamble away the benefit money they have collected the day before. The reason is that society has failed them.

'Lazy, stupid and worthless'

Right wing politicians take a different view .... Often, the teenagers themselves are criticised for being lazy, stupid and worthless – for having no pride, no desire to do anything with their lives other than to 'sponge' off the state and spend their time creating and causing trouble for the rest of society.

This argument is unbelievably arrogant because ... of course there is more to it than that. Rather than blaming and attacking, which is easy to do, it might be good to finally see someone doing something practical and realistic to deal with the issue of youth unemployment and crime.

It might be good to see some sensible suggestions, some support and some enthusiasm. It is easy to judge. It's not so easy to do something to help.

It must be possible to motivate these youngsters, to give them a sense of self-worth. They are our country's future. They are our present failure ... and it is vital to the future success of our country that we start looking for practical, long-term solutions that will enable young people to feel valued, supported and looked-after in our modern society – regardless of class or income bracket.

'It's easy to judge'

What the politicians should be doing is offering policies which will stem this tide of youth disaffection, not criticising, blaming and judging – and then turning their backs.

> Picks up original viewpoint and offers possible solution

> Second pull quote suggests more should be done to help young people.

> Picks apart the alternative viewpoint still further

Task

What is the writer's point of view in this article and how are language and presentational features used to convey this viewpoint?

Reading reports

Key points

- A report is a particular type of **information text** usually written for a specific audience.

- The **purpose** of a **formal report** is to **pass on specific information** about a particular issue, or investigation, so that others may **take action** using the findings of the report.

- A **newspaper report** usually gives information about an event that has just happened and may also explain why it happened.

- It is highly likely that you will find a question on a newspaper report in the exam and that it will focus on the use of **language** and **presentational features**.

Types of report

Here are some examples of different sorts of report:

- A **newspaper report** about the previous day's earthquake in Japan

- A group of scientists' **formal report** of their findings from their research project

- A **fact-finding report** to a school Governing Body on the results of the Student Council's survey

Formal reports

- **Formal reports** usually follow a clear **structure**: introduction; explanation of the research undertaken; summary of findings; conclusions or points for action.

- The style of a report is usually **formal**, using the **third person** and **past tense**.

Take a close look at this formal report and the annotations that consider its structure and style.

> First paragraph sets out the details of what was required

The Student Council was asked to conduct a survey to find out exactly what our students feel about the recent changes in school policies. In particular, it was required to focus on:

- uniform
- the new school day
- lunchtime arrangements.

The work had to be completed before the end of term.

> Second paragraph explains the methods used

We devised questionnaires (see Attachments A, B and C) and issued them to form tutors, so that they could be completed in pastoral time. Since the responses were all anonymous, students were asked to be honest about their opinions, but to take the survey seriously, so that a thorough analysis could be carried out. Because of other priorities, it took several weeks for all the forms to be returned but, eventually, 95% of them came back.

> This paragraph begins to work through details

The results were quite startling. Although there had been a full consultation on what new school uniform should be introduced, over 69% of students complained about it. Despite their initial enthusiasm, 45% of girls no longer liked wearing a blazer; and over 90% of boys would prefer to wear a sweatshirt. 96% of students think that school uniform should be abolished all together.

> Percentages to emphasise the strength of feelings

Although everyone likes the new school finishing time of 2.30, over 70% of students wish the lunch break could be longer, and would even consider starting school earlier, if that meant they could have an hour-long break in the middle of the day, as in the past.

> In each case, results are summarised for the reader

| Relevant detail taken from the survey throughout | The idea of a staggered lunchtime, with different year groups eating at different times, was not popular. 68% said they did not like having to wait until 1.15 for lunch and many pointed out that they had breakfast before 7 o'clock each morning, so they were unable to concentrate in the pre-lunch lessons. There was also concern about the noise, with some having lunch and others still in lessons... | Presumably the report would go on to sum up the results and then offer suggestions for further action |

This is how one student responded to the following question:

What impression of the students' ideas is given by the report.

The responses to the survey are described as 'startling', which immediately alerts the reader to the fact that the answers were unexpected. Almost all the findings are negative. For example, the percentages complaining about the school uniform are high: 69% complained, 45% of girls dislike blazers, 90% of boys would prefer a sweatshirt and 96% of students want school uniform to be removed. This creates the impression of a very unhappy student population.

However, there is some balance in the students' views. They like the change in the school finishing time and, amazingly, would be happy to start school earlier if that meant they could have a longer break in the middle of the day. This is another example of a 'startling' result. You would expect that students would prefer to stay in bed in the morning...

(A)

Examiner's tip

Using words and phrases from the question at key points in your answer shows the examiner that you are bearing the question in mind throughout and have a clear purpose.

REMEMBER

Questions about reports may ask you to:

- Retrieve information or find evidence from a text
- Comment on the language used and, possibly, on what is being suggested
- Comment on whether the style and tone are appropriate.

Task

Improve and continue the student response by adding:

- Further direct evidence from the report
- More detailed comments on the effects of the language, structure and style of the report.

Newspaper reports

- News reports are usually written in an impersonal style.

- The writer will provide facts – opinions will often come from 'sources' or people whose words are being reported through direct quotation.

Read the news article on page 18, which is from the BBC website. The annotations highlight some important features of article writing.

Choice of quote in headline indicates bias

Emotive language used to engage reader interest

Article reports what has been said

Quotations from the band involved

Phrase to introduce an element of impersonal tone

Inclusion of sarcastic quote again indicates bias

Final paragraph sums up and looks forward into the future

First paragraph sums up the basics of the article

Typical length of paragraph for this type of news report – single-length paragraphs referred to as 'tabloid paragraphs'

Quotation from 'other side' in order to offer a little balance to the article

Bias apparent again at the end

Rage Against The Machine: 'We want to wipe the smug grin from Simon Cowell's face'

The hotly contested battle for the Christmas number one reached boiling point today after Rage Against The Machine told how they wanted to 'wipe the smug grin from Cowell's face.'

The American group, which is currently set to beat Joe McElderry's single 'The Climb' to the top spot tomorrow with 'Killing In The Name', have been the subject of a powerful internet campaign against the X Factor winner's record.

The group's guitarist Tom Morello said of the movement: 'It's trying to save the UK pop charts from this abyss of bland mediocrity.

'I don't believe it has anything to do with Simon Cowell personally. I like that guy. He's a great entertainer. He's going to do fine with his No. 2 this Christmas. What you're seeing is real democracy.'

He added that the band would be donating the unexpected royalties to the homeless charity Shelter.

'We graciously extend the same invitation to Simon Cowell,' he added.

McElderry is said to be furious about the rival group, and said of the track: 'It is dreadful and I hate it. How could anyone enjoy this?'

He was also pictured throwing darts at a picture of the rock band's frontman Zack de la Rocha.

Morello had sympathy for the 18-year-old however: 'The campaign has nothing to do with that nice young man, and his parents are going to be proud of him when he comes second.

Task

Look again at the news report about the battle for the Christmas Number one.
What is the writer's viewpoint and how is it revealed?

Reading articles

Key points

- An article from a journalistic source – a newspaper, a magazine or a web page – is likely to be one of the texts you are asked to consider in the examination.

- **Feature articles** tend to offer more than just information; they often provide more of a **considered view** or an **interpretation** of an event or issue.

- Exam questions on feature articles may focus on the **language** used as well as the effects of **layout** and **presentational features**. They might also ask about the **writer's viewpoint** or ask you to retrieve information.

(See pages 38–39 for more on Analysing presentational features.)

Feature articles

- Whereas news reports usually have an impersonal style, feature articles may contain opinions and be written in the **first person** (I/we). They provide the writer's and others' views and interpretation, as well as information.

Read the following article which is a feature on homelessness from *The Big Issue*. The language and techniques of feature writing are presented in the annotations.

Annotation (left)	Article text	Annotation (right)
List of three emotive verbs to emphasise the violence	Thousands of people live rough in our public streets and parks. Rough sleepers are more likely to be attacked, abused and robbed than any other group. Yet, they are subject to harassment from the authorities and the public.	Strong opening sentence introducing the topic
Deliberate choice of verb to show detachment from homeless people	There are those who believe that the homeless people, who sleep rough, should be eliminated. They should somehow be swept from our streets and placed in unappealing hostels. Some believe they are a danger to society .... that they are thieves and murderers.	Emotive language used to reinforce point of view
Clear topic sentence stating the writer's viewpoint	The above view is far from the truth. In fact, those who are forced to sleep rough are often the ones in danger. *Big Issue* vendor Ralph Milward was kicked to death in the quiet Dorset suburb of Westbourne. The fact that there are rough sleepers in our streets and parks is evidence of our failure as a society.	Implies that the homeless are worthless, like rubbish
Use of pronoun 'we' to involve the reader and suggest their need to act	What we need to do is to deliver social care interventions that really work. We need to build bright new hostels for the unfortunate homeless. We need to give them relevant education concentrating on functional skills, so that they can, if possible, find work in the future. How much better it would be, if the homeless were housed and employed.	Includes the reader suggesting a shared responsibility
		Concluding sentence – presenting an unarguable vision for the future

Here is how one student analysed the use of language in the first half of this article:

Good points

- The first paragraph addresses the question directly as well as demonstrating an understanding of the form, audience and purpose.

- The second paragraph focuses on the specific use of language, identifying features for detailed comment.

This feature article uses a variety of language and structural techniques to strongly suggest that homelessness has reached a crisis point.

The writer employs emotive language when painting a vividly negative description of the way the homeless are treated. The use of the rhetorical list of three; 'attacked, abused and robbed', strongly suggests that the homeless are in danger. The use of 'eliminated' implies the homeless are a form of vermin rather than human beings, and something we should get rid of. It is a cold, heartless verb. This technique is reinforced with the idea that some want them 'swept away', which presents an image of people as nothing more than waste products, rubbish to be cast aside.

A*

Task

Complete the response to the homeless article using the student answer above as a starting point.

Reading advertisements

Key points

- An advertisement, either from a magazine, web page or newspaper, is quite likely to be one of the texts in Section A of your exam.

- You may need to be able to **identify** features of presentation and/or language, and **evaluate** the effectiveness of each one.

- If the **form** is an advert, the **purpose** will clearly be to persuade, but you will need to carefully consider the target **audience** for the advert.

Presentational features

Presentational features are essentially the way the text is set out to appear on the page. These aspects include:

- Use of images
- Use of colour
- Font style, size and colour
- Use of text – layout and organisation as well as language
- Logos, slogans, shapes

Notice how these features are used in this advert.

How to begin analysing an advert

You need to show that you are able to **evaluate** the presentational features, not just identify them. In other words, focus on *why* features have been used, considering the effects on the target audience at all times.

Add to these notes which one student made in response to the advert above.

Clear focus on the effects of the image	**Notes**
Links the image to the overall purpose	Main image – huge towering skyscrapers viewed from below. This suggests that the person is looking up, possibly aiming high? This would link to the main idea of the advert. The image seems to be suggesting that aiming for 'big business' is very hard, possibly too hard to achieve. The perspective of the photograph makes the viewer seem trapped at the bottom.
Infers meaning from the angle of the image	Audience and purpose – it's clearly aimed at graduates who are looking for employment – the name of the company explains this. There's a lot of direct address – 'not what you're looking for' etc. This personalises the advert and therefore the company – makes them seem friendly which is the overall message they appear to be selling.
Does not just identify features but evaluates them	Text – very friendly tone, use of white font makes the main messages stand out – the tone links to the idea that working for 'big business' would be anonymous and unfriendly. What this company is promoting is a smaller, more friendly working environment.
States effect of choice of font colour clearly	

Identifying and evaluating presentational features

When looking at adverts, it is really important to focus on the effects of the images.

A typical question you may be asked could be:

How do the layout and presentational features of this text help to achieve its overall purpose?

Use of 'commands' to appeal directly to reader

Main header text in red links to the image of footprints

Full page photo of a deserted beach – suggests lovely weather, peace and relaxation

The couple are walking towards the sunset, suggesting exploration and romance

Body text is presented with wavy borders suggesting relaxation

Footprints in the foreground – draw reader's eye into middle of image – the couple

Logo also in red placed at corner in line with footprints.

Leave a smaller footprint on holiday, escape to Devon.

A trip to Devon is definitely a step in the right direction. You could start by exploring our two National Parks or maybe our World Heritage Sites. Want more? We have enough protected land to cover Paris and Madrid combined, and a network of cycleways and footpaths that could stretch from Devon to Florida. Not tired yet? Head for the coast, either of them. Uniquely we've got two, so stretch your legs. After all that you'll want a good meal. Well, with more organic food producers than anyone else, you may have travelled far but your food won't have. So, if you want to lessen your carbon footprint on holiday, make tracks for Devon.

Call 0870 608 55 31 or visit www.naturallydevon.com

Devon

REMEMBER

Good readers 'read' the *whole* text, not just the words. Think of reading as 'de-coding meaning' – there are many ways, including presentational features, to provide meaning.

Here is part of a student response to this question.

Links purpose to presentation

Analyses features and their effects

Explains effect on reader

Connection between presentational features and written text

This advertisement is designed to lure holidaymakers to Devon, and the presentational features are intended to fulfil that purpose. The sandy colour of the beach and background, which is also mystical and, apparently, stretches into infinity, gives an immediate impression of the beach and its endless possibilities. The couple could be anyone and they are meandering across the beach. It seems they have all the time in the world, because their footprints – which lead us from the bottom of the picture to the lovers – take our eyes up to the horizon and to the heading: 'Leave a smaller footprint...', linking the presentation to the written text, with its mention of Devon...

Good points

- Elements of text are analysed.
- A range of features is dealt with in detail.
- The features are integrated into a general understanding of what the text is setting out to achieve.

Task

Complete the analysis of how the presentational features help achieve the text's overall purpose.

Reading leaflets

Key points

- Leaflets can serve a variety of **purposes**: to give information, to offer advice, or to persuade the reader to act or think in a particular way.

- Leaflets tend to organise their information in short sections, allowing them to be read very easily.

- Presentational features such as sub-headings and bullet point lists are often used to break the information down into short pieces of text. Use of image and colour also helps convey the message.

Reading a leaflet

- When writing about leaflets in the exam, you will need to consider what the writer aims to achieve, focusing on the layout, design and presentational features. Leaflets use presentational features in order to allow the information to be read very quickly.

- You may also be asked to focus on the way language is used to achieve this aim and what can be inferred from the language. This means reading between the lines.

Look at this leaflet from an airline company.

Here is how one student began their analysis of the use of presentational features in this leaflet.

Explanation of how the colours are intended to affect us	This text is dominated by the colours red and blue: red to emphasise the important selling-points and blue to remind the reader that this is all about flying. The blue makes us think of the sky; and red is for excitement. 'Jet2.com' is in red, and after reading that our eyes notice the £5 lure, the fact that the in-flight entertainment they are advertising is 'Easy to use' and
How we respond	'Available today...'. The red is unavoidable and carries our eyes around the text. Then, the £5 bubble is repeated at the end, so it is what we remember.
	On the front, the phrase 'brand new in-flight entertainment' is angled up as if it is a plane taking off, above the image based on the inside of a cabin. We cannot fail to see the long image of the aircraft and at the back it is as if we are looking into the plane to see the
Understanding the text's purpose	traveller being offered the mezzo system. It clarifies exactly what is going on...

Examiner's tip

Commenting on the effect of individual language choices and layout features is necessary but if you can demonstrate how elements of the text, use of colour and image, etc connect and work together, you will gain more marks.

Good points

- Clear evidence of understanding and analysis of the effects of presentational features.
- A range of features identified and analysed.

A

Analysing leaflets

- If you are given a leaflet to analyse, start by considering the leaflet's **purpose** and **audience**.

- You might be asked to write about how the presentational features, or the language, are used.

Read the leaflet below. What do you notice about the way it has been presented?

SWINE FLU
INFORMATION
0800 1 513 513
www.nhs.uk
www.direct.gov.uk/swineflu

IMPORTANT
INFORMATION
ABOUT
SWINE FLU

This leaflet contains important information to help you and your family – KEEP IT SAFE

Large image showing swine flu 'germs' being sprayed into the air

Important information at the top

Black background suggests possible grim results of flu

Hand features large in foreground – useless in preventing germs from spreading

The key purpose of the leaflet is written in capitals

Colour scheme simple – blue, white and black – and makes image stand out

The words 'keep it safe' also in capitals, for emphasis

Task

Write an analysis in response to this question:

> **How have presentational features been used for effect in this leaflet?**

Use the annotations as a starting point.

Reading diaries and blogs

Key points

- Diaries are factual accounts, usually organised **chronologically**.

- A blog (or 'web log') is also a form of diary, but written for and read online by a wider audience.

- If a diary extract comes up in the exam, you will most likely be asked to comment on its language features and their effects or the writer's viewpoint, as well as simple information questions.

Diaries

- Personal diaries are written in the first person and are informal in style, usually written for the writer's eye only. They include personal recollections as well as facts about daily events.

- Diaries written for publication, by celebrities or politicians, record events of public interest and can be more formal in style but are usually in the first person.

Below is an extract from the final diary entry of Captain Scott, whose famous *Discovery* expedition to the Antarctic ended in the tragic death of himself and his whole party in 1912.

As you read it, use the annotations to help you identify the particular language features he uses.

> Clear purpose to the diary entry – to provide an account of the expedition

> Numerical list creates a factual tone

> Gives a personal opinion after the list of facts

> Powerful adjective amongst this factual account makes a strong impact

> Emotive language used to show extreme circumstances

> Use of first person throughout – 'we' more often than 'I'

The causes of the disaster are not due to faulty Organisation, but to misfortune in all risks which had to be undertaken.

1. The loss of pony transport in March 1911 obliged me to start later than I had intended, and obliged the limits of stuff transported to be narrowed.

2. The weather throughout the outward journey, and especially the long gale in 83° S., stopped us.

3. The soft snow in lower reaches of glacier again reduced pace.

We fought these untoward events with a will and conquered, but it cut into our provision reserve...

Every detail of our food supplies, clothing and depots made on the interior ice-sheet and over that stretch of 700 miles to the Pole and back, worked out to perfection. The advance party would have returned to the glacier in fine form and with surplus of food, but for the astonishing failure of the man whom we had least expected to fail. Edgar Evans was thought the strongest man of the party.

The Beardmore Glacier is not difficult in fine weather, but on our return we did not get a single completely fine day; this with a sick companion enormously increased our anxieties.

As I have said elsewhere, we got into frightfully rough ice and Edgar Evans received a concussion of the brain – he died a natural death, but left us a shaken party with the season unduly advanced.

But all the facts above enumerated were as nothing to the surprise which awaited us on the Barrier. I maintain that our arrangements for returning were quite adequate, and that no one in the world would have expected the temperatures and surfaces which we encountered at this time of the year...

> Understandable use of exaggeration – again emotive?

On the next page you can see how one student responded to the following question about the Scott's diary extract:

What do we learn about Scott's thoughts and feelings in this diary extract?

Scott's feelings are obvious right from the start. There are words like 'misfortune', 'disaster' and 'risk', which make us understand the desperate situation that he recognises they are in. Obviously, Scott has an organised approach to life, as he lists the problems they have encountered, but that list in itself implies that a whole range of events have militated against them. It is clear that Scott does not feel he could have done anything differently, because he blames other events: the late start due to the loss of pony transport, the weather and the soft snow. What is more, he wants to make it known that they have made heroic efforts ('We fought ... with a will and conquered').

However, he lays great emphasis on the fact that Edgar Evans let them down by falling in rough ice. They did not get fine weather, so their 'sick companion' proved a great burden.

Even despite all this, Scott is of the opinion that everything had been properly planned and they were thwarted by the 'temperatures and surfaces' that were unexpected. Right through the extract, he seems to be justifying his own role and claiming that the fates were against them, so that what happened was unavoidable and certainly not his fault.

> Identifies significant vocabulary

> Interprets what is presented

> Interprets character from what is written

> Retains focus on Scott's thoughts

> Prioritises what Scott blames

> Understands Scott's thoughts

> Summary to conclude

Blogs

- Blogs are also written in first person and organised chronologically but they can also be more 'talk-like' than most personal diaries.

- The writer has an idea of the wider general audience and the content and tone of the blog matches this, rather and being more personal and private.

Read this blog, written by Glenn Morris, the leader of an educational Arctic expedition. Identify the language that shows his awareness of his wider audience.

Who might the audience be for this blog? Consider:

  – Family   – Friends   – Fellow Arctic explorers

Northern Lights offer a stunning midnight display

March 28th 2009

+ AUDIO MP3

Hi it's Glenn here. Here's an update. We've reached a fish camp on the way back to Iglulik and going very well now. Last night we camped on the ice very late and it was pitch black when we set up the tent.

It was absolutely astounding because I'd never seen a sight like it. The Northern Lights were just stunning like green inverted curtains shimmering over the entire sky. It was very cold and it was absolutely stunning and as well as that the stars were just numerous in this great black expanse of the Arctic winter. So it was really quite entertaining watching the Northern Lights. We should reach Iglulik all being well sometime on Saturday.

REMEMBER

- Identify the purpose and audience of the blog or diary extract first.

- Then, if the question requires it, comment on the language features that deliver that purpose to the intended audience.

**Task**

Read the two items: *Captain Scott's Diary* and Glenn Morris's blog.
Compare the way language has been used in the two texts.
For more on Comparing language see pages 46–49.

Reading biography and autobiography

Key points

- Biographical writing is a type of non-fiction text which is about the life, and possibly work, of a real person possibly a public figure or someone who has had a significant impact on the world.

- **Biographies** are written *about* the person concerned and **autobiographies** are written *by* the person concerned.

- A biography will be written in **third person**, an autobiography in **first person** and their **structure** and organisation is normally **chronological**.

- The **purpose** of biographical writing is usually a mixture of entertaining and informing the reader. Exam questions you may see on this type of writing are most likely to focus on how effectively the language is used to meet this purpose. You may also be asked to infer meaning from the extract, or find some information.

Examiner's tip

Focus clearly on the use of language in a text like this. Look particularly at the way language has been used to present the person and the events they are recounting.

Autobiographies

- An autobiography is the story of someone's life – or a significant part of their life – written by the person themselves (even though sometimes 'ghost writers' actually write the book).

The following extract is from the autobiography of footballer Steven Gerrard, who plays for Liverpool FC.

Annotation (left)	Text
Striking image in first sentence	Cut my veins open and I bleed Liverpool red. I love Liverpool with a burning passion. My determination to reach the heights at Anfield intensified when poor Jon-Paul passed away. Also fuelling my drive to succeed was an accident I suffered during my school days. My career was nearly destroyed before it started. All my dreams of starring for Liverpool and England, of lifting European Cups and shining in World Cups, rested on the skill of a surgeon when I was only nine.
Dramatic sentence to highlight strong feeling	
Dramatic language for effect	

Annotations (right):
- **Short sentence for dramatic effect**
- **List of aspirations to intensify danger of potential disaster**
- **Mention of age highlights the life-long ambition**

Anfield was already my first love and my second home. I'd been there a year, training with Michael Owen at the Vernon Sangster Sports Centre, learning my trade, when a calamity hit me that left me in hospital fearing for my future. Even now, I shudder at the memory of what took place on a patch of grass near my house on the Bluebell Estate of Huyton, Merseyside.

It was just a field, surrounded by bushes, a mess really. The type of place where people threw their rubbish without a second thought. Me and my mates didn't care. All that mattered to us was the grass was half-decent for a game of shootie. We were on it night and day, summer and winter. To us kids, that scrap of wasteground was Anfield, Goodison and Wembley rolled into one – a heaven on earth. One Saturday morning, early doors, I was kicking about on the strip with a kid from our street, a boy called Mark Hannan. We'd sorted out the pitch. It wasn't exactly the Bernabeu, but it was home. A mate nicked some nets from his Sunday League team, cut them in half, and rigged up two seven-a-side goals. Perfect.

Annotations (left):
- **Use of colloquial language reminding reader that it is a childhood anecdote**
- **Hyperbolic description**
- **Anfield, Goodison and the Bernabeu are all football grounds**

Annotations (right):
- **Phrase intensifies the idea that his whole 'world' is football**
- **Single word to end the paragraph and emphasise his enjoyment of playing**

Here is one student's approach to this question on the text:

How does the writer use language to engage the interest of the reader?

In this extract, Gerrard uses dramatic language from the outset with the use of the phrase 'cut my veins open', which speaks directly to the reader and therefore invites them to share more closely in the story. Closely following this is a strong image of blood: 'veins', 'blood' and 'red' all of which foreshadow the event to be described later on as well as inviting the reader into the story with its hints of danger and violence. The language of 'calamity' 'fearing for my future' and 'shuddering at the memory' reinforces this sense of danger by building up tension, as does the mention of 'Liverpool', 'England', 'European Cups' and 'World Cups'. All of this is what Gerrard potentially stands to lose through the injury he is going to describe. It is as if he is suggesting that this enormously successful career, intensified with the listing in the sentence of all the teams and events he has played in, might never have happened to him at all.

B

Good points

- Clear engagement with the language of the text.
- Picks out particular language features which will gain the reader's interest.
- Uses appropriate quotes to support ideas.

Biographies

- Biographies contain events from the person's past, designed to give the reader a clear picture of what their life was like and how they have been influenced by the life they have led.

The extract below is from a biography of Victorian artist and poet, Dante Gabriel Rossetti. Rossetti was a member of the Pre-Raphaelite movement – a group of nineteenth century artists, writers and critics.

His paintings and poetry have been liked by some and disliked by others. Their popularity changes all the time. Currently, his pictures of beautiful long-haired sirens can be seen on countless everyday items that we buy in the shops. His poems were once highly acclaimed – not least because they were so sexual – but now languish, largely unread. Perhaps they are simply unfashionable.

His private life also causes much discussion, even today. It was linked closely to his artistic life. The two seem to be inextricably entwined. He adored his model, Elizabeth Siddal, but postponed their marriage and pursued other women. In a grandly romantic gesture, he even went so far as to bury his poems in Lizzie's coffin; but later he wanted them back, and dug them up seven years later…

> First paragraph summarises the differences in how his artistic life is viewed

> Second paragraph focuses on his love life

> His life cannot be separated from his work – they are both equally interesting

Here is how one student has responded to the lfollowing question about this extract:

How is langauge used in this extract to influence our impression of Rossetti?

> General impression of Rossetti, detailed by what follows

The biographer makes us think of Rossetti as a man who loved but was not faithful and who wrote poems which are not well-read today.

> Impression extended and developed

We are told of the 'long haired sirens', who sound attractive and, as sirens, might well have lured Rossetti to his problems. We can imagine him surrounded by beautiful women. There must have been large numbers of them because they are now on 'countless' items. Obviously, his poems must have been popular, because the word 'acclaimed' makes it

> Focus on important vocabulary

seem they were award-winning and highly treasured. Nowadays, we are told they 'languish, largely unread', so we think of them lying back like resting, carefree but idle

> Links ideas

women – maybe like the women he used to paint.

In that Rossetti's private life and his art were 'inextricably entwined', it is as if the elements are linked

Examiner's tip

If you are asked about language, make that your key focus: for example the vocabulary chosen, the use of exaggeration, quotations, imagery.

| Analysis and effect | like a knotted ball of string. They cannot be pulled apart. His love for Elizabeth Siddal must have been genuine because he 'adored' her, as if she was like a goddess, and he must have been close to her because later she is referred to by the loving abbreviation, 'Lizzie'. |

| Links language back to general impression | ——— Still, there are some interesting contrasts in the vocabulary: he 'pursued' other women but when Lizzie died he made a 'grandly romantic gesture'. These seem to sum up his character and his inconsistency pointed out in the extract. |

(A*)

Authors of biographies need to research a great deal into the person or **subject** they are writing about.

Below is an extract from a biography of John Wilson, founder of Sight Savers International.

First, read this **synopsis** (short summary) for the biography – it is the sort of synopsis often found on the back cover of a biography. Notice how much information it contains about the life and work of John Wilson.

| Positive opening comment about the subject | John Wilson did more than anyone else to prevent and cure blindness, and help blind people, throughout the world between the 1940s and his death in 1999. He also made a significant contribution to the cause of disabled people in general. His achievements deserve comparison with those of other charismatic figures like Helen Keller and Albert Schweitzer. ——— | Compares the subject with other figures |

Now read this extract from John Wilson's biography.

The day's timetable included a chemistry class. The pupils were to carry out an experiment. Wilson later described what happened:

'There was a rubber tube leading into a retort filled with water. The idea was that oxygen, when it was produced, would come bubbling up into the water. It was my turn to heat the test-tube with a Bunsen burner. I was sitting on a high stool very close to it, playing the blue flame from the Bunsen burner on to the test-tube when it suddenly exploded. The chemicals had been wrongly labelled and produced an explosive mixture. It must have been quite an explosion because they say it shattered whole rows of bottles and wrecked part of the room.'

A classmate confirms this: 'There was a huge bang. We got peppered with glass. Everybody was bleeding. I got some glass in my face, but they managed to remove it.'

One boy present was blinded in one eye. John Wilson was blinded in both.

Here is how a student began their analysis of the language used for effect in this extract from John Wilson's biography:

The long quote from John Wilson is very matter-of-fact. The use of the word 'playing' when talking of 'Playing with the blue flame' reminds us that this is an anecdote from his childhood. It also highlights the difference between the fun of this 'play' and the devastating result. However, he does inform us that it 'was quite an explosion' and that 'it wrecked part of the room.' His words almost seem like understatements, considering the way the accident changed his life forever.

John's comment about the colour of the 'blue flame' is particularly poignant because he will never see colour again. This adds to the impact of the accident, as mention of the colour reminds us as readers that something so fundamentally taken for granted is to be taken away from him.

He also uses 'they say' because he would never see the damage done to the room; he reports what others 'saw' because he can no longer see for himself, which adds pathos to the description.

The classmate uses some powerful imagery in their account of the tragic event: for example 'peppered' with glass suggests it was dotted all over them. He also states that 'everybody was bleeding' to explain the full horror of the scene. The fact that this person also got glass in their face, 'but they managed to remove it', contrasts shockingly with Wilson's own fate and adds to the impression of chance and misfortune about the whole event. The writer's decision to include both John Wilson's first-hand account and his classmate's is successful as both add impact to the retelling of this event which was such a turning point.

The extract ends with a short sentence, confirming that John Wilson was blinded in both eyes. The short sentence is effective in that we are aware of the impact upon John's life as he 'was blinded in both' eyes. The ending of the extract is bleak, matter-of-fact and very simply-phrased, suggesting that nothing more needs to, or can, be said to make the facts of the matter any better. Things would never be the same for Wilson again.

(A*)

Good points

- The student quotes specific words and phrases that are used for effect.
- First-hand accounts and their effect are commented upon.
- The use of language is analysed, with meaning being inferred.

REMEMBER

When you are writing about biography and autobiography, the examiner wants you to concentrate on the effects created by particular language choices, not on retelling the story even if it is fascinating!

Task

Using the extracts from the biographies of Rossetti and John Wilson, compare how language is used in each text to gain and keep the interest of the reader.

(See pages 46–49 for techniques on Comparing language.)

Reading travel writing

Key points

- Travel writing is a particular genre of non-fiction writing. It is not to be confused with a 'guide book' – the two have differences in purpose and form.

- Travel writing tends to have a narrative element to it – often a **chronological account** of a visitor's experiences whilst travelling.

- It is usually in the **first person** as it is one person's account, from their point of view.

- Although **factual** in content, there will be an **element of bias** in travel writing – the writer will often include their opinions on their experiences within their writing.

- It is likely to be the language and perspective of travel writing that will come up in exam questions but you may also be asked to retrieve information.

REMEMBER

- Look for different language techniques that the travel writer uses to convey information to the reader.

- Be aware of the attitudes or feelings that the travel experience causes in the writer.

Travel writing

- Travel writing involves describing travel experiences. It can be factual but can also give individual interpretations of the experience. The very best travel writing allows the reader to feel as though they are participating in the journey!

- Generally, travel writing entertains and informs the reader whereas a guide book would contain more facts and information and may also advise the reader.

Now read this extract from *Notes from a Small Island* in which American journalist, Bill Bryson, describes his first time in England.

My first sight of England was on a foggy March night in 1973 when I arrived on the midnight ferry from Calais. For twenty minutes, the terminal area was aswarm with activity as cars and lorries poured forth, customs people did their duties, and everyone made for the London road. Then abruptly all was silence and I wandered through sleeping, low-lit streets threaded with fog, just like a Bulldog Drummond movie. It was rather wonderful having an English town all to myself.

The only mildly dismaying thing was that all the hotels and guesthouses appeared to be shut up for the night. I walked as far as the rail station, thinking I'd catch a train to London, but the station, too was dark and shuttered. I was standing wondering what to do when I noticed a grey light of a television filling an upstairs window of a guesthouse across the road. Hooray, I thought, someone awake, and hastened across, planning humble apologies to the kindly owner for the lateness of my arrival and imagining a cheery conversation which included the line, 'Oh, but I couldn't possibly ask you to feed me at this hour. No, honestly – well, if you're quite sure it's no trouble, then perhaps just a roast beef sandwich and a large dill pickle with perhaps some potato salad and a bottle of beer.' The front path was pitch dark and in my eagerness and unfamiliarity with British doorways, I tripped on a step, crashing face-first into the door and sending half a dozen empty milk bottles clattering. Almost immediately the upstairs window opened.

'Who's that?' came a sharp voice.

I stepped back, rubbing my nose, and peered up at a silhouette with hair curlers.

'Hello, I'm looking for a room,' I said.

'We're shut.'

'Oh.' But what about my supper?

'Try the Churchill. On the front.'

'On the front of what?' I asked, but the window was already banging closed.

A typical question you could be asked would be:

What does Bill Bryson think of England when he first arrives?

Here is one student's response.

There is a lot of hustle and bustle as Bryson first arrives; the port is 'aswarm with activity', like a beehive or another crowded, busy place. Soon, though, everything changes as 'abruptly all was silence.' This contrast with the previous 'activity' intensifies the silence.

The description of the foggy streets is almost out of a horror movie with its 'fog' and 'low-lit streets', creating a gloomy, oppressive atmosphere. Bryson appears to enjoy the experience of being alone; he asserts that it is 'wonderful having an English town all to myself.'

His mood soon changes to one of 'mild dismay' when he observes that everything is shut for the night. His choice of words convey this frame of mind, as words like 'dark' and 'shuttered' carry negative connotations. They suggest being shut out, as if the country he is trying to get into has closed its doors against him. Despite these signs, his hopes are still high for a good reception. Humour is added by the stark contrast between his imagined experience (a 'roast beef sandwich...') and the reality of the guest house.

The humour continues as he describes his 'unfamiliarity with British doorways', creating a slap-stick image of Bryson stumbling and crashing into the door. The ensuing dialogue and the description of the guest house owner as a 'silhouette with hair curlers' help us to see the English as others see us: unfriendly, far from glamorous and ready for bed at an early hour.

Bryson is as unfamiliar with his surroundings as he is with some English usage, interpreting the word 'front' in a literal manner: 'on the front of what?' This lends a certain pathos to the situation as we sympathise with Bryson, alone, late at night, in an English town with nowhere to stay. 'The window was already banging shut,' as was his hope of finding food and a room for the night.

Good points

- Identifies contrast of bustle and quiet, which changes the atmosphere of the piece.
- Recognises the effective use of sympathy or pathos in our perception of Bryson's experience
- Recognises humour in writer's portrayal of his thoughts and actions.
- Identifies the writer's feelings and discusses inferred message about England and the English.

Read the following extract from the travel journals of George Orwell, taking note of the annotations and this question.

What do you learn about the industrial landscape of Sheffield in the 1930s, from Orwell's journal?

| Negative first sentence – sets tone for the whole account | Had a very long and exhausting day (I am now continuing this March 4th) being shown every quarter of Sheffield on foot and by tram. I have now traversed almost the whole city. It seems to me, by daylight, one of the most appalling places I have ever seen. In whichever direction you look you see the same landscape of monstrous chimneys pouring forth smoke which is sometimes black and sometimes of a rosy tint said to be due to sulphur. You can smell the sulphur in the air all the while. All buildings are blackened within a year or two of being put up. Halting at one place I counted the factory chimneys I could see and there were 33. But it was very misty as well as smoky – there would have been many more visible on a clear day. I doubt whether there are any architecturally decent buildings in the town. The town is very hilly (said to be built on seven hills, like Rome) and everywhere streets of mean little houses blackened by smoke run up at sharp angles, paved with cobbles which are purposely set unevenly to give horses etc, a grip. At night the hilliness creates fine effects because you look across from one hillside to the other and see the lamps twinkling like stars. Huge jets of flame shoot periodically out of the roofs of the foundries* (many working night shifts at present) and show a splendid rosy colour through the smoke and steam. When you get a glimpse inside you see enormous fiery serpents of red-hot and white-hot (really lemon coloured) iron being rolled out into rails. | Implies that he has seen more than enough |

Annotations:
- Implies that he has seen more than enough
- Powerful adjective – 'monstrous' – creates image of a daunting industrial landscape
- Expression 'I doubt' actually enforces this opinion
- 'Monstrous' imagery continued to create hell-like atmosphere

* **foundries**: places where metal is cast (shaped) using intense heat

Task

Using the following suggestions, write your answer to this question:

How does Orwell use language to demonstrate his feelings about 1930s Sheffield?

You could include:

- How Orwell feels about Sheffield
- How he creates a sense of danger about the city through his use of language

Reading reviews

Key points

- A review is **form** of non-fiction text which provides a **description** and an **evaluation** of an event, an object or publication such as a book or film.

- The **purpose** of a review is to provide a clear overview and an evaluative judgement or **recommendation**.

- A review is often written for a clear **audience** with a shared interest in the topic

- Reviews are often, but not always, written in the **first person**.

- They tend to place their topic in context, comparing it to similar events, objects or publications. They often 'rate' the topic in terms of its appeal to the audience.

- The focus in exam questions about reviews may be on language choices, how these link to the writer's viewpoint and with what effects. You might also be asked to find information.

REMEMBER

- The purpose of a review is to give an overall evaluation.

- Focus on the language and structure and how they are used to present a particular point of view.

Analysing reviews

- When you read a review, make sure you notice the ways in which it is structured and the way language is used to express a clear **point of view**. So one of the first things to consider when reading a review is the standpoint of the reviewer – whether their view is **biased** or **unbiased**.

Read this review for a video game, taking note of the annotations.

> Introductory sentence sets the review in context.

The beloved adventure game franchise Monkey Island set sail on a new episodic journey earlier this year and has recently come into port with its fifth and final episode. Tales of Monkey Island chronicles the further adventures of Guybrush Threepwood—Mighty Pirate— as he pursues his often-imperiled wife, Elaine, and tries to vanquish his nemesis, LeChuck. Yet this tale is no heroic cliche, and it takes some amusing twists and unconventional turns. The relationships between lead characters are the engaging heart of the story, while the supporting cast and wacky environments provide ample opportunity for humor. This is a funny game, and though there are some lulls in the otherwise lively pace, the clever puzzles and the playful ways you have to go about solving them will keep you entertained for the duration. Tales of Monkey Island is a lengthy adventure that's easy to enjoy and easy on your wallet, as well as sure to please both newcomers and veteran insult swordfighters alike.

> Short summary of the game's content

> Clause focuses the reader's attention and offers the writer's first personal view.

> Positive comments clarify the writer's opinion.

> Summative statement provides the writer's overall evaluation.

This next review is for a film.

After all the hype surrounding the release of *Teddy's Magic Christmas*, I must confess to feeling like the hero of the hour when I proudly presented the last-minute surprise tickets to my kids. Their almost tearful gratitude had all of us damp-eyed with festive emotion and warm with Christmas spirit. Unfortunately, this completely evaporated within the first ten minutes of this dreary, derivative and quite frankly dire excuse for a film.

The basic plot, as I'm sure you are aware from all the advertising, is that poor Teddy (voiced by the hot new talent of Zak Valance), is the last remaining 'proper' toy in Mr Muggins' toyshop, and has to fight a lone crusade against the rising tide of high-tech toys swamping the market, thereby 'saving' the children of the world from cynical, plastic gadgetry and hard-edged sales pitches, reminding us all (sniff sniff) of the magic of Christmas.

While I'm not suggesting that films aimed at the very youngest of filmgoers absolutely have to have a plausible plot-line, they surely do need to have some kind of story to carry them along, at least. Otherwise you simply don't care. Which, I'm afraid, is exactly what happened to us – we simply didn't care, because the major flaw of the film in my opinion was that Teddy had all the personality of…well…a stuffed toy!

Overall judgement: don't waste your money

Rating: ★★ *(and that's just because it's Christmas)*

Here is an extract from one response analysing the language of this film review:

The first sentence of this film review doesn't immediately let the reader know what the writer thinks of the film. It does seem a little bit over the top from the start, however, which makes us wonder whether the reviewer is serious: 'the hero' of the hour'. It is only when we get to the word 'unfortunately' that we know that the review is going to be negative.

There are descriptions of how the children reacted which sounds emotional and as if the event actually happened, for example 'tearful with gratitude'. This contrasts with the fact that everyone was let down when they actually saw the film ('simply didn't care' and 'major flaw' – this is vocabulary intended to reveal disappointment and the critical view). The writer uses some language techniques such as listing and alliteration to add to the idea that the film was disappointing: 'dreary, derivative and dire'. This alliteration of depressing 'd's is intended to show how dismal the film was...

(B)

Examiner's advice for improvement

- Include more direct evidence – embedding quotes into the body of the response.
- Add more detailed analysis of specific effects – say a lot about a little.
- The review often uses irony – go into detail about how this ironic tone is created.

Now, read the second response to this question. The student has adapted their work, taking into account the suggestions for improvement.

The writer of this review uses the first sentence to create a sense of expectation in the reader: we are not immediately sure whether the review will be positive or negative. The use of 'hype' might be thought critical, but being 'the hero of the hour' offers a positive image and suggests there are good things to come. This links with the concept of 'tearful gratitude', the emotive phrase 'festive emotion' and the comforting 'warm with Christmas spirit'. The reader might expect the text to move on to spell out exactly why this is a film to engage and 'warm' us.

However, next comes 'Unfortunately': it opens the sentence, contrasts with what has gone before and introduces a striking tone of disapproval. The positivity has 'evaporated', like something temporary, disappearing like steam.

Even within the synopsis of the story, the use of apostrophes around 'proper' and 'saving' gives an ironic effect, as the writer mocks the film's attempt to employ traditional and stereotypical ideas, whilst the '(sniff sniff)' makes the reaction seem artificial and forced, undermining the message of the film and amusing the reader...

(A)

Task

Write a response to the Monkey Island game review, commenting on how the writer has used language to express their point of view.

Reading web pages

Key points

- Web pages are designed to provide, and navigate through, a lot of information.

- Web pages are usually designed according to specific conventions.

- In your exam you may be asked to comment on the language used, the organisation or the presentational features of the web page.

Reading a web page

- Reading web pages requires different kinds of reading skills to printed text. You are reading quickly, often skimming and scanning in order to find specific information on the page straight away. A web page uses particular layout conventions and presentational features to help you do this.

- Also, a web page has to be immediately appealing and accessible otherwise the reader will just skip to another site. Designers and writers take this into account when they create web pages.

Look at the different features and devices used on this web page.

Photograph is appealing and eye-catching

Central images use colour to suggest sand and sun. The rhinoceros suggests exotic locations

Telephone number in a prominent position

Prominent 'Quick search' panel research a trip

Orange used to highlight Special offer and 'pay later' messages

Lists of the range of experiences the company provides, suggesting it has something for everyone

Bookmarks to a range of social networking sites and links to other areas of site

Live links picked out in thematic colours to enable the reader to find the relevant information easily

Nine separate task bars at the top to help easy navigation

Red used to highlight important information as well as linking to the company logo

Destinations map offers a different way to access specific information

Photographs highlight the experiences on offer

Pink highlighted text shows more active links.

Here is one student's analysis of this web page. They have responded to the question:

How does this web page use presentational features to attract readers?

This is a successful web page, designed to interest those considering taking a gap year and tempt those who had not previously considered taking one. The top picture looks breathtaking and will attract any potential traveller; the smaller pictures are varied and look exciting with the photographs of places, people and adventurous activities. These photos and captions such as 'Volunteer Work' and 'Adventure Travel' convey the range of exciting experiences on offer with this company, and the people look relaxed and as if they are having a really worthwhile experience.

The organisation of the text is clear and demands attention; the six navigation panels are clear and accessible, drawing the eye towards the whole range of experiences on offer such as volunteer work, travel and adventure. The 'Quick search' panel and Destinations map with active links provide other routes to access specific information from the site, for example for those wanting to travel to a particular place.

The picture of the rhino suggests danger and exotic locations, highlighting the interest and drama on offer with a gap year from this company. The page uses colour to link to the different experiences; for example the green of adventure is linked to the top navigation bar and to the green information links so that any reader can quickly navigate around the page to find what they need. The company invites readers in with repetition of 'Buy now, pay later' highlighted in orange, and the 'book now' message is repeated, highlighted in red to draw the eye which is because it is, as far as the company is concerned, one of the most important messages to get across to the reader.

A

Good points

- There is clear analysis of the effects achieved from particular presentational and organisational features in relation to the site's purpose and audience.
- Precise details and textual references are offered in support of the analysis.

Read the following example of a web page from the World Wildlife Fund's website.

Clear, recognisable logo used at the top of the home page, stands out from other colours used on the page

Interactive globe graphic suggests that the charity's work is international

Main colours are earthy and natural browns and greens and blues, linking to the central purpose of the charity

Main photos work together with the two dates, making message about climate change ultra clear

Succinct text summarising latest news on key issues

Provides more detail of what the site offers

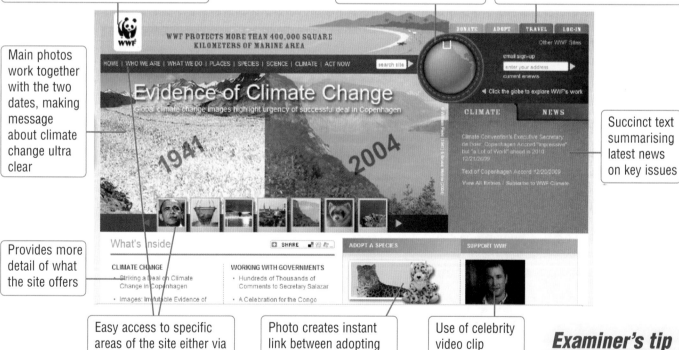

Easy access to specific areas of the site either via navigation bar or thumbnail images

Photo creates instant link between adopting an animal and receiving a gift for doing so

Use of celebrity video clip reinforcing the charity's appeal

Examiner's tip

When 'reading', do not think just about the actual words. Reading means 'de-coding' and can include the effect of pictures, fonts, colour, logos – in fact, any design feature can contribute to your overall 'reading' of a text.

Task

Using the annotation boxes to guide you, comment on the way presentational features have been used to appeal to the readers of the WWF web page.

Reading information texts

Key points

- Texts whose main **purpose** is to provide **information** come in a wide variety of **forms**: leaflets, web pages, instructional texts such as DIY guides or recipes, guide books and reference texts or texts giving hints or advice.

- The language of an information text is usually impersonal, quite direct and clearly organised.

- Most information texts will have a **target audience** in mind, even if it is a 'general adult' audience. Target audiences can be categorised by age, background, gender, interests, location, beliefs and many other factors.

REMEMBER

Target audience is the term used to describe the group of people the text is written for and designed to be read by.

Information texts

- Information texts, like the one below, often use **subheadings** or other **clear organisational features** to guide the reader easily through the material.

Read the following information text from the Chester Zoo website and the annotations. Find three pieces of information intended to suggest that elephants have some almost human features.

Asian Elephants

Asian Elephants are smaller than African elephants and have much smaller ears. Their backs are also more rounded than the African elephant and they have an extra toenail on each foot – four per foot in all. The tusks, which are specially adapted incisor teeth, are only found on males, although some males, especially in Sri Lanka, have no tusks. They have stout bodies and thick legs, with a thick, wrinkled, dry skin, grey to brownish in colour. The long sensitive trunk comprises of the nose and upper lip and is used to feed, plucking at grasses and passing them into the mouth. They also use the trunk to wash with and to vocalise. The trunk has a single prehensile 'finger' at its tip, unlike African elephants which have two.

Uses the present tense

Lots of information in the form of facts about Asian elephants

What do they eat?
Chiefly grasses, but also scrub and bark, fig leaves and some fruit. They have also been known to eat banana or rice crops if they roam into plantation areas. They eat an average of 150kg of vegetation a day and drink 80 to 100 litres of water a day.

Subheadings divide the material, making it easy for the reader to find information

How long do they live?
Up to 70 years

Did you know?
Elephants use infrasound to communicate, which is a sound level with a frequency too low to be detected by the human ear. It is also used by whales, alligators, giraffes, rhinoceros and hippopotamuses.

Direct question, simply worded, suggests a younger audience

List the three features you have found which make the elephants seem to have almost human qualities.

Explain your decision.

Features	Explanation

Giving more than information

- Some information texts combine presenting facts with other purposes, such as giving tips or advice. This has an influence on the language features of these texts.

- Hybrid information-advice texts like these are likely to have a highly specific target audience.

For example, look at the following text from a conservation website:

Who do you think is the target audience for this text and are any pieces of information/advice not particularly appropriate for them?

Preserving a greener world

Rhetorical questions to engage a response

It is time we took the world more seriously. Yes, yes, of course we all know that, but how often do we do anything to change our bad habits or make a difference to what we will leave behind for our children?

Colloquial tone

It's time for each of us to take responsibility: recycle our glass, send back our newspapers, re-use our plastic bags and stop everybody turning up the thermostat! Is it asking too much to expect people to put a brick into the toilet cistern, so they use less water? Why don't we offer people a ride so there are fewer cars on the road? In any group of people, how many have a clockwork mobile phone re-charger? Do we have to have Facebook running all evening? How many people make sure there are no red lights still showing on all their electrical equipment when they go to bed at night?

Listing for effect

Range of advice with information on what we could do to help

Information on how to improve the situation throughout, with advice clear

Humour included

How many have ever considered sharing a bath…?!

> **REMEMBER**
> In your exam, the first question will always ask you to find specific pieces of information. This helps you to focus on some of the key information in the text before you move on to more challenging questions.

Examiner's tip

Practise comparing information texts with other text types, such as persuasive texts, as their contrasting language features mean they might come up in the exam.

Task

How is language used in this text to simultaneously and successfully inform and advise the reader?

Analysing presentational features

- There will be a question in the exam to test your understanding of how the **layout** and **presentational features** are used in media texts.

- You will be expected to write about what the writer is hoping to achieve, and how particular presentational features have been used to support the writer's **purpose**.

Examiner's tip

For top grades, always use the correct terms for any presentational features. Even more importantly, always explain the intended effect of the device on the reader. Keep asking yourself while reading; 'why has this device been used? What is the effect?'

REMEMBER

Skilful 'reading' is about much more than simply 'reading the words'. Our eyes draw meaning from everything on the page, not just the text. Good designers use this to their advantage. In your exam answer it is your job to analyse the presentational features they use.

Identifying the features

- You need to be clear that **layout** means the way the text has been designed, or organised on the page whereas **presentational features** are individual aspects used to create the layout, such as pictures, headlines and use of colour.

- When you comment on presentational features you need to explain how they work with each other to create an overall effect, not just what effect they have individually, for example choice of colours, fonts, images and language of text.

Here are some key presentational features used in media texts to refer to in your answers:

Headline	the main heading in a newspaper story, designed to draw the reader's attention
Strapline	a second, introductory headline, below the main one, adds more information to the headline
Subheading	often used to summarise sections of the text or break it up into smaller sections, allowing the reader to skim over the whole text and see the overall point
Font	style and colour can vary throughout a text. Often it is possible to draw conclusions from the choice of colour-scheme or font style
Capitals	capitals (used other than as standard) are often used to stress and reinforce particular words or phrases
Caption	the text under a photograph or diagram which explains it
Standfirst	the introductory paragraph in an article or report, which could be in bold print or with the first word capitalised
Pull-quote	a quotation which is lifted from the article and set apart, in larger or bold type
Bold, italics, underline	different ways of making certain words stand out
Slogan	a memorable word or phrase, designed to create interest
Logo	emblem to represent a product or company
Photographs and graphics	used to add depth to the story or more information.

Analysing how features have been used

If you just describe what is on the page you will be working at a simple level. Instead, you should aim to say **why** the text has been designed in a particular way – what **effect** the writer is hoping to achieve.

Read the article opposite.

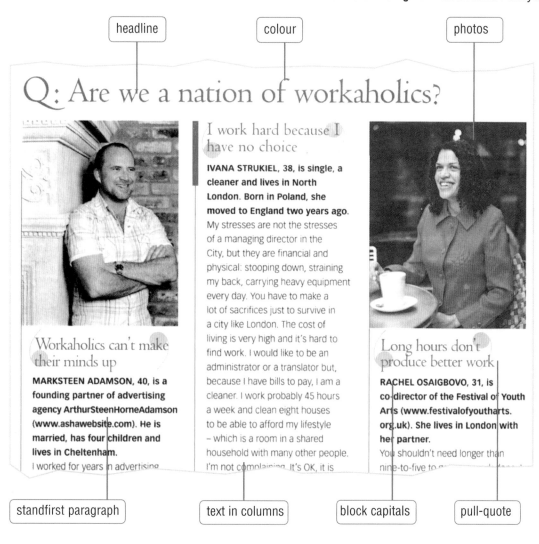

headline

colour

photos

Q: Are we a nation of workaholics?

I work hard because I have no choice

IVANA STRUKIEL, 38, is single, a cleaner and lives in North London. Born in Poland, she moved to England two years ago. My stresses are not the stresses of a managing director in the City, but they are financial and physical: stooping down, straining my back, carrying heavy equipment every day. You have to make a lot of sacrifices just to survive in a city like London. The cost of living is very high and it's hard to find work. I would like to be an administrator or a translator but, because I have bills to pay, I am a cleaner. I work probably 45 hours a week and clean eight houses to be able to afford my lifestyle – which is a room in a shared household with many other people. I'm not complaining. It's OK, it is

Workaholics can't make their minds up

MARKSTEEN ADAMSON, 40, is a founding partner of advertising agency ArthurSteenHorneAdamson (www.ashawebsite.com). He is married, has four children and lives in Cheltenham.
I worked for years in advertising

Long hours don't produce better work

RACHEL OSAIGBOVO, 31, is co-director of the Festival of Youth Arts (www.festivalofyoutharts. org.uk). She lives in London with her partner.
You shouldn't need longer than nine-to-five to get

standfirst paragraph

text in columns

block capitals

pull-quote

Here is how one student commented on the way presentational features are used in the article:

The article is designed neatly in three columns because it gives three different answers to the question posed in the headline. Two of the accounts are livened up with photos – the people are happy, and this reflects their points of view. Also, we home in on 'real people'. A glance at them makes them look 'ordinary' and approachable – so we might be more inclined to accept their views. The first paragraph of each account is in bold, to mark that it is an introduction, and the person's name is in block capitals to make it stand out. We are drawn to the fact that the names are very different (Adamson, Strukiel, Osaigbovo), so we register that they might have different backgrounds. We feel we are getting a spread of opinions. The pull-quotes summarise the key points that the interviewees are making; they are bigger because they 'answer' the question posed in the headline. The 'question and answer' format tries to simplify the information for the reader, whilst the use of orange gives a positive effect – which ties in, successfully, with the smiles of the people pictured.

(A)

Good points

- The different presentational features are identified, including the overall design.
- The effect of the features is explained.
- There is some evaluation of how effective the design is.

Examiner's tip

If you can evaluate how effective the layout or presentational features are, you will gain a higher mark. Don't be afraid to give your opinion but always explain it!

Task

Choose an article from your favourite magazine. Write about the presentational features used, explaining their effect. Give your evaluation of the effectiveness of the overall design.

Dealing with inference

Key points

- One of the questions in the exam will ask you to show you can **read between the lines** or **infer** meaning from a text. Good readers know that 'understanding' a text works on more than one level. There is the **literal** level of meaning – what is actually stated – but often you automatically 'read between the lines' – *inferring* meaning. Skilful readers use **inference**.

- You can **infer** meaning in a variety of ways: from the **language** chosen, the structure and organisation of the text, the pictures and from other presentational features.

REMEMBER

The reader **infers** meaning from the text but the writer **implies** it. Use both terms accurately when writing about inference.

Inferring meaning from language

- There are a variety of ways in which language can be used to infer meaning other than the surface meaning. One of the techniques to look for is **irony** – when what is being literally *said* is different to what is actually *meant*. Irony can be created by:

  - **Rhetorical techniques** – rhetorical questions, the repetition of words and phrases: *'Can we allow ourselves to continue with the mindless, senseless destruction of the earth's precious natural resources?'*

  - **Exaggeration and understatement** – making a point seem ridiculous either by using larger-than-life detail or by underplaying it. *'Of course we all know for a fact that every single teenager in the country, if not the world, is a hoodie-wearing, knife-wielding thug.'*

  - **Quotations** – for example, quoting someone to show it is clear that we disagree with them or to question their truthfulness: *The Minister said that 'he had done nothing at all wrong' by claiming £175,000 on his expenses for a new lawnmower.*

Using humour

- Often we infer meaning as much by what is **not** said as by what **is** said.

Read the following text, which is an extract from journalist Bill Bryson's *Notes from a Big Country*. Use the annotations to help you identify what is not said!

> People sometimes ask me. 'What is the difference between baseball and cricket?'
>
> The answer is simple. Both are games of great skill involving balls and bats, but with this crucial difference: baseball is exciting and when you go home at the end of the day you know who won.
>
> I'm joking, of course. Cricket is a wonderful game, full of deliciously scattered micro-moments of real action. If a doctor ever instructs me to take a complete rest and not get over-excited, I shall become a fan at once. In the meantime, however, I hope you will understand when I tell you that my heart belongs to baseball.

Annotations:
- Implying that cricket is hard to understand
- Implying that cricket is not exciting to watch
- Implies that cricket is boring
- Uses understatement to imply there is very little action

Analysing inference

- Of course inference is not always for humorous effect.

This is an article from *The Times* by the journalist, Libby Purves. She is writing about the rate of changes to the education system.

Annotations:
- Suggests that children were happier when their education was not being interfered with
- Use of the word 'scored' links with the idea of 'assessment' later on
- Description suggests that the Government papers have no importance or meaning
- Simile used to suggest humour and mockery of the work of the politicians

Pupils Will Never Learn Unless We Make It Fun

In their seven cheerful years of primary school – mostly in a small village – my children got through three Secretaries of State for Education. If they had been born 20 years later they could have scored four in even fewer years. And seen the Education Ministry itself bisected. In UK education policy, everything accelerates except improvement.

Report follows review, white papers flutter weightlessly down as if from some celestial pillow fight, government initiatives sprout like mushrooms round a cow-pat. Infants who once footled around happily with Play-Doh, songs and stories are now formally assessed against 69 government targets, to the loud dismay of experts in child development.

Here is how one student has responded to the question:

What does the writer of this article want us to think and how is the meaning made clear to the reader?

Libby Purves wants us to think there have been too many changes in education and too many education secretaries. She implies that education secretaries are not around long enough to get to grips with the problems in education, so there are rapid and regular changes but no improvement: 'everything accelerates except improvement'.

She suggests that there are too many reports and reviews. She mocks them, saying they 'flutter weightlessly down as if from a great height'. This makes them sound lightweight and meaningless. 'Flutter' implies they are flimsy and more like birds than valuable documents. She also says they come as if 'from some celestial pillow fight': they are not serious, therefore, but come as if from gods playing in heaven - not important, therefore. There is also the implication that ministers have their heads in the clouds and are far removed from normal people and their concerns. She says government initiatives 'sprout like mushrooms round a cow-pat.' They sound numerous, are like fungus and come from manure - hardly pleasant images.

Finally, she offers the opinion that experts in child development, who should know about children and their needs, are 'dismayed' by the 69 government targets...

Annotations:
- Summarises some views
- Identifies inference
- Aware of attitude
- Extended analysis
- Retains focus on question
- Covers the whole text

A*

Inferring meaning from presentational features

- Images and the layout of text items can imply meaning in the same way that language does.

Take a careful look at this picture, which is part of an advertising campaign for PETA, an American organisation which campaigns for cruelty-free fashion.

Task

How does this photograph help the campaign organisers get their message across to their readers? Consider:
- possible meanings for the slogan 'fur is dead'
- the colours and fonts used for the slogan and 'Made in the USA'
- how the slogan relates to the image of the dog.

Examiner's tip

Inferring meaning is a high-level skill and demonstrates your ability to 'read between the lines' and work at a more sophisticated level. For example, in a text which includes images, paying attention to the messages implied by these and relating them to the messages implied by the text itself will gain you higher marks.

Analysing language

Key points

- One question in the exam will always focus on **comparing the language** in two of the three texts.

- Having a clear understanding of the kinds of things to cover when analysing language will help you tackle this type of question with confidence and skill.

- Once you have scanned the text and identified its form, audience and purpose, concentrate on its prominent **language features**.

Examiner's tip

Focus on elements in the text which are typical of it or its form, such as use of short sentences or touches of humour for a particular effect.

REMEMBER

- There is no need write about absolutely everything in the text – you simply won't have time.

- It is always better to write 'a lot about a little' rather than 'a little about a lot'.

Key language features

You will be asked to compare language in two texts. These language features might include:

- Sentence and paragraph types
- Significant vocabulary
- Punctuation
- Imagery (similes, metaphors and personification) and other linguistic devices
- The style of the language

Sentences and paragraphs

- Look out for the **length of sentences** and how they are **constructed**. Writers achieve a huge range of effects by varying use of the following:

  - **Short sentences** can suggest speed or excitement, e.g.

    He ran forward. The ball fell at his feet. He shot.

    They can also indicate surprise or despair, e.g.

    Her inspiration stopped. Her career ended.

    Long sentences can indicate calm, e.g.

    The sergeant reported that right along the river, teams of men and women were resting at last and preparing to return to their headquarters for a much-needed break.

    Or they can build to a climax, e.g.

    The crowds gasped as the top of the mountain blew away, clouds of ash shot hundreds of feet into the sky and rivers of lava, terrifying in the early daw, shot upwards, then cascaded down into the valley.

- **Paragraphs**, too, can create different effects:

  - Very **short paragraphs** can be used to attract the reader's attention, to pick out the main details in an article or to offer a 'punchy' idea. Popular newspaper articles often have short paragraphs so that they can be read more easily.

  - **Longer paragraphs** can provide more detail and analysis. Articles in more serious newspapers often have longer paragraphs

Significant vocabulary

- The kinds of words used in a text can also tell you a lot about the **purpose** of the text:

  - **Imperative verbs** such as 'follow' and 'begin' suggest **instructional** or **advisory** writing.

  - **Connectives** like 'since' and 'because' are typical of **explanatory** writing that because these connectives link ideas together.

  - Connectives such as 'however', 'nevertheless' and 'indeed' tend to be used in **persuasive** or **argumentative writing** where a point of view is being expressed.

- The words or **vocabulary** chosen can also tell you about the **audience** for a text:

  - **More complex vocabulary** indicates that the text is aimed at a more intelligent readership

  - A text containing **specialist vocabulary**, for instance scientific vocabulary, will be aimed at those with a special interest in that area.

  - A text including **slang** and **colloquialisms** could indicate a teenage target audience.

Punctuation

The punctuation of texts can clearly indicate the writer's intention, as in these headlines:

TEENAGER 'TORTURED TO DEATH'

The inverted commas indicate it may not have happened, but show that someone has offered that opinion.

Let's focus on ... improving your home

This ellipsis (…) indicates that there are many things we could do. An ellipsis can also end a sentence leaving the conclusion to our imagination.

HOLLY HITS OUT!!

The double exclamation mark is to attract attention and suggest excitement, humour or even surprise.

Examiner's tip
When considering the audience for a text, take note of the way punctuation has been used in the body of the writing. For example, more sophisticated punctuation, like example semi-colons and colons, are normally used in more complex sentences – making them more likely to appear in texts aimed at a more educated reader.

Similes, metaphors and linguistic techniques

You will be familiar with writing about **simile**, **metaphor**, **alliteration** and **onomatopoeia** from working on poetry but writers also use these techniques in non-fiction texts.

This extract from an autobiography includes effective examples of all of them.

They held us in a small room. We felt like condemned men and smelt like battery hens. We had no idea of the day or the time and dreaded the dull echoes of sharp boots and the crank of the lock on the door. It was an eternity of torture…

similes

alliteration

onomatopoeia

metaphor

One student analysed the use of language in the extract like this:

The writer makes their captivity vivid by using a series of linguistic devices. First, two similes are used: to stress their desperate situation ('like condemned men') and the inhuman conditions in which they were kept ('smelt like battery hens'). Deadly 'd's introduce alliteration as their jailors approach – 'dreaded the dull…' – and then there is onomatopoeia which captures the sound as the key turns and their horrors are about to begin again: 'crank'. The primitive sound helps us understand their situation. Finally, the metaphor 'eternity of torture' is used to express how long and painful it must have seemed to them at the time.

Good points
- The analysis focuses on precise aspects of language, rather than generalising.
- Linguistic devices are discussed, not just identified.
- There is an awareness of how the effects are linked to create an overall impression.

Style

- A text may be **formal** and written in standard English or **informal** if the audience would respond more readily to that style (for example, in some letters, articles or advertisements).

- You need to start by identifying the **essential features** of each text. For example, if you were asked to compare a formal and an informal text, you might write:

The first text is formal, using sentences like 'The government has taken a stance which...' while the second text is less formal and targets drug users; 'Get real...'.

Stylistic techniques or linguistic features

- A variety of stylistic techniques may be used, depending on whether a text is devised to inform, explain, persuade, advise, argue, review or comment. For instance:
  - **rhetoric**, especially **rhetorical questions**, used for added impact:

    Can this be acceptable?
  - **emotive language**, which touches the readers' feelings:

    They are tiny and cold and they are starving.
  - **irony** (subtle mockery):

    I have always thought it is a good idea to make the poor starve...
  - **exaggeration**:

    The Royal Family eats nothing but caviar for breakfast.
  - **contrast**:

    The seabirds sing, while the fishermen starve.
  - **colloquial language**, as if people are chatting:

    If you want to pull, you have to impress the lads.
  - **ambiguity**, where there can be more than one interpretation:

    Bird watching is a really exciting hobby.
  - **inference**, where things are suggested rather than clearly stated:

    He met the girl of his dreams. He didn't come home that night.
  - **examples, quotations or anecdotes**, giving credibility to what is written:

    Only yesterday, a shop assistant said to me...
  - **humour**, to get the audience on the side of the writer:

    There was more life in my popcorn than in this film.
  - **lists**, for emphasis:

    She packed the potatoes on top of the bananas, the bananas on top of the tomatoes and the tomatoes on top of the eggs.

This extract from a newspaper article is short, but uses several of the techniques above.

> Who can fail to notice the Prime Minister's excellent track record when it comes to improving all areas of British life?
>
> We all recognise that approach which claims 'I'm a man o' the people', and don't the people just love him? Especially those paying taxes they can't afford, waiting in traffic that never moves, facing ever-mounting debt and an impoverished old age...

Here is what one student wrote about what the writer is suggesting:

The writer begins with apparent irony. The rhetorical question asks the reader to consider the PM's record, and suggests the track record may not be so good. Later, there is the implication that the people might not actually love him, while the colloquial 'I'm a man o' the people' might be poking fun at him, implying that his 'approach' is a pretence which 'we all recognise'. Then there is a list of problems, which form a critical commentary on the government. It uses emotive detail ('they can't afford') and exaggeration ('traffic that never moves') as it moves to a cutting climax, with the elderly 'facing ... an impoverished old age.'

Good points

- Language is analysed to explain the style.
- The writer's point of view is interpreted through the detail.
- Quotations are used effectively to support the points being made.

Task

This extract comes from *Take a Break* magazine.
- Comment on the ways in which the writer has used language features for effect in this text.
- Give some examples and explain the intended effects on the reader.

Gaze and laze

Take a break where the sun always shines

All eyes turn to the sea on this 30-mile stretch of Italy's western shore, considered one of the most beautiful coastlines in the world, where Campania gazes out into the Tyrrhenian reaches of the Mediterranean.

It takes in Sorrento, Positano, Salerno and Amalfi – which gives it the local name *Costiera Amalfitana* – and even extends into the sea.

Sitting off the coast like a satellite at the end of the peninsula, the island of Capri is just a 20-minute cruise away from Sorrento. Fram the port of Marina Grande it's a short ride by funicular railway to the labyrinth of narrow alleyways that make up Capri town.

But it is at Anacapri, the island's second town, that you'll find Capri's very own Garden of Eden, where mythological statues sit like sentinels surveying the deep blue waters. Or where classically draped figures from Italy's past appear to hold command over clouds fleeing across the contrasting blue of the sky.

Comparing language

Key points

- One question in Section A of your exam will ask you to **compare language** in two of the three texts you have been given.

- One text will be identified for you from the three available. You are allowed to **choose the other text** that you want to compare with this one.

- This question will be worth **double the marks** of the other three questions so you will need to be prepared to give more time to this question.

Comparing language

- Your examiners are looking at your work to see if you can **collate material from different sources**, making **comparisons and cross-references** between the two texts you are being asked to compare, providing **evidence** to support your points.

- When you compare language, consider:
  - the levels of difficulty, for example between a text written for an adult audience and one written for younger people
  - the different tones, for example between a light-hearted, humorous text and a serious text
  - the different kinds of language features required for different purposes, for example an account of a holiday for a brochure when compared to a diary account of a visit to that destination.

Have a look at the question below.

> **Compare the ways in which language is used for effect in Source 2 with the way it is used in one of the other texts. Give some examples and explain what the effects are.**

This is the 'key word' in the question – the most important instruction

Notice how the question is specifically asking you to use direct evidence and comment on the effectiveness

This means 'effect on the reader' – what it makes the reader think or how the reader might react to it

- Remember your key approach to any non-fiction text:
  Decide how the writer has used **language** to meet the needs of the form, purpose and audience. Think about:
  - sentences and paragraphs
  - significant vocabulary
  - punctuation
  - imagery and linguistic features.

REMEMBER

Showing your ability to analyse and compare how **both** texts have been written – *what* has been done and *why* – will get you the marks.

Making clear cross-references

- The vital element is to compare the texts. It is not enough to write an analysis of one, then an analysis of the other. In fact, if you do this you may end up repeating material from your other answers!

- Here are two possible ways to construct a comparative response:

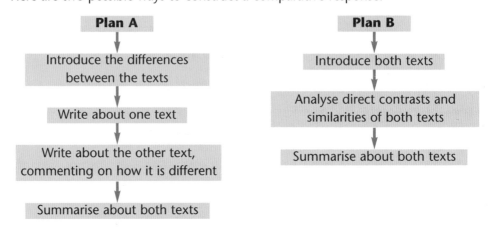

Plan A
Introduce the differences between the texts
Write about one text
Write about the other text, commenting on how it is different
Summarise about both texts

Plan B
Introduce both texts
Analyse direct contrasts and similarities of both texts
Summarise about both texts

- In making reference to the texts, you must link one to the other clearly. Notice how the second response below does this successfully, while the first one simply refers to each text in turn.

The first text uses language which is suitable for younger people, including slang and colloquialisms. The second text targets parents, so the tone is advisory and goes into the kinds of details they might appreciate.

C

> Second text dealt with in separate sentence. No attempt to actively contrast the texts

. The first text encourages teenagers to be more healthy, using catchy appeals which would suit younger people, like 'Betta for yer'; and exclamation marks to make it seem more exciting. In contrast, the second text is formal and clearly produced for a more mature audience. The language is impersonal: 'It is better to send a piece of fruit for break time...'

A

> Identifies evidence from the text that appeals to audience and the effect of this

> Uses a connective to link the texts by contrasting them

Comparative introductions and conclusions

- A focused response is important from the start to the finish. Your introduction and conclusion should work just as hard as the rest of your response in answering the question. Remember 'Every Word Counts' in this type of exam.

Have a look at this **introduction**. It is from a response to a question asking for a comparison of the ways in which language has been used to appeal to the target audience.

Examiner's tip

The best marks are achieved by making detailed comparisons, using quotations from both texts in support.

The two texts deal with a similar purpose but use language in very different ways. The leaflet is aimed at primary school children and uses vocabulary appropriate for that age group: they might not be interested in healthy eating, but they will love the nursery-rhyme-style approach. They will also respond well to the shorter sentences and simple punctuation. The article is different. It seems almost academic as it analyses eating habits and their outcomes, using words like 'pulmonary thrombosis' and 'desensitisation', which are aimed at a more mature and educated audience...

> Straightforward introduction

> Audience and linguistic approach

> Clear comparison which will lead in to next paragraph

The **conclusion** need not be long, but it should demonstrate your ability to sum up your ideas and that you are still clearly focused on the question.

Both texts are effective, but each for its own audience. The leaflet hopes children will 'Be a better boy or girl', stressing healthiness through humour and the use of rhyme and never forgetting its readers are so young; whilst the article's dense text and polysyllabic language will probably have a positive impact on broadsheet readers.

> Draws to conclusion

> Generalises on language style

A

> Final comparison

- Comparative connectives are extremely useful when it comes to this type of question. Here are some of the most useful ones.

Similarly	In contrast	While the first text
Just as	Whereas	The second text
Likewise	On the other hand	When we turn to
Also	But	In comparison
So	However	The second text, though

Use these connectives to link ideas about both texts within and between paragraphs.

As you compare, have a list of key questions in your head:

- Are there different target audiences for these texts? How do I know?
- Is there a difference in the difficulty of the language? Vocabulary, sentences, paragraphs?
- Is the type of language different? Descriptive or informative, for instance?
- What do I notice about any differences in tone between the two texts? Why is it there?

Practising comparison

Read the following texts, which are both about the way elderly people are viewed by our society. Then have a look at the following question:

Compare the ways in which these two texts use language to appeal to their audiences.

Item 1

This extract is from a blog written by a man living in Manchester.

> I think it's time some people got their head around the fact that most of the kids out there are as good as kids have always been and no worse than the worst that have gone before them. Face it, most people just want to moan, and who better to moan about than children who never have a chance to answer back?
>
> I caught two of my neighbours' youngest kids in my back garden last week. I was surprised and they suddenly looked terrified. Frozen. Rabbits caught in the headlights. All that. I certainly didn't expect to find them there. I was going to start shouting – I was certain they were after my apples – but went for a quieter: 'What are you two doing here?' They looked relieved.
>
> 'Bird...,' the little boy muttered. 'It's hurt... Bird... Look!'
>
> Sure enough, there was a bird with a broken wing and two little boys setting about rescuing it. That is what boys have always done. In this case, their efforts to bandage it with a football sock were not ideal, but you couldn't fault their motives.
>
> We should cut kids like these some slack. They can only be as good as we let them be. So isn't it time we just let them be?

Item 2

This newspaper article focuses on the way one elderly person feels about where they live.

A pensioner's life made a misery by 'young vandals'

Frank Blackburn, 78, who lives on the Albany Estates, has been a prisoner in his house each evening for over a year. Groups of children, many as young as 7 or 8, have made him fear for his life and the safety of his property.

'They gather every night,' says Frank. 'The police don't do anything about it.'

Stones have been thrown through his windows, excrement has been pushed through his letter box and he cannot sleep. Gangs roam the area, shouting and drinking. Other older residents are just as fearful.

A police spokesman said they are currently dealing with the matter.

Task

Using Item 1 and Item 2, answer the question opposite in as much detail as you can. Remember to:

- make cross-references between the texts
- use detailed evidence from both the texts
- focus on the language that has been used.

Examiner's tip

People often think that comparing texts means 'finding similarities' or 'things in common'. In fact, it is often more useful to think about 'differences' rather than similarities!

How to tackle the exam

What to do with the exam paper

1 Spend 5 minutes skim reading the three texts. Decide what they are about.

2 Read through the questions.

3 Focus on Question 1: underline the important words in the question, then spend 10 minutes answering it.

4 Do exactly the same for Question 2 and Question 3.

5 When you get to Question 4, spend 20 minutes on it, because it is worth twice as many marks as the others.

These timings reflect the number of marks available; and you will have enough spare time at the end to check through and improve your work.

Examiner's tip

If you read the questions before you read the texts, this can save you time because you are reading *purposefully* – you already know what you should be looking for as you read.

Types of questions

- You will be asked **one** question on **each of the three** texts. The **fourth question** requires you to compare two of the texts.

- The questions will test your ability to:
  - find information (this is **information retrieval**)   (8 marks)
  - write about **presentational features**   (8 marks)
  - analyse what is being **suggested** or **inferred**   (8 marks)
  - **compare** how **language** is used in two texts   (16 marks)

When you read the sample questions below, highlight the key words in each question. This will help you focus on exactly what you have to do.

Read **Source 1**, the magazine article called *The Last Polar Bear* by Paul Parry.

1 What do you learn from Paul Parry's magazine article about where he has been and what he has been doing?   *(8 marks)*

> This question wants you to show that you have understood the text and can identify some evidence to demonstrate your understanding of the content.

Now read **Source 2**, the leaflet called *Our Shrinking Planet* by the conservation society Save the Earth.

2 How does the presentation of the leaflet add to the effectiveness of the overall text?   *(8 marks)*

> This question wants some comments on how the leaflet has been presented, so you are being asked for your evaluations here. The question focuses of presentation, not language.

Now read **Source 3**, *The Journey Home*, which is an extract from a travel book by Martina Fellows.

3 What are some of the thoughts and feelings that Martina Fellows has on her journey?   *(8 marks)*

> This question is asking you to infer from the text or read between the lines and show understanding of what is being suggested.

Now you need to refer to **Source 3**, *The Journey Home*, and *either* **Source 1** or **Source 2**. You are going to compare the texts, one of which you have chosen.

4 Compare the ways in which language is used for effect in the two texts. Give some examples and explain what the effects are. *(16 marks)*

> This question requires more evidence that you can read and understand and find supporting evidence - this time by comparing the language used in two texts.

See pages 46–49 for more on the technique of comparing texts.

Task

Below you will find four questions which are typical of the ones you will find in Section A of your exam.

1 Read **Source 1**, the article *The Flight of the Eagles* by Helen Dunham.
  What do you learn about how eagles live from reading this article? *(8 marks)*

2 Now read **Source 2**, the magazine article and the picture that goes with it called *Our Life in Their Hands* by Simon Middleton.
  How are the headlines and photograph intended to affect the reader? *(8 marks)*

3 Read **Source 3**, the text *One Boy's Journey*, which is an extract from an autobiography.
  What impression do you get of the forest? *(8 marks)*

4 Now you need to refer to **Source 3**, *One Boy's Journey* and either **Source 1** or **Source 2**.
  You are going to compare two texts, one of which you have chosen.
  Compare the way language is used in these two texts.
  You need to give some examples and explain what the effects are. *(16 marks)*

Using a grid like the one below, tick which Assessment Objectives you think are being covered in each of the four questions.

Assessment objective	Question 1	Question 2	Question 3	Question 4
Read and understand texts				
Select material appropriate to purpose				
Collate material from different sources				
Make comparisons and cross references as appropriate				
Explain and evaluate how writers use linguistic and grammatical features to achieve effects and engage and influence the reader				
Explain and evaluate how writers use structural and presentational features to achieve effects and engage and influence the reader				
Support comments with detailed textual references				

Raising your grade

Key points

- One of the questions in Section B of Paper 2 lets you **write to describe**.

- You will probably have to describe a **person or place**.

- When writing to describe, you should:
  - describe what you know
  - plan and structure the description
  - write an effective introduction and conclusion
  - use your five senses, as appropriate
  - go into detail.

Answer all parts of the question

- Read the question carefully and answer it exactly.

- If the question asks you to comment on only part of a text then don't comment on all of it.

- If it asks you to comment on the language then don't comment on the presentational features.

- If bullet point 'prompts' are provided, use them to structure your answer.

Show your overall understanding of the text

- Make sure you refer to the **purpose** of the text, as this demonstrates your understanding of why it has been written or presented in the way that it has, e.g.

  The article describes prisons as 'waste-paper baskets' and 'cess pits'. These are negative and unpleasant images <u>which reinforce the writer's argument that prisons should be abolished</u>.

- Make sure you refer to the **audience** of the text as well. This demonstrates your appreciation of how the language has been chosen to appeal to a particular group of people, e.g.

  <u>The writer is appealing to an intelligent audience so he uses long sentences and quite difficult ideas.</u> The article has a great deal of text, <u>which would not appeal to someone thumbing quickly through the newspaper</u>.

- Give an **overall interpretation** of the text to show that you grasp the text as a whole. Being able to develop a detailed analysis based on clear appreciation of the content will earn high marks.

REMEMBER

- Always **be aware** of the **question type** you are answering.
- Use **direct evidence** from the texts to support your comments.
- **Analyse** and evaluate the **effects of language**, as well as **presentational** and **layout features**, where appropriate.

Show that you can analyse and evaluate, not just comment

- **Analyse** the writer's use of language, presentation and structure. This means explaining in some detail how certain features have been used, e.g.

  The writer suddenly throws in a short sentence, 'No good'. <u>This reflects how the runaway has come to the end of the road and has nowhere to turn. He is stopped short, just as the reader is.</u>

- Read between the lines of the text, so that you are interpreting it. Using **inference** shows a high-level skill but your inferences need to be supported by **direct evidence** to gain high marks, e.g.

  The style of the second extract is softer, <u>which suggests that the writer has some sympathy for the children in the unit</u>. For example, he uses words like…

- **Evaluate how successfully** the writer has used language or presentation. Don't be afraid of giving your opinions, as long as you provide **reasons** for your them, e.g.

  The final paragraph of the article is <u>less successful because</u> we are expecting a full-scale conflict, whereas Martin just backs down and disappears into his office. The writer could have chosen a more powerful example to illustrate bullying in the workplace.

Make good use of the text in your answer

- Remember the advice: **Write a Lot About a Little**.
  In other words, providing **detailed analysis** of the effects of **some features** of the text will get you more marks than making sketchy comments on everything.

- **Choose your quotes carefully**, and try to **integrate or embed** them into your sentences. The quotations should be brief and relevant, e.g.

  Davidson is presented as a rather pathetic figure; he 'waves ineffectually' at the taxi and gets splashed as it passes him.

- **Link texts** together when you are comparing them, e.g.

  The second text also uses strong language, but this time for a different purpose. Whereas the first text is aimed at selling a product, the second is…

How to develop your skills

- Good quality texts are all around you. A great way to prepare for this exam is to read as much as you can. Remember that this exam is assessing your skills with reading a range of non-fiction texts, so your preparation can involve reading magazines, newspapers and web pages. We're not talking about revising by reading a whole novel every week!

- Remember that 'reading' means 'de-coding' in terms of this exam paper. Get yourself into good reading habits by being aware of the purpose, audience and form, of every non-fiction text you read.

- Junk mail can be annoying – however for your exam preparation it's a gift of free resources! Get your hands on every leaflet and free magazine that comes through the letterbox. You could keep a bag by the door just for this purpose; your family will think you've gone re-cycling crazy! Notice how leaflets are organised – look back at *Analysing presentational features* on pages 38–39 to see how images, colour, layout and organisational features are designed specifically to appeal to a range of target audiences.

- Analyse and evaluate when writing about language and presentational features.

Producing non-fiction texts

Section B: Producing non-fiction texts

- **Section B** of your English exam will assess your **Writing skills**.

- You will be asked to complete **two non-fiction writing tasks**. The first task is shorter and is worth 16 marks; the second task is longer and is worth 24 marks.

- You will have an hour to complete this section, and must answer **both** questions.

- You should aim to spend around 25 minutes on the shorter writing task and 35 minutes on the longer writing task. This should include 5 minutes to check your work once you have completed each task.

Examiner's tip

In Section B, one third of the marks are awarded for your use of sentence structure, punctuation and spelling. Be aware of this and leave some time to check your work for accuracy as well as choices of vocabulary and paragraphing.

The tasks

- The **first writing task** will ask you to produce a relatively short non-fiction text, for example, a letter or e-mail. It is likely to be a functional task, such as writing to inform or explain.

- The **second writing task** will ask you to produce a longer non-fiction text in which you have a chance to develop your ideas in more detail, for example, an article for a magazine or newspaper. This might involve writing to argue or persuade.

- You will be given a clear **form**, **purpose** and **audience** for each task. Usually the audience of the text will be mentioned in the task, for example, 'Write an e-mail to a friend to let them know about...' If an audience is not given, you will be writing for the examiner.

- The tasks you are asked to write may have a connection with the theme of the texts you read in Section A, and it may sometimes be possible to use some of the ideas from these texts in your own writing.

REMEMBER

The analytical skills you have developed in your preparation for Section A: Understanding Non-Fiction Texts will come in handy when you need to write non-fiction texts for yourself!

The exam paper – Section B

Higher Tier
Section B: Writing

Answer **both** questions in this section.
You are advised to spend about one hour on this section.
You are advised to spend about 25 minutes on question 5.
You are advised to spend about 35 minutes on question 6.

---

5 Write a letter to a friend who lives in another part of the country, encouraging them to visit and telling them why it would be a good idea.

(16 marks)

6 Statistically, young drivers are more likely to have accidents.

Write an article for a magazine in which you argue for or against the idea that people should not be allowed to drive until they are 21.

(24 marks)

The skills you will be assessed on in Section B

The questions that you will be asked in Section B will also be based on Assessment Objectives. All the Assessment Objectives will be tested in both answers.

Assessment Objective	What this means in detail
Communicate clearly, effectively and imaginatively, using and adapting forms appropriate to task and purpose in ways which engage the reader	This means you must know how to write for a specific **purpose** (e.g. to inform) and in a specific **form** (e.g. a letter), as well as how to target a specific **audience** (e.g. teenagers). You must be able to produce ideas relevant to the task that are appropriate to that particular **form**, **purpose** and **audience**.
pages 76–93	
Selecting vocabulary appropriate to task and purpose in ways which engage the reader	The quality of your vocabulary is often a clear indicator of your overall English ability. If you are deliberately choosing quality **vocabulary** that is appropriate to that particular **form**, **purpose** and **audience**, you will get more marks.
pages 68–69	
Organise information and ideas into structured and sequenced sentences, paragraphs and whole texts	It is not enough to have a number of ideas. The way you **structure** and **organise** them is very important and gets you marks. Having a clear **opening**, a clear sequence of paragraphs for the **main section** and a powerful **conclusion** are ideal. Your ability to construct effective **paragraphs**, and use **sentences** to help your ideas flow more easily, will score highly with your examiners.
pages 60–61 and pages 74–75	
Use a variety of linguistic and structural features to support cohesion and overall coherence	Your ideas should flow together and have an overall sense of purpose and connection. If you have planned ahead, this will show in your writing.
pages 56–59	
Use a range of sentence structures for clarity, purpose and effect, with accurate punctuation and spelling	One third of your writing marks are awarded for **SSPS** – sentence structure, punctuation and spelling. The words 'range' and 'variety' are useful to remember here – the more variety of sentence structures you use, the more interesting your writing is. Using a range of more sophisticated punctuation is one of the signs of a good writer. Accurate spelling of more complex vocabulary is also a way of impressing your examiner.
pages 62–65	

Planning for purpose and audience

Key points

- You have two writing tasks to complete for Section B – Writing. The shorter task is worth 16 marks. The longer task is worth 24 marks.

- You will often be given a **form**, a **purpose** and an **audience** for each task. If a task does not mention a specific audience, it will be for the examiner.

- Planning your response will be useful as it will help you to decide on what ideas to include and the order to arrange them in.

- There are three main stages to planning: **generating ideas**, **structuring** and **developing** your ideas.

Examiner's tip

Don't think that you have to write masses for these tasks. As a rough guide, the shorter writing response might be 1–1½ sides of A4 and the longer writing response might be 1½–2 sides of A4 in length. Don't worry about not writing enough – quality is more important than quantity.

Making good use of your time

- How you use your time during the exam can make all the difference to your final grade. You should be busy and productive throughout the exam – either planning, producing answers or checking your work.

- Every minute counts on this paper and it is really important to use your time effectively.

Shorter writing task

- Ideally, you want to spend around 25 minutes on the shorter writing task, including around five minutes planning and checking.

- The examiner will expect your writing to be around 3–4 paragraphs in length.

- Purposeful, appropriate, well-structured writing is the key to success in the shorter writing task. It is vital to stick to the point and not go 'off-task' – you don't have time.

Longer writing task

- Spend around 35 minutes on the longer writing task, again including at least five minutes checking your work.

- Your response will be longer than the shorter writing task – about 5–6 paragraphs in length. You might write up to two pages if you have average-sized handwriting.

Purpose and audience

The **task** is the question or problem you have been set. It might be, for example, to write part of a travel brochure or to write an article for a newspaper about animal cruelty.

- The **audience** is the reader (or readers) – the people who will read your brochure or article. A specific audience is often called a **target audience**, e.g. people who are looking for a package holiday. A broader audience might also be given, e.g. readers of a newspaper or a magazine.

- The **purpose** is the reason why you are writing your brochure or article. You might be trying to **persuade** your audience to travel to a place you have described or to donate money for a particular cause, or to campaign against animal cruelty. You might just simply want to inform your audience about cruelty to a certain species of animal or inform your audience about global warming.

- The **form** is the type of writing – for example, a brochure, a newspaper article or a letter.

- When you read the task you need to **identify** the audience (reader) the purpose (why am I writing this?) and the form (what am I writing?) in any writing task you are set.

- Think about the kind of **language**, **structure** and **tone** that will fit the form you are writing in.

Here is how one student made notes around a task to identify form, purpose and audience.

Form – a letter: remember to get layout right

Audience – a friend, so tone is informal and fairly chatty

Write a letter to a friend explaining why you would like him or her to join you in a campaign to stop bull fights in Spain.

Purpose – persuading friend to your view on an issue of animal cruelty, so use persuasive techniques

Notes

Form – letter (needs to have an address and greeting)

24 marks – longer writing task – needs to be about one-two sides of A4, so I need to make at least three clear points and develop them

Audience – can be quite informal as it's a letter to someone I know, but will need to be quite serious in tone because of the topic

Purpose – to persuade – need good reasons to persuade my friend to my point of view so that she supports the campaign. Use persuasive techniques like list of three, direct address and rhetorical questions

Identify the form, purpose and audience of these writing tasks:

Write an article for a newspaper persuading more people to adopt a healthy lifestyle.

Write a review for a magazine about a film or TV programme you have seen recently.

Write a letter to your local council which argues for more facilities for families to be made available in your area.

Write a report for your local newspaper which gives advice on how to improve your town centre.

Task

Look at the question below and identify the form, audience and purpose – as in the example above.

Some people believe there should be a curfew from 10pm – 8am for young people to help to stop vandalism. Write a letter to a newspaper arguing either for or against this idea.

(24 marks)

Then sketch out some notes for how to produce your answer, using the example above.

Generating and organising ideas

- Once you understand what you have to write about and who you are writing for, the next thing to do is to get your ideas into some kind of order, or plan.

- The plan will not be marked but the examiner will be able to see that you have thought about the question.

  Your plan needs to:

  - Answer the **main purpose** of the task.

  - Cover the **main things you want to say**.

  - Put your ideas into an **order** or **sequence** to provide a **clear structure** for your writing.

  - Include, if you wish, **key words**, **phrases** or **sentences** you intend to use.

Look again at the idea of a curfew for young people. You can generate ideas by using a spider diagram like the one below.

Of course, you do not need to use a spider diagram like this example. A list or a flow chart would be fine!

Developing your ideas

- The next step is to develop your first ideas by adding a little more detail to your plan.

Here is one student's first attempt at a plan.

1   Why I think a curfew should not happen
2   More reasons why a curfew should not be brought in
3   Some examples of things you'd have to do instead if there was a curfew
4   Sum up my argument against a curfew for teenagers

Examiner's advice for improvement

- This plan isn't very balanced – it only considers one point of view.
- The points are far too vague – they need to be specific.
- It would be better if both viewpoints were represented.
- Although it has a conclusion it also needs a proper introduction.

The improved example below is based on the spider diagram:

1   Introduction – set out as a newspaper letter 'Dear Editor,'.
    Make reason for writing clear.
2   Advantages of a curfew
    – Reduce vandalism in residential areas.
    – Those on streets easily dealt with (fewer of them).
    – Police want curfew.
    – Curfew a success in parts of U.S.A.
3   Disadvatages of a curfew
    – What happens to early morning workers? Newspaper boys/girls?
    – Abuse of young person's freedom – denied their personal choice.
    – Unworkable, not enough police to enforce it – cost of recruiting more.
    – Unfair to the young people who do not vandalise – might lead to resentment.
4   Clear conclusion – summing up my main argument, perhaps adding a new point: make up a quote by Obama.

Good points

- The notes are broken down into sections which, in some cases, might represent the paragraphs in the letter.
- If working on the longer writing task, the student could turn some of the sections into two or more paragraphs.
- The ideas have been ordered logically.
- There is a 'core idea' for each section, with more detailed ideas in note form.

Examiner's tip

You do not need full sentences in your plan or to explain the points fully. The plan is a tool to help **you** to write your response.

Task

- Identify the key elements in this task – form, purpose, audience and important ideas.

> **Write the text of a speech for your year group, in which you attempt to persuade them to show more interest in what school offers out of lesson time. You might want to think about:**
> - **advantages to them from joining activities**
> - **the kinds of activity in which they might become involved.**

- Make a plan of your ideas – a spider diagram or a list – that you could use to answer the question. Choose the type of plan that best helps you to organise your ideas and to write them up in the time available.

REMEMBER

The way you organise your writing will be assessed – so it is important to think of the order of your points to make sure your response is clearly structured.

Structure and paragraphs

Key points

- You will be awarded marks for how well you structure your writing. So organising your work clearly is important.

- A well-structured piece of writing has a clear **introduction**, developed ideas in the **main section**, and a strong **conclusion**.

Examiner's tip

You will have around 25 minutes to respond to the shorter writing task. Ideally your writing should be only three or four paragraphs long, although you may write more if you need to.

Examiner's tip

Varying the length of your paragraphs for effect will gain you marks. A short paragraph, for example, will really stand out from the rest.

Overall structure

- As you plan your response, think carefully about its **overall organisation**, e.g. how will you begin, how many main paragraphs will you need, will your conclusion refer back to the introduction?

- Create a clear structure, using paragraphs accurately and effectively to put across your main points or ideas. Making sure each paragraph has a **topic sentence** will help this.

- Use **connectives** to link paragraphs together, making the shift from one idea to the next smoother.

Organising and linking paragraphs

- Start each new paragraph with a topic sentence. Topic sentences act like sub-headings, signposting the main idea in each paragraph.

- The remaining sentences in the paragraph then develop the idea in more detail, for example:

  The government has its priorities wrong… – you then say why, or what the priorities should be

  There are three steps to perfect happiness… – which you then name and discuss

  Please attend to these safety requirements… – you then list the safety requirements.

- Link your paragraphs using **connectives** – words or phrases that show your reader how your ideas link and work together. Here are some different types of connective:

  time order (chronological), e.g. *At first, Then, Later*

  logical order, e.g. *Therefore, Consequently, As a result*

  contrast, e.g. *On the other hand, In contrast*

  simple ordering of ideas, e.g. *Firstly, Secondly, Finally*

  development of ideas, e.g. *Because of this, Also, What is more, In addition*

Look at how this student organises and varies the length of paragraphs in her response to this writing task:

Explain in a letter to a friend why a holiday was memorable.

Longer paragraph – starts with topic sentence that sets the scene for the detail given in rest of paragraph

Direct address – fits the audience

Short paragraph, making the most important point stand out

Powerful linking word to introduce next paragraph, changing the focus

Sun, sea, sand... sooo boring! In the past, if ever I was asked to choose an ideal holiday, of course I would rave about gorgeous beaches, great sun tans, fabulous night-life – but all that changed after that trip to Wales I told you about. If ever I am asked to choose my ideal holiday now, I'd say 'adventure holiday' every time!

It was the most fantastic experience of my life: life-changing, in fact.

Suddenly, I felt like the kind of person who did, rather than the person who watched. I was the one up to my waist in freezing water, the one hanging off a rope on a cliff-top, the one sailing down the river in a red canoe... me!

Too many exclamation marks – use no more than one or two per response

A

Task

Look through a magazine to find an article at least three paragraphs long. Identify:
- the topic sentences
- the linking words and phrases.

Notice how they help you to follow the stages of the article.

Structuring your writing

- Start by introducing what you intend to discuss in your writing in a way which engages the reader.

- Develop your response in the next three to four paragraphs, expanding your ideas.

- Make sure you **sustain** your viewpoint.

- Keep to the same style throughout.

- End by emphasising your viewpoint. You could also save a new idea for your conclusion.

Here is how one student has planned their paragraphs for the following shorter writing task:

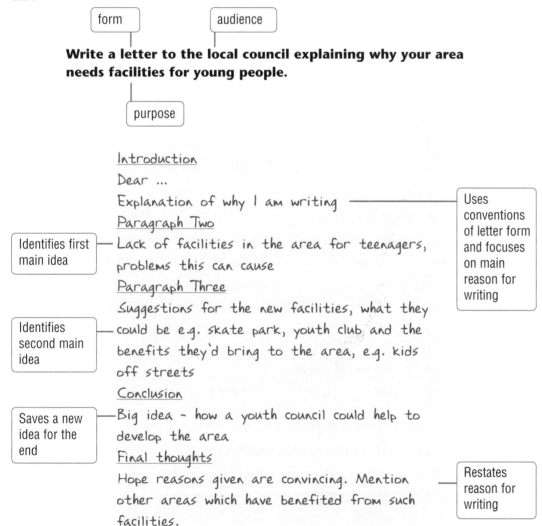

Good points

- The writing is going to be controlled and purposeful, because there is a clear introduction and conclusion.
- The paragraphs follow on from each other very clearly and cover a range of relevant ideas.

Task

Using the example plan above, write the letter to the local council.
Stick to the points outlined for each paragraph.

Sentences

Key points

- The way you use sentences in your writing is one of the things that the examiner will be assessing.

- Sentences should be used to make your meaning clear, but they should also be used deliberately to create the right **tone** for the **form**, the **purpose** and the **audience** of your writing.

- Include a mixture of sentence types: statements, questions, commands and exclamations, as appropriate.

Using a range of sentences

- Sentence variety makes high-quality writing stand out: so make sure you use **simple sentences**, **compound** and **complex sentences** and **questions** or **exclamations** for effect.

- Injecting this variety into your writing will help make it varied, interesting and engaging for the reader.

Simple sentences

- A **simple sentence** contains **one main idea**, with one **subject** and a **verb**. It is a sentence which is complete in itself:

The dog trotted into the room.   *The car moved off quickly.*

- Although simple sentences seem almost childlike in their simplicity, they are used by well-known writers to create effects. Look at this example from *A Farewell to Arms*, by Ernest Hemingway:

   'Mrs Henry has had a haemorrhage … the doctor is with her.'
   'Is it dangerous?'
   'It is very dangerous.' The nurse went into the room and shut the door. I sat outside in the hall. Everything was gone inside of me. I did not think. I could not think. I knew she was going to die.'

Notice how simple sentences have been used here to add to the sense of shock – as if the narrator cannot feel anything. This is an example of simple sentences being used deliberately for effect.

- Simple sentences can be used one after another to **add excitement**:

   He began to run. The man followed. His heart was racing. The man was catching him. He had no choice. He plunged into the icy water.

- Simple sentences can also **build tension**:

   The scratching noise was coming from the left of the room, near the fireplace. Sarah moved closer. She put her ear to the wall. She tapped on the bricks. The fireplace was hollow. Sarah looked desperately around for a tool, something to make a hole in the wall.

- However, short sentences can also **relieve tension**:

   Back and forth he paced, through the living room, the hall, the kitchen, back through the hall again, to and from the window, to and from the letterbox, waiting, pacing, endlessly…

   <u>*And then the knock at the door. At last.*</u>

- A simple sentence after a series of longer sentences can pull the reader up short and **make a quick but powerful point**.

   Time after time, the Government promises to listen to the public sector, to provide funding so desperately needed for our hospitals, our schools, our social services – and time after time those promises are not kept. <u>Something has to change.</u>

Compound and complex sentences

- Complex and compound sentences contain more than one idea, subject and/or verb.

- A **compound sentence** is two simple sentences joined together with either a semi-colon or a conjunction (a joining word). Each part of a compound sentence could stand on its own as a sentence. For example:

    It is now or never. We need to do something today.

becomes

    It is now or never <u>and</u> we need to do something today.

    It is now or never <u>so</u> we need to do something today.

    It is now or never; we need to do something today.

> Each half of the compound sentence is balanced by 'and', 'but or 'so' or by a semi-colon.

REMEMBER

If punctuation is used to link the two parts of a compound sentence, it will always be a **semi-colon**.

The second part of a compound sentence is linked to the first part by the **subject matter** as well. It is used to add extra information about the first part of the sentence. This is a good way of showing **development of ideas** in your writing.

- A **complex sentence** has one **main clause**, which contains the main point of the sentence, and at least one subordinate clause. A **subordinate clause** links to the main clause but cannot stand on its own as a sentence. It often starts with a word like 'who' or 'which'. For example:

    The boy walked across the field. — Simple sentence

    The boy, <u>who was alone at last</u>, walked across the field <u>that led to the farm</u>. — Complex sentence containing two subordinate clauses

Complex sentences use punctuation and connectives to link all the clauses and phrases in the sentence together. The subordinate clause can be removed and the main sentence will still make sense. For example:

| Adverb | Adverbial phrase | Subordinate clause | | Main clause |

    Finally, after years of debate, which involved seemingly endless meetings, our Government has decided to act: too little too late?

- You can 'expand' a sentence by adding extra detail to make the writing come alive for the reader and enable them to picture what you are writing about. Take care, because too much expanding can sound ridiculous!

Look at that first simple sentence again:

    The boy walked across the field.

| Subject noun | Verb | Object noun |

Examiner's tip

Take care not to over-use adjectives. Used sparingly, they have more effect.

At the moment, it is rather dull and flat. To make it more interesting, it could be 'expanded' with some more descriptive vocabulary. The rule is:

- Adjectives link to nouns
- Adverbs link to verbs

One student expanded the original sentence like this:

    The thin pale boy walked slowly and cautiously across the muddy field.

| Adjectives | Adverbs | Adjective |

Notice how this expansion adds much more detail and interest to the sentence.

Examiner's tip

When you are checking your writing, ensure that your sentences make sense and are well punctuated, especially if you include many long complex sentences.

Advertisers use this technique all the time. Here is an example from a travel brochure:

'Come to Portugal, where you will spend long, warm, lazy days happily wandering through glorious, green, picturesque countryside.'

| String of three adjectives | String of three adjectives | Adverb |

Task

Look for a leaflet or a magazine article. Choose two paragraphs and count how many sentences they have. How many are simple, compound or complex?

Sentencing for effect

• Compound and complex sentences can create a range of effects, for example grouping ideas together:

If the Government doesn't act quickly to do something about the crisis in public funding, there is going to be disastrous consequences for the whole of the public sector, including schools, hospitals and social care.

> The use of long clauses adds weight to the feeling that there is a long list of services that will be affected badly.

• You can also **add detail** to an idea with a complex sentence:

Frustrated, the man snatched his coat and left; he was a solitary figure as he marched up the street.

Look at this example of a good student response. Notice how a variety of sentences have been used deliberately for effect:

Good points
• The first three sentences are long, complex sentences, which create an impression of length, so that the reader empathises with the description of the journey
• The final sentence is short to show how the narrator has to separate herself from what is going on – as if it is for survival!

Being enclosed with my family on a long car journey – the slow, tortuous imprisonment of motorway traffic, motorway holdups, motorway views, dad's motorway tantrums – sounds like a version of hell rather than the start of our annual holiday excursion. My brother, rattling the seat next to me with his constant jiggling about, wriggling and writhing like an annoying, sticky and very loud snake, moans constantly. My mother insists on supplying the journey as if it were some army field trip, complete with flasks, sandwiches, sausage rolls and those awful chocolate cakes that my brother whines for but which will no doubt make him sick by the time he's had his fourth... and not a piece of fruit in sight.
I stare out of the window.

(A)

Questions, commands and exclamations

• Questions and exclamations should be used **sparingly**, so that they have an impact.

• They can be used very effectively in writing to argue, persuade or advise.

Examiner's tip

Different effects suit different audiences and purposes. For example, rhetorical questions are useful in writing to argue or persuade.
• **Rhetorical questions** don't require an answer. Their job is to gain the reader's attention or to make a powerful statement.

Can you imagine the effect of this lack of public funding on our society?
This really means: 'the effects are going to be terrible'.

Examiner's tip

- Try beginning or ending a piece of writing to argue, persuade or advise with a rhetorical question:

  Is it ever acceptable to value animals more than humans?

  This really means: 'it is never acceptable to value animals more than humans'.

- **Commands** are a way of addressing the reader directly:

  Buy this book and your life will change overnight.

- **Exclamations** show strong emotional reactions, for example humour or anger:

  This is a disgrace!

  The results were stunning!

Using adverbs

- An **adverb** is a word or phrase that tells you more about a verb. For example:

  Janice shouted <u>loudly</u>.

  Francis marked the children's books <u>carefully</u>.

Adverbs and actions

- Adverbs can tell you **how**, **when** and **where** actions happen. For example:

  The event ran <u>smoothly</u>. (how)

  The swimming race will take place <u>tomorrow</u>. (when)

  There are many ambitious runners <u>here</u>. (where)

Adverbs of manner

- Adverbs of manner show comparison. For example:

  Her handwriting was <u>more</u> legible than his.

  She finished this race <u>much</u> faster than she thought she would.

Placing adverbs

- Adverbs are often found next to a verb, but they can occur at almost any point in a sentence. For example:

  Clara walked <u>quickly</u> to school.

  Clara walked to school <u>quickly</u>.

  <u>Quickly</u>, Clara walked to school.

  Try varying the position of adverbs in your sentence to create more variety in your writing.

Task

Look at the following story extract which uses only simple sentences.
Rewrite it so that the sentences are more varied and interesting. You can alter the order and add extra words if you need to.

> The day finally came. It was time to put the plans into action.
> We had been waiting for a long time. Everyone was very excited.
> We had one final meeting. The plans were looked through again.
> We wanted to make sure we had made all our preparations. We
> wanted to be certain that we hadn't missed anything.

Punctuation

Key points

■ To obtain top marks, you will need to use a range of punctuation.

■ The examiner will expect you to use the following, as appropriate: commas, apostrophes, question marks, exclamation marks, speech marks, brackets, dashes, ellipses, colons and semi-colons.

Examiner's tip

Although you are unlikely to be writing a narrative in your exam, you might want to include some direct speech in a piece or writing, so you need to be aware of the rules about its punctuation.

Commas

Use commas to:

1 separate the **items in a list**:

> When I was only a young boy I was <u>battered, bruised, scalded</u> and totally neglected.

2 add **clauses or phrases** to the main part of the sentence:

> I escaped my uncle's tyranny, <u>as soon as I was old enough to think for myself</u>, making friends with the Cohen family.

> <u>Relying on my own abilities,</u> I was planning, <u>step by careful step</u>, <u>during my childhood</u>, to work my way out of that situation.

3 separate a phrase that adds **extra information or detail** to a sentence:

> Ralph O'Hara was a very rich man, <u>as far as I could tell</u>.

Speech marks

Follow these guidelines for punctuating direct speech.

- Speech marks go around the actual words spoken. They show the beginning and end of direct speech.

- Punctuation at the end of speech is placed before the final speech mark.

- There should be only one speaker for each paragraph

'Is that your wallet?' asked the policeman.

'Yes, it's mine,' answered Jake.

The policeman replied, 'That's very strange because the name on the wallet is Christine.'

'Easily explained,' said Jake, 'that's my surname.'

'I think you'd better accompany me to the station,' said the policeman. 'A lady by the name of Christine Withers has just reported her wallet was taken by a boy of your description.'

> If details of the speaker follow the speech, punctuate, close speech marks, use a lower case letter to continue.

> If the speaker is placed between two complete sentences of speech, add a full stop, open speech marks and start the next speech with a capital letter.

> If the speaker comes first, put a comma, then open speech marks and start the speech with a capital letter.

> When the speaker comes in the middle of a sentence of speech, add a comma and open speech marks and use lower case to continue the speech.

Apostrophes

Use apostrophes to:

1 show **possession**.

If the 'owner' is singular the apostrophe goes before the 's':

> Terry's watch

> the snail's trail

If the 'owner' is **plural** and **does not** end in an 's', you add an apostrophe and an 's':

> the men's hats

> the children's toys

If the 'owner' is **plural** but ends in an 's', you just add the apostrophe after the 's'.

the parents' views

the boys' bikes

2 show where a letter or letters have been removed (an **omission**):

'Do not talk!' ➡ *'Don't talk!'*   *'I am going to the shop'* ➡ *'I'm goin'...'*

Colons and semi-colons

- Use **colons** to:

  1 introduce **a list**, following a general statement:

  This country has been involved in many wars: the Civil War, the Boer War, World War One and World War Two.

  2 introduce an **explanation**:

  'I'm sorry I didn't show up: I had a heavy cold and my head hurt.

- Use **semi-colons** to:

  1 indicate **a short pause** between two clauses or simple sentences that are equally important:

  I was uncertain what to do next; I couldn't let them down.

  2 **separate phrases** in a complicated list:

  I love my aunts for many reasons: Auntie Rachel because she's so kind; Auntie Kate because she's so funny; and Auntie Zulema because of her generosity!

> **REMEMBER**
> If you know how to use a wide range of punctuation, you are more likely to be using a sophisticated range of sentence lengths and types. All this adds interest to your writing and can boost your grade.

Brackets

- Use **brackets** to mark off extra information in a sentence:

  The gloomy teachers (<u>including Mr Morse and Mrs Tutty</u>) trooped on to the stage.

  The BAFTA (British Academy of Film and Television Arts) awards were well worth watching.

> **REMEMBER**
> Brackets are to be used sparingly. They can often be replaced by commas or dashes to give further variety to your writing.

Ellipses

- Use an **ellipsis** (...) to:

  1 create an idea that a situation will continue forever.

  It seems that this cycle of bullying will run on and on...

  2 allow the reader to decide what might fill the space:

  Out on the moors, the beast began to howl for something ancient, howl for ...

Task

Rewrite this extract so that the punctuation is:

- Correct
- More interesting and effective.

The problem with family life today is that people do not spend enough time together they are all busy working playing and leading active lives spending time together is not valued any more and that is why family holidays can be stressful and difficult.

It is time to act says Mrs Helen Smith from the Family Society it is time to make more effort in supporting families so they can spend more time together and offer them financial help so that work stops becoming the most important aspect of parents lives.

Language to engage the reader

Key points

- Choosing language that is appropriate to the **form**, the **purpose** and **audience** of the writing task set is very important in Section B of the exam.

- Using words in **imaginative**, **interesting** ways will be rewarded by your examiner.

- This means using a **wide vocabulary**, linking your ideas with **connectives**, and choosing the most **precise** word for your purpose.

Examiner's tip

Informal writing tends to use more colloquialisms and shortened forms than formal writing. However, you are still expected to follow the rules of standard English.

REMEMBER

Variety in your choice of words gets you marks. So avoid using the same word. **Repetition** should only ever be used deliberately for effect.

Examiner's tip

When you come across unusual words in your reading, look them up and find out what they mean. This is another way of increasing your vocabulary.

Using appropriate vocabulary

- Selecting vocabulary appropriate to the **form**, the **purpose** and the **audience** of your writing is vital if you want to gain a good mark. It is one of the things your examiner will be looking for.

- Adapt your **style**, **tone** and **register** to suit the form, purpose and audience for your writing. For example, a letter to a Government Minister would be **formal**:

    'I sincerely hope that you think carefully about the points that I have offered for your consideration.'

However, a letter to a close friend giving them advice about how to deal with moving home would be informal:

    'Don't you worry – you'll soon be chatting and laughing with everyone. They won't be strangers for long!'

Widening your vocabulary

- If you want to achieve really high marks, you need to show that you can use a wide **vocabulary**. This means aiming for **variety** and **interest** with the words you choose.

- Regular use of a **thesaurus**, which offers alternatives for word choices, gives you more practice at using wider vocabulary.

    Your letter to a Government Minister might substitute 'think about' with:

    consider/contemplate/deliberate over/take into account

    Your letter to a close friend might substitute 'worry' with:

    be anxious/lose sleep/agonise/fret

- Using subject-specific or **technical vocabulary** that is linked to the topic you are writing about shows that you have clearly understood the **purpose**. For example, if you were writing about the elderly, you might use terms like 'social services' and 'primary carers'. If you were dealing with 'education', you might include language such as 'vocational courses', 'academic potential' and 'extended curriculum'.

Connectives

Connectives are used to link paragraphs and ideas together. These might be to:

- order ideas, e.g. *Firstly, Secondly, Finally, To begin with, Then*
- give logical reasons, e.g. *Therefore, Consequently, As a result, Accordingly*
- contrast/offer alternatives, e.g. *On the other hand, In contrast, Nevertheless, Whereas*
- develop an idea, e.g. *Because of this, Also, What is more, In addition, Taking this further*

Connectives make your writing flow and demonstrate that your ideas are well thought out. Examiners call this type of language '**markers**' and will look to see that you know how to use them.

Look at how this student uses wide vocabulary and connectives to ensure that their writing is appropriate to the form, purpose and audience:

| Use of linking phrase to introduce first point |
| High-level vocabulary |
| Connective to develop an idea |

One of the main reasons the Government should engage in this debate about educational funding is to ensure that future generations of school-leavers are not being hampered by second-class exam results. Firstly, if students are being challenged to compete in an increasingly choked higher-education system, they need be in the best position. For this, they need high-quality examination results. What is more, the country is increasingly taking on expertise from abroad to address the lack of talented medics and scientists being produced by our out-dated university provision. As a result, less funding is being provided by these institutions and therefore...

| More formal than 'make sure' |
| Connective to order idea |
| Connective to summarise ideas |

(A)

Good points

- This response uses a range of connectives to organise ideas and clearly mark them out for the reader.
- It avoids repetition, for example substituting 'students' for 'school leavers'.
- It includes high-level vocabulary.

Using more precise words

- Use adverbs to provide more information about what happens and to make the sentence more precise:

  He created the model.

  Meticulously, he created the model.

- Try to avoid nouns and verbs that sound very general. For example:

  She ran to the shops.

  improves when the words become more precise:

  She jogged all the way to the newsagent's on the corner.

- Be aware that the specific noun, verb or adverb you choose creates a particular effect, in this case saying something about both character and setting:

  Ali leaned against the wall.

  Ali lounged nonchalantly against the conservatory wall.

Try inserting some more interesting verbs, nouns and adverbs into these sentences:

- Michael walked towards the bus stop.
- Hannah picked up her homework from the desk.
- Paul leant against the wall.

Task

Look up the meaning of the following words in a dictionary. Practise stretching your vocabulary by choosing a few at a time and writing a sentence using each of the words:

abundant	archaic	benevolent
caustic	dejected	exuberant
exertion	fallacious	gregarious
jaunty	lackadaisical	myriad
nostalgic	proverbial	reminiscent
stationary	verdant	wrench

Using language creatively

Key points

- **Engaging** the reader's interest is really important in your responses to the writing tasks – it is something the examiner will assess!

- Manipulating language for effect, for example by using **imagery**, **stylistic techniques**, **irony** and **rhetorical devices** is an effective way of improving your written work.

- Using language in **interesting** and **imaginative ways** will help you to achieve marks.

Creative language in non-fiction

- Creative and engaging language has a place in non-fiction texts just as it does in stories and poems or other works of fiction. In terms of the exam, if you use imaginative and interesting language you are likely to achieve better marks.

Using imagery

- Using imagery, such as similes and metaphors, will bring your writing to life and make the examiner take note. You don't have to be a poet to use imagery – writers of non-fiction texts often use it in their work.

- **Similes** make a comparison using 'like' or 'as': e.g.

  The chance of working for that company might seem <u>like a ticket to paradise</u> right now, but…

  Her lessons do sometimes seem <u>as dull as ditchwater</u>, but you can still learn something.

- **Metaphors** state things that are not literally true, but the comparison has a strong effect: e.g.

  Even though your teachers come <u>from the time of the dinosaurs</u>, they can teach you important lessons….

  You <u>exploded</u> when I last suggested this, but, at the risk of causing <u>another full-frontal attack</u>…

- **Personification** is a particular type of metaphor, giving inanimate objects 'live', often human, characteristics: e.g.

  <u>Greedy, hungry</u> flames <u>licked</u> the sides of the building ferociously.

In this extract from an autobiography, the writer uses imagery and stylistic techniques to communicate their feelings to the reader:

Engages reader – makes them want to read on.	Filled with disgust and remorse, I threw the bottle onto the hard concrete floor. It shattered, and shards of glass scattered; they formed a pattern in a circle like some mystic fortune teller's handiwork. → **Uses semi-colon to link two vivid images together** / **Effective simile**
Overused simile – a cliché?	I lurched towards the window and glanced downwards. Below, cars crawled along the busy road like ants. Dizziness overcame me – whether from vertigo or the booze … I wasn't sure. → **Ellipsis used to indicate uncertainty**
Personification – 'yawning'	I was on the top floor of a deserted tenement block and somehow I made my way to the wrong doorway. I opened the door and there was a yawning gap – a nothingness. I knew something profound and knew it in an instance. That was my life! My life!! → **Short sentences, pulls reader up, keeps their interest**
Metaphor – again overused?	Only I could do something about it, step back – take back my life. Be in control! It was at that moment, when I teetered on the edge, that I decided to do away with the demon drink. I haven't touched alcohol since that day. Never! → **Continues metaphor of the 'yawning gap'**

Single-word sentence to reinforce writer's feelings'

Avoiding clichés

- A **cliché** is an over-used phrase that has become so common that most people have heard of it. Clichés tend to be similes and metaphors that have been so repeated that they have almost lost their meaning. Try to avoid using these in your own writing.

Take a look at how this student has over-used clichés in the start of their account of a family trip to a theme park.

> By the time we got to the theme park my little sister was as white as a sheet. She had been as sick as a parrot in the car and still wasn't feeling well. She looked the spitting image of a patient in a hospital bed, to be honest! Anyway, I was climbing the walls by then because we'd had to stop the car three times for her. Even though she was as pale as a ghost, we'd got rides to go on and I was sick to the back teeth of waiting.

Stylistic techniques

- **Onomatopoeia** is a way of capturing sounds in words. It is the term we use when a word sounds like the sound it is describing: e.g.

  Imagine the <u>dull thud</u> as the university's door to opportunity closes behind you.
  The leaves <u>crunched</u> and <u>crackled</u> deliciously underfoot.

- **Alliteration** is when words begin with the same letter or sound: e.g.

  <u>W</u>hat a <u>w</u>eary <u>w</u>ay you <u>w</u>ill have to tread without further qualifications.
  The <u>q</u>uiet <u>q</u>ueue <u>c</u>rept forward.

Task

Describe the effect of the alliteration in each of these examples. How does it affect the way you read the sentence?

> **REMEMBER**
> Alliteration can create different effects. In the sentence 'the sensuously slippery snake slithered silently over the silvered rock', the alliteration of the 's's makes us imagine the movement or even the hissing of the snake.

Emotive language

- Writers use **emotive language** to make the reader respond with a particular feeling: for example, sympathy, anger, passion, guilt…

- Emotive language is often a feature of writing to argue or persuade.

Read this short extract which includes several examples of emotive language:

> If we don't try harder to encourage more people to think carefully before buying a puppy from these <u>unscrupulous</u> breeders, the animal shelters are going to be even further crammed to the rafters <u>with unwanted, abandoned, helpless</u> dogs – dogs that could be given <u>happy</u> homes with <u>loving</u> families instead of being <u>discarded, forgotten and abused</u>.

Task

Write a paragraph about an issue about which you feel strongly, using emotive language to make your views clear.

Irony

- **Irony** can be when a writer means the opposite of what they are saying. It is a good technique to use – but don't over-use it. Include, at most, two or three examples in a piece of writing: e.g.

  'Oh, great, I really wanted a bruise on my arm.'

  It can be used in a humorous way:

  'That lump on my neck will really improve my looks.'

  It can also be used for serious effect:

  The robbers were really brave people – beating up a defenceless 98-year-old pensioner.

Task

Re-write the three ironic sentences above, making them literal – in other words, saying exactly what the writer meant.

Look at the following diary extract to see how the writer has used irony to make a clear point in a humorous way:

> Dear Diary,
>
> I'm feeling great today. I'm meeting friends I haven't seen for almost six years and I've woken up with a sore throat, a headache and I feel sick! Perfect timing, as usual.

REMEMBER

There may be some relevant evidence, facts or statistics in the reading extracts from Section A. It is fine to include some of this material in your writing responses as long as it is appropriate.

Evidence, statistics and quotations

- Using material which seems factual and the result of research really makes your writing sound powerful.

- However, your examiner does not expect you to be an expert on all the topics you are asked to write about. It is fine to invent 'evidence' but it must make your writing sound more believable.

Have a look at how this student has used evidence in order to make his article about the RSPCA more powerful:

> If over 42% of this animal shelter's intake comes during the month of January, that is a startling statistic. It seems that virtually 50% – that is half – of the pets that are bought for Christmas presents are abandoned within two weeks of them being received.
>
> We spoke to a representative from a local shelter. 'We are dependent on the public for financial contributions. It is only through donations that we can maintain our services. Unfortunately, it is largely through a much sadder type of donation that we are needed in the first place. Personally, I would prefer less charity giving and more thought being given to whether to buy a dog in the first place.'

Good points

- The use of two numerical statistics makes the article sound believable and accurate, as if the material has been researched.
- Using a quotation from a 'representative' is a common technique in articles. In this case it makes the student's work seem authentic.

(A)

Rhetoric and humour

- Using humour engages your reader. It also is very effective in writing to argue and persuade, because it helps to 'break down' any barriers between you and your reader. This increases your chance of persuading them to act or think in a particular way.

- Rhetoric has been used throughout history to engage and persuade. Politicians learn 'the art of public speaking', as do any public figures whose job it is to persuade people to think differently.

Rhetorical techniques include:

- Rhetorical questions
- Lists of three – sometimes adjectives for powerful impact
- Direct address with use of the inclusive pronoun 'we' and 'us'
- Assuming your audience's agreement
- Appearing to agree with, or flatter, your opposition to help win them round
- Repetition of key words or phrases
- Exaggeration to make your point more strongly

Look at an example of work below. The student is writing in response to the question:

Should teenagers be taught to drive at school? Write a letter to your Headteacher persuading them that this is a good idea.

Good points

- The response has a strong personal voice – remember the examiner does not have to agree with the message of the essay.
- Rhetorical questions appeal directly to the reader.
- Clearly structured argument
- This is a successful response because it engages the interest of the reader, using a range of sentences and rhetorical techniques for effect.

Dear Headteacher,

Once upon a time, schools were places of rigid academic learning: the three R's – reading, writing and 'rithmetic. If a teacher from a Victorian school were to travel forward in time, what do you think she'd make of the subjects modern teenagers study? Boys doing food technology... Girls being taught electronics rather than needlework... Mixed PE lessons...

My point is, of course, that schools must, and have, adapted to suit the changing times. And another change, or adaptation that needs to be considered, is whether we could be preparing students for the outside world even better than we are now. Therefore, they should be taught to drive while at school.

Now, I can fully understand your concern. Teenagers are not to be trusted with three tonnes of metal, I hear you cry. Teenagers, when put behind the wheel of a car, will only be interested in ploughing into as many groups of pedestrians as they can find, laughing wildly as their music blares out of their stereo systems.

We all know that this is a stereotyped view. And, for the minority who may need more guidance on how to undertake sensible, careful and safe driving, where better than school for them to start to learn?...

Engaging start, using humour for effect

Uses two techniques – list of three and rhetorical question – to draw reader in

Assumes reader's agreement to encourage them to agree with own point of view

Agrees again with opposition

Uses exaggeration for effect

Uses rule of three adjectives – to drive point home

Rhetorical question to pose sensible question

Ⓐ*

Task

Complete the letter to the Headteacher begun above. Use rhetorical effects and humour to make your viewpoint clear.

Openings and endings

Key points

- Your examiner is looking for clear structure and organisation in your writing.

- The **opening** and **closing** paragraphs of your writing are very important – they are the first that your examiner reads, which creates an immediate impression; and the last thing she reads, just before giving you a mark.

REMEMBER

Your examiner is a real person! They want to read responses that interest them from beginning to end.

The opening

- The first paragraph in your writing has an important job – to grab the reader's attention.

- Don't 'play safe' with your opening. Try to avoid:

  In this essay I am going to...   ✗

  I am writing to you because...   ✗

  I think that...   ✗

- Try a more effective start. What about:

  A short piece of conversation   ✓

  An anecdote (a story about someone or something)   ✓

  A description?   ✓

Here are two examples of how students have begun their response to the task:

Write a speech for your teachers arguing for the school's homework policy to be changed.

So, what are we here for today? I can hear you asking. Well, I'm here to put forward some ideas about our school's homework policy – from the students' point of view. It's important that you know how students feel about the kinds of homework set at our school and listen to some suggestions for how we could change our homework policy.

Ⓒ

Examiner's advice for improvement

- The style is engaging but the opening could be improved.
- It could perhaps adapt its tone better to the audience.
- The final sentence lacks subtlety.

The second response is instantly much more engaging as the Good points explain:

'I'm not accepting that, Robert, it's copied from Melissa.'
    'Samantha, I asked for your thoughts on the fourth marriage of Henry VIII, not Mrs Wikipedia's!'
    'So, Michael, mum 'helped' again, did she? Good old mum, she's on her way to a good GCSE in Chemistry at this rate!'
    Sound familiar? I'm sure it does. We all know there's a problem with homework – and we all accept that something needs to be done about it. What I'm aiming to do is outline some suggestions that might ensure that Robert, Samantha and Michael – and the rest of us – spend time undertaking work of real value, rather than responding to the tasks set under the current homework policy.
    When I was asked to write a speech to you all about the value of homework, what did I do? No, Mrs Hussain, I didn't 'google' homework – well, not at first, anyway!

Ⓐ*

Good points

- This is a very skilful opening, which uses quotations for humorous effect.

- It uses a natural-sounding rhetorical question to signal real start of speech.

- Direct address involves the audience – 'We all know...' and ' No, Mrs Hussain'.

- The student makes the audience 'wait' for the main point of the speech, sustaining their interest.

Different openings

Look at three different opening paragraphs to the question:

> **Write an article for a school magazine which argues either *for*
> or *against* banning mobile phones in school.**

A I'm not in favour of banning mobile phones in schools. Some teachers think they are a nuisance and can disrupt a good lesson. In my view, mobile phones do have their benefits. They allow students to communicate effectively – an essential skill in the world of work.

> Responds directly to the question, communicates a basic point of view clearly

B Banning mobile phones in school? This should never occur. I know teachers feel they can disrupt lessons … but think of the benefits! What if a parent needs to contact a student urgently? Perhaps there has been an accident or illness in the family? Maybe a student needs to contact a parent …. a younger brother has been taken ill. What then?

> Rhetorical questions engage reader right from the start.

> Offers several examples – perhaps too many

C Last month, a young boy was sitting in a science lesson when his mobile phone rang. The teacher was fuming and cursed the use of 'these modern toys'. He ordered the boy to leave the classroom immediately. The phone was confiscated. If only the teacher had waited a few valuable seconds. The boy was me and the text message was to 'meet me outside the school gate now. Your dad has had an accident. We are going to see him in hospital. Love mum.' So, no, I don't think mobile phones should be banned!

> Uses an anecdote to engage the reader's interest

> Then finally reveals the main point of the argument

Look at the three answers and consider their different approaches:

A Takes a direct approach, putting across a clear view from the start.

B Uses rhetorical questions to engage the reader and then offers a good reason to support the opinion. Does it really sparkle? Is it too like many other answers might be?

C Opens with an anecdote to engage the reader, offering an inventive approach.

The ending

- Your final paragraph should always leave your reader with a clear impression of your ideas and your point of view.

- It should also link back to the introduction to round off your writing.

Here is the concluding paragraph of the speech about homework.

The most important message I want you to take away from today is that a radical review of the purpose and effectiveness of homework is absolutely necessary. In its current format it is outdated, ineffective and, quite frankly, a waste of time. Please take time to reflect on the points I have outlined today, and, in conclusion, I hope I have managed to convince Mrs Hussain (and the rest of you) that, this time at least, I didn't 'google' my homework!

> Clear summing up of the views expressed

> Uses a rhetorical technique – list of three

> Summarising connective

> Links to the humour in the opening paragraph

Examiner's tip

Adapt your tone and style to suit your audience. For example, using an anecdote could suit a persuasive piece but will not suit all non-fiction writing tasks.

Task

Read some magazine articles. See if you can identify some of the different techniques the writers use to engage the interest of the reader in their first and final paragraphs.

Writing letters

Key points

- A letter is one of the forms you may be asked to write for either the **shorter** or **longer writing tasks** in Section B.

- A letter will usually be a functional piece of writing. Produce exactly what the task demands.

- During your GCSE course you will have studied a variety of different forms of **functional writing**. In the exam, you can expect to find any of the following forms to write, for example a **letter**, a **report** or an **article**.

REMEMBER

- This part of the exam is assessing your writing skills. So focus carefully on the text of your letter but also make sure that you get the opening and signing off conventions of the letter right.

- The same applies if you are asked to produce a web page or a leaflet; it is still the text that you should focus on. You are not expected to design a web page or a leaflet.

Adapting your style

- If you are asked to write in the **form** of a letter, your **purpose** could be to inform, to explain, to argue or to persuade, to describe or review. Look carefully at the question to identify what your purpose is.

- The **audience** is a very important part of letter writing. If your audience is someone you don't know, or to someone in authority, such as your head teacher, a Government Minister or local council representative, your writing will need to be **formal**: e.g.

> Form   Audience
>
> **Write a letter to the Minister for Education explaining your views about the current education offered to Key Stage 4 students and suggesting ways in which it could be improved.** — Purpose

If your audience is someone you know, such as a friend, a family member or to a group of people your own age or younger, your letter will need to be **informal**: e.g.

> Form   Audience
>
> **Write a letter to a friend who has recently moved back to your area, informing them about the things to do where you live.** — Purpose

Setting out letters

- Your letter needs to **look like** a letter. There are some important things to remember when setting out a letter. They don't take much time but they show the examiner that you understand the form.

Look at the following response to this longer writing task:

> **Write a letter to a mobile phone company complaining about the contract they asked you to sign.**

123 School Road
Baschurch
Kent
TN3 OBX

29th January 2011

Customer Services Department
Anyphone Ltd
Long Road
Basingstoke
Hampshire
BS1 9KP

Dear Sir/Madam,

    I recently purchased a new mobile phone from your Basingstoke branch after being attracted by the advertising on your website. Initially I was certain that a purchase from your company was a sound decision; the deal presented on the website detailed a package including free evening and weekend calls to all other networks, as well as an attractive offer of 200 free text messages per month. As this appeared to be a highly competitive offer, I was keen to purchase both phone and deal from yourselves.

When I came into your store to make the purchase, I was impressed by the customer service. The advice was clear and helpful and the store assistant friendly and very quick to deal with my purchase. I got the model of phone I wanted and, unlike previous experience, the paperwork was straightforward and not time-consuming.

It was only when I got home that I realised that the contract I had signed was not, in fact, the same as the online offer. Far from it. The offer on your website made it clear that the free tariff applied to <u>all other</u> networks, whereas the paperwork I received indicated it was only the <u>current</u> network; calls to other networks were not covered by this free offer. This is clearly a fundamental difference in service and you can understand my disappointment.

When I rang the store to query the discrepancy, I was told that the 'offer' only applied to online purchases. However, this was not made clear to me when I bought the phone; in fact quite the reverse, as when I asked the store assistant assured me that all website offers were matched in store.

Therefore, I would like you to either change my contract to the free tariff offer or cancel it immediately. I feel that I was misled by your sales assistant and would appreciate it if you could contact me in writing to let me know what you intend to do.

Yours faithfully,

Moniza Hussain

(A)

Good points

- The purpose of this letter is very clear.
- The letter includes relevant detail.
- The letter is well structured with each paragraph making a clear point.
- The writer uses the right greeting (Dear Sir/Madam) and signing off phrase (Yours faithfully).
- This is an effective functional letter.

Examiner's tip

- A letter is to a **specific person** unless it is a 'general audience' letter, for example to a magazine letter page.
- A letter needs to **look like** a letter – address, greeting, signing off phrase.
- Think of a letter as an essay in a different package – it's the **content** that matters most but basic **layout** must be right too.

Signing off

- There are clear rules to signing off at the end of a formal letter.
  If you are writing to someone you don't know, your letter would use the greeting:

  Dear Sir or *Dear Madam*

  then, you *always* end with:

  Yours faithfully

- If you are writing to a named person or someone you know formally, for example:

  Dear Mrs Jones or *Dear Customer Services Manager*

  then, you *always* end with:

  Yours sincerely

Remember: **never have** double 's' – 'Sir' and 'sincerely'.

- If you are writing to a friend or someone you know well, you can sign off with:

  Yours, Best wishes or even *Love*

Task

Imagine you have been having problems with neighbours.
Write a letter to the local council asking for help and support. Set out your letter formally.

Writing reports and articles

Key points

- **Reports** usually have a **functional purpose**: to inform, explain and sometimes to argue a point of view.

- **Articles** tend to be more **'open'** in **purpose**: to discuss ideas and issues.

- You may be asked to write for a *specific* **audience**: for example a report to your Year Group. However, you may be asked to write for a more *general* **audience**: for example an article for a magazine.

- This type of writing task will be based on facts but you might be expected to offer your own **opinions**.

Writing reports

- A report is usually a mainly **factual account** of a recent event or set of circumstances, for example:

  Write a report for the school magazine on a recent sporting event.

- The information you supply will usually be a mixture of facts and opinions:
  - **facts** provide the basic content on the event or issue
  - **opinions** provide more of an assessment of the material, making it more lively to read as well as more personal.

Here is one way you might plan the response to this task:

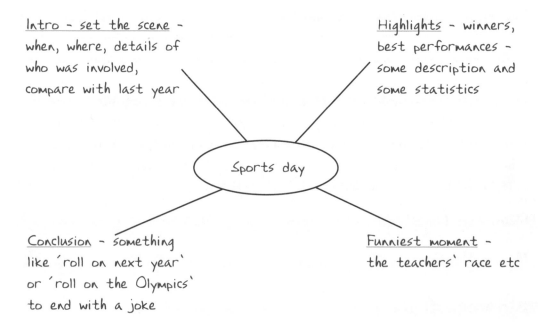

Intro – set the scene – when, where, details of who was involved, compare with last year

Highlights – winners, best performances – some description and some statistics

Sports day

Conclusion – something like 'roll on next year' or 'roll on the Olympics' to end with a joke

Funniest moment – the teachers' race etc

This student has used no opinions at all in the start of their response to the task:

The Sports Day was held on Friday rather than mid-week as it has been in previous years. The weather was fine all day, which meant that no events were cancelled unlike last year when some of the Year 7 races had to be postponed until the following week. This time all year groups were able to take part in the whole day and all the awards could be given out at the ceremony afterwards, with Mr Scott providing his usual jokes. **(C)**

Examiner's advice for improvement

- The student responds to the form and purpose, but could offer more detail to engage the interest of the reader.
- The style is dry and although technically accurate, this response could benefit from the addition of more opinions.

Here is the same student's rewritten version which now includes a mixture of facts and opinions:

Sports Day was held last Friday, <u>which is a perfect arrangement because participants get plenty of time to recover over the weekend</u>. The weather was <u>beautiful</u> all day – not a cloud in the sky – unlike the torrential rain we had last year which caused some of Year 7 <u>such disappointment</u> when their races had to be postponed until the following week. This time all year groups were able to participate in the whole day and all the awards could be presented at the ceremony afterwards. Mr Scott provided <u>his usual hilarious commentary, entertaining everyone</u> and nearly causing Matthew Oldham to fall off his block as he was accepted his medal!

Standout performances this year included the now predictable sight of Naomi Brown winning the 100m, the 400m and heading up the relay team. What would Year 10 do without her? And, of course, the staff race was as thrilling as usual (though as a comedy event rather than a sporting one).

Of course, it was a shame that the planned trip to our new venue – the all-singing-all-dancing sports arena – had to be cancelled at the last minute. We were really looking forward to a Sports Day in a more professional setting on a proper all-weather athletics track and even under floodlights. Never mind – there's always next year!

(A)

Good points

- This is an engaging response with a good mixture of facts and opinions.
- The inclusion of opinions creates a lively tone which is appropriate for the student audience.

REMEMBER

Detail is just as important in non-fiction as in creative writing. Setting the scene for your reader is a very important, effective part of good non-fiction writing.

Examples of the good points have been underlined in the first paragraph. Underline some more in the rest of the response.

Sports Day can be competitive – and fun.

Examiner's tip

Journalists always try to answer these standard questions when they are writing reports: **who, what, where, when, why** and **how**. Make sure any report you write answers them too.

Task

Write a report of a recent school event that you have taken part in. You are writing for your school news bulletin. Try to include:

- Facts and details about the event
- Your own opinions.

Writing articles

- Articles are normally written for magazines or newspapers.

- An article has a clear **purpose**: to discuss or express ideas, usually from a particular **point of view**. This may involve elements of writing to persuade and argue as well as to inform or explain.

Here is one student's plan produced for the following writing task:

Write an article for your school magazine explaining your ideas for ways schools can address the issue of bullying.

Plan

Paragraph 1: <u>Intro</u> – different types of bullying, introduce idea of anti-bullying charter

Paragraph 2: <u>Types of bullying</u> – physical violence, blackmail, verbal, cyber

Paragraph 3: <u>How schools can make a difference</u> and what they can do – anti-bullying charter, review own policies on bullying

Paragraph 4: <u>What I believe</u> – need to act now, all staff act on student reports of bullying as part of charter, work with other schools

Paragraph 5: <u>Conclusion</u> – what schools must do now ... sign up, prevent further pain and anxiety of victims/help change behaviour of bullies

Look at the following extract from the same student's response to this writing task:

Good points

- The response is clearly organised, using topic sentences effectively.
- Rhetorical techniques and emotive language emphasise point of view.
- Paragraph structure makes the arguments clear and powerful.

Rhetorical question to open – engages reader	What is bullying and how can we help prevent it? I would like to explore the different ~~types of bullying~~ and discuss ways in which schools can make a difference ... by signing up to an anti-bullying charter.
Clear explanation of main purpose	
Topic sentence introduces this paragraph	All types of bullying are harmful. The most obvious is physical bullying when the victim is subjected to actual physical violence. Verbal and written threats are, of course, also forms of bullying which cause distress and can involve blackmailing the victim for money or possessions. New forms of cyber bullying, via text messaging and internet chat room sites also appear to be on the increase.
Detail added and range of bullying identified	
Main point of discussion emerges – topic sentence to begin	Schools can make a difference to all of these forms of bullying by signing up to an anti-bullying charter. This act alone demonstrates to staff, parents and students that a school stands firmly against all forms of bullying. Schools should also review their anti-bullying policies to check they are working in practice. From desperate messages sent to 'Childline' and letters to magazine advice pages, it is obvious that some fellow students view school as a violent, brutal and frightening place.
Opens sentence with emotive language to gain reader's sympathy	
Rhetorical rule of three to enforce point	
Restates student's opinion using emotive language	I passionately believe ....
Final paragraph starts with connective phrase, before going on to state solutions	To sum up, it is vital that our school and other schools in this area...

Task

Using ideas from the plan above and some of your own, write the last two paragraphs of the article on anti-bullying.

Layout and presentational features

Read the student response below to this longer writing task.

> **Some people think schools should be closed and all subjects should be taught via computers.**
> **Write an article for a school newspaper, arguing either for or against this idea.**

Headline – grabs reader's attention

Strapline – a second level heading gives more information than the headline

Subheading – summarises first part of the text

HOME ALONE?

Experts suggest that students learn better at home

SCHOOL DAYS OVER FOR EVER?

A group of educational advisers are suggesting that students can be taught better at home via computer-link. They claim students can learn more from a computer than they do from a teacher. Apparently, school is soon to be a thing of the past!

Some educationalists believe they can save money by bulldozing and flattening school buildings – no doubt selling the land to development companies so we have yet more housing estates in our towns.

If that happened, we would lose so much. Think of all the nurturing school gives us – mad and funny teachers, our mates, all that gossip potential ... seriously though – most of us are lucky enough to have some very good teachers, dedicated, friendly and talented at their job. We all know that there are one or two who we would cheerfully never see again, but in the main, they're not a bad bunch. And they care. When we don't understand something, they take the time to explain it to us.

Nobody wants to learn on their own, without the fun and friendship that goes with the school package. Why would anyone bother to switch on their computer to watch someone analyse a Shakespeare play? Where's the motivation? And what about supervision? I know I'd be more motivated to flick a button or click a mouse and go on some entertaining games, check my Facebook page or see what Amazon has to offer.

These misguided educational advisers might wish to revolutionise the education system, but surely a better way to achieve this would be to invest in and improve current facilities rather than crushing the system we have. What is wrong with schools at the moment is that they are underfunded – not that they exist at all.

(A*)

REMEMBER

Magazine articles use a range of layout and presentational features. You don't have to design these in the exam, but, as this example shows, you can include a **headline** and a **strapline** to prove your understanding of these features to the examiner.

Good points

- The style and tone are appropriate to the audience.
- Presentational devices are used to show it is an article.
- The headline and strapline encourage the audience to read on.
- The ideas are well organised and the detail is convincing.

Task

Using the plan below:
Write a report for a travel magazine about places to visit near you, explaining why the area is interesting for everyone.

Intro: set the scene

Main points of interest (2 paragraphs): good things about the area
– things to do, the shops, where to go

Conclusion: give recommendation – why it's a good area

Writing to argue

Key points

- One of the questions in Section B may ask you to argue *either* for or against something.

- When you write to argue, you need to **present and develop a point of view**. Your aim is to convince the reader of this view.

- Your answer should refer to the **other point of view**, be **well structured** and use a range of **techniques** to convince the reader.

Good points

- The Grade A introduction is lively and imaginative, capturing readers' attention.

- It makes immediate mention of work experience as the subject of the article.

- The style is appropriate for purpose and audience.

- The writer presents one side – their fears – at the start. They can then declare their real point of view later.

| Short effective opening sentence |
| Use of humour to engage reader |
| Longer and shorter rhetorical questions for effect |
| List of three – drives point home |
| Writer's real point of view is revealed |

Including both points of view

- Your main aim when you write to argue is to present your point of view. For example, it could be that students should not have to wear school uniform.

- List the 'arguments for' and the 'arguments against' your point of view. That will help you think about what to include when you are writing.

- There are different ways in which you can organise this type of writing:

  - Take each idea in turn: present one idea then contradict it, present another then contradict it, and so on.

  - Present one side of the argument briefly, at the start, before arguing at length for the opposing argument, which is your point of view.

  - Develop your own side of the argument in detail, referring briefly to the other point of view as you make your own points.

Structuring your argument

- It is vital to structure your argument carefully – remember, it is assessed as part of your overall mark in Section B of the exam.

  You will be expected to include:

  - An introduction – a paragraph which presents the subject and probably suggests your attitude, or point of view

  - Your argument, presented in a way which uses paragraphs to put across your main ideas in a structured and systematic way

  - A conclusion – a paragraph which sums up your overall point of view

Introductions

- Take a look at these two introductions of different grades. The students are writing an article for an employer's magazine, arguing either for or against work experience.

> In my opinion, work experience is a good thing. Some people argue that it is a waste of time, but I am going to prove that it helps students get to know what real life is like. There are many things in its favour...

C

Examiner's advice for improvement

- This writer expresses their view at the start and makes a simple reference to opposing view. A more sophisticated response might reveal the writer's point of view at the end of the introduction.

- The response shows how the argument will develop – as a simple list of reasons why work experience is a good thing. The ideas might be organised in a more complex way to interest the reader.

> I am not afraid to admit that the prospect of work experience terrified me. How would I cope with new people, a new working environment and having to get up at six o'clock each morning? Would the fortnight be worthwhile? I guessed not, and feared I would be bullied, put upon and, probably, bored for most of the time. I felt certain I would be better off learning maths in a classroom, rather than draining oil in a local garage.

A*

Conclusions

- The most important job of a good conclusion is to remind the reader of the main point of view. It should link back to the way you started, if that is appropriate.

- Try and write an ending which will stick in the memory. This might include a new idea to support your argument that you haven't already mentioned.

Here is the way the Grade A* response concluded their piece of writing:

So, incredibly, in just two weeks it was all over. My initial fears had all evaporated and I had made good friends that I was sorry to leave – even though I did have a lot of sleep to catch up on! Any problems were only minor. I loved almost every minute, learnt a great deal, and they have offered me a Saturday job. I now believe that work experience is a vital part of the KS4 curriculum. If it comes to a choice between doing maths or cleaning a filthy engine, I've learnt there is no real comparison. Roll on next Saturday!

> Summary of the experience

> Clear link to the purpose of writing

> Ends on enthusiastic note to back up argument

Techniques of argument

- You might want to include some of the following to engage the reader in your argument and to emphasise your key points:
  - reasons for your argument
  - evidence (if possible)
  - short anecdotes (where appropriate) or quotations
  - facts and figures
  - rhetorical questions
  - direct address to the reader
  - lists and sentences varying in type and length

Have a look at the following extract, which uses some of these techniques. It is the start of a student response to the question:

REMEMBER

Of course, it would be tricky to include all of these techniques in a 30 minute response. Instead, use a range of techniques relevant to the task. Examiners will reward an appropriate selection of techniques.

> **Write an article for a magazine arguing for or against this idea:**
> **The government should give grants to ensure that every home in the UK has high-speed broadband access by 2016.**

The government have promised to make sure that everyone in the country will have access to high-speed broadband by 2016. Will they achieve it? It's a very impressive promise. However, good internet access is one of the rights of modern society, proven to improve the quality of life. And looking after the quality of our lives – yours and mine – is one of the government's responsibilities.

At the last count, 77% of homes in the UK had broadband access. Of these, over 60% have high-speed connections. However, the majority are still in densely-populated areas such as towns and cities. Over a third of rural households are still without access to high-speed broadband.

> Rhetorical question – engages reader

> Inclusive pronoun – addresses the reader directly

> Use of figures and statistics

Task

Write a letter to a newspaper arguing either for or against this idea:

The internet is a great resource and does more good than harm.

Writing to persuade

Key points

- One of the questions in Section B may ask you to **write to persuade**.

- When you write to persuade, you are trying to get the **reader** to **do something** or **believe something**.

Good points

- The response uses some persuasive language techniques effectively.

- It is clearly structured with a strong introduction and use of topic sentences in following paragraphs.

- Ideas are presented in a logical and coherent way.

Persuasive techniques

- There are certain techniques that you can use to make your persuasive writing stand out:
  - effective **structuring of ideas**
  - **emotive language**
  - **examples** and **anecdotes**
  - **rhetorical techniques**.

- Make sure you use these for particular effect in your work, selecting the techniques that best suit the purpose and audience of your task.

Structuring ideas

- There are different ways of persuading people, and different ways of organising what you are going to say.

- The main difference between writing to **argue** and writing to **persuade** is that a piece of **argument** involves the presentation of two **different points of view. Persuasive writing** does not usually present the alternative point of view. More often it presents **one view** on a topic of issue using a logical argument.

A student was asked to write a letter to the Headteacher suggesting how the school could be improved.

Dear Headteacher,

Your request for students to offer suggestions about how we should spend the new buildings budget was both surprising and very exciting. Obviously, all the students in the school have opinions, and we are very grateful for this opportunity to have our views taken into account.

But where to begin? Well, firstly, I imagine we would all agree that the exterior of the buildings needs to be improved. The paintwork is peeling and the caretaker seems to have almost lost the war against graffiti. There is no doubt that potential new students and their parents would be much more impressed with a cleaner and better presented façade. It is fair to say that most people consider outward appearance to be a good representation of what is going on inside. In the case of our school, this is certainly not true, but visitors are not to know that.

The area around the school is also desperately in need of attention. There is always litter and debris, some of which arrives at weekends but lingers longer than anyone would like. St Gregory's School had a similar problem and when they addressed it as a priority, it apparently had a marked effect on both student attitude and student achievement: that would be something I am sure the governors would welcome here....

Concerning our classrooms...

Positive opening to win round the Headteacher

Good sense of structure

Well used metaphor for effect

Persuasive idea

High level of vocabulary

Saying what the Head would like to hear

Offers good example to persuade

Extends the idea: the governors would approve too

A*

Emotive language

- **Emotive language** is language which makes the reader feel something strongly, such as guilt or anger. It can be a very effective technique in persuasive writing.

Look at how the student continues their letter about the state of their school:

> Concerning our classrooms; these are uninspiring and dull. There has been no attempt to provide any positive climate for learning for many years, with the result that classrooms are dull, dreary and downright miserable places to be. They are often freezing in winter and breathlessly hot in summer, making any kind of proper concentration incredibly difficult. It is the younger students who are particularly affected by this, coming as they do from their bright, sunny and colourful primary schools. It must be a monumental shock for them.

List of three drives home this point.

Use of emotive language creates feelings of guilt and encourages changes to be made.

Second list of three provides contrasting description with 'dull, dreary and downright miserable'.

Examples and anecdotes

- Using **examples** and real-life stories can make a point you are making more persuasive, if used occasionally and appropriately.

- An **anecdote** is a short story which supports what you are trying to say. The reader is more likely to be persuaded if you write about something that has actually happened.

Consider how this student has used examples and anecdotes to illustrate her points:

> As we know, there was a good deal of concern after the last Open Evening – several parents expressed anxieties about the state of the temporary classrooms, and one parent in particular asked you some very challenging questions, about the last plan to replace them, in front of prospective students. We need to ensure that this doesn't happen again.

REMEMBER

You are allowed to invent your own examples and anecdotes in the exam – they don't have to be true!

Example given, as if from real life

Very short anecdote used in context

Rhetorical techniques

- **Rhetoric** is 'language used for effect' originally in 'the art of public speaking'.

- You have already seen some examples of rhetorical techniques in the response above, including an example, an anecdote and emotive language.

Examiner's tip

Rhetorical touches like these can improve your grade.

Now read the final paragraph of the student's response. Notice how she finishes her piece of writing:

> We all know the school is a mess, Mrs Smith. We all know the budget is limited. We share your concerns about finances. But if we don't attract new, enthusiastic and eager students to our school because of the disastrous state of our buildings, we soon won't have a school at all. Surely none of us want that outcome?

Pronoun 'we' makes reader feel involved

Repetitive phrasing emphasises points and builds to main conclusion

List of three adjectives

Powerful vocabulary for emphasis

Ends strongly with rhetorical question to make Mrs Smith think

Use of exaggeration to persuade reader to act

Task

Write a persuasive letter to your Head of Year about a part of your school that needs updating or improving. Use the persuasive techniques you have learnt about on these pages.

Writing to inform

Key points

- One of the questions in Section B of your examination may ask you to write to inform.

- The question is likely to focus you on a particular form, and audience as well as purpose.

Examiner's tip

An information text does not need to be dry or dull; it can be more than a list of facts and figures. Try including some personal response (for example, a well-chosen anecdote, example or comment). This will raise your grade as your writing will immediately be more interesting.

REMEMBER

You don't need to *be* an expert in your chosen subject, but it helps if you *sound like* one! Make up some survey results, include some figures and numbers – this gives your writing more credibility.

Good points

- The plan is clearly divided into separate paragraphs.
- The ideas within each paragraph are connected which should give a strong sense of purpose to the article.
- The information from the spider diagram has been developed well in the detailed plan.

Effective information writing

- When writing to inform, you should concentrate on:
  - **choosing information** to suit your purpose
  - organising your ideas into **clear paragraphs**
  - writing an effective **opening** and **ending**
  - including **facts** and **opinions**
  - creating the right **tone** for your audience and purpose.

Selecting the information

- Focusing on the main purpose, think first about the types of information you will provide to your reader. Come up with 5-6 main ideas and produce a clear plan. Spider diagrams work well for this but it could also be a simple list.

- Better answers will develop some of these main ideas in detail rather than include lots of undeveloped material.

Look at this spider diagram that one student produced for the following task:

Write a report for a teen magazine to inform readers about a topic you are interested in.

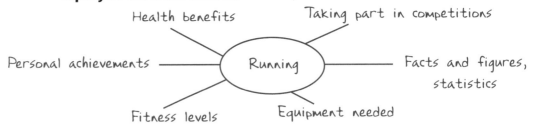

Developing the structure

- **Group** your ideas together and **link** them effectively. Unless you plan carefully, you run the risk of writing disjointed pieces of information which lack direction.

Here is the same student's **detailed plan** for a response to the question above. Notice how each main idea is given a new paragraph and how then a few points of information are covered within each paragraph.

Plan

Intro: why I have chosen this topic
- background information - why I like it, when I started
Para 2: what running involves
- time commitment, equipment needed, how to start
Para 3: making progress
- health benefits, how to make progress, how running improves fitness (stats/ figures)
Para 4: taking it further
- getting into club running, training for races, competitions
Conclusion: passing the baton
- why starting running changed my life, why I recommend it to others

Making the information clear

REMEMBER

The longer writing task should only take you 35 minutes. So aim to complete between 5 and 6 developed paragraphs in this amount of time. Any more might lead to some ideas being undeveloped.

- When you are writing to inform, you must make the information clear and accessible for your audience. You can assume the reader knows nothing about the subject about which you are providing information.

- The more details you can give, the clearer your information should be.

Decide how well these two different extracts from the 'How to start running' article offer clear, relevant information to an audience who have no knowledge of the subject.

It is really important to take it easy when you first start running. Don't go for a run too often and don't go out every day. Depending on your fitness level and your previous sporting history, you need to adapt your training to suit your body.

C

Examiner's advice for improvement

- The information doesn't really provide any detail about why it is important to do what is being suggested and offers advice rather than information.
- More precise information is needed.

It is really important to take it easy when you first start running. For instance, deciding on running every day is not a good idea and can lead to injury, as your muscles will not have the chance to recover and get stronger between runs. Think 'time on your feet' rather than 'distance covered' – running for fifteen minutes without stopping, at a steady pace, is far more beneficial than aiming to run for four miles if you have never run before. Lots of elite runners began their careers by adopting the '10% rule' – in other words, increasing their weekly run time by 10%. For example, if you are starting from a position of never having run before, aiming to run three times a week for fifteen minutes each time is a fantastic goal in itself! Keeping that up for two weeks and then adding two minutes to each fifteen minute run in the third week is a sensible target. Your body needs time to adapt and listen to the new messages you are giving it.

A

Good points

- Although the information is more or less the same, this response provides much more detail about why each piece of information is important.
- The direct address to the reader ('you' and 'your') makes the information personal and engaging.
- The occasional use of exclamation marks helps create an appropriately friendly tone.

Creating a strong opening

- A **vivid opening** will immediately attract the attention of the examiner. Unusual or inventive approaches can gain you marks.

- For example, when writing to inform, you could start with:
  - Some **humour** to engage your audience, for example a description of you at the end of a run: *I heave myself up the road, gasping, dripping in sweat, legs trembling with the effort it takes to make it to the front door…. Yes, you've guessed it – I've been for a run.*
  - An account from **personal experience** which gives a context for your writing, for example: *The day I started running was the day that the TV remote broke. Flat batteries. Unable to move from the sofa, too flabby to stir…*

Examiner's tip

Sentence control also impresses the examiner. The student makes good use of a range of punctuation and sentence variety to add depth to their writing.

Task

Write an article for a Year 7 student brochure informing new students about their first term at your school, from the perspective of an older student.

Writing to explain

Key points

- One of the questions in Section B of your examination may ask you to produce an explanation text.

- Explaining does not just involve supplying information. It requires you to explain **how** or **why** something happens not just **what** happens.

- The question is likely to focus you on a particular form and audience, as well as purpose.

REMEMBER

Functional writing is any writing that could exist in the real world and has a clear transactional purpose – for example to provide information. Types of functional writing could include letters, reports, articles and reviews.

Examiner's tip

Students often confuse writing to explain with writing to inform. Remember that writing to explain requires more than just information. Think about feelings and background and reasons as well as the facts.

Types of explanation task

- When you write to explain, it is vital to give reasons for what happened, or how you feel, or why something is important.

- You are likely to be asked to respond in one of these ways.
  You may be asked to **write an account from personal experience**. For example:

  Most of us have a mixture of good and bad memories from our past. Choose a memory of an event in your past and explain why it was so significant for you.

  > The examiner doesn't want a long detailed story – your focus should be an explanation of why it was significant.

  or

  Write about a time in your life that you felt particularly proud of yourself. Explain why you felt so proud of yourself during this time.

  > Here, the examiner is interested in why that time was significant, not just what it was that made you proud.

- You may be asked to **write a functional non-fiction text**. For example:

  Write a letter to a relative explaining why they should visit a place you think is very special.

  > This task is asking you to explain why this place is special to you, rather than just information about the place.

  or

  Write an article for a school magazine explaining why it is important to take regular exercise.

  > This task asks you to explain why and how exercise is important, not just supply information about exercise.

Presenting the explanation

- The most effective explanation texts present a situation, then explain **the cause(s)** of it (why it came about) and **the effect(s)** it had.

- Sometimes an explanation text might explain how someone feels about what has happened.

- All the way through, an explanation text gives **reasons**. This is the key part of writing to explain.

Look at this example introduction from a response to this writing to explain task:

| Form | Audience | Purpose |

Write a letter to a friend explaining why a recent holiday was so memorable.

As you know, we went on holiday to Greece last year. It was very memorable. We stayed in a place called Milos and there were not many British people there. I am sure we could have had a good time and then it would have been 'just another holiday'. However, it was memorable because of the bad moments we had there not because of the good ones.

Ⓒ

Examiner's advice for improvement

- Good direct address reader in opening in sentence – could have been continued.
- The range of sentences used could be more varied to sustain the reader's interest.
- It could introduce the reasons why the holiday was memorable in a more engaging way.

Here is the student's improved response:

As you know, our last family holiday was to the island of Milos in Greece: a holiday that will take some beating! Our resort was stunning, the beaches were picture-postcard – all of which you know already from some of the panoramic shots that dad took that you have already seen. However, it wasn't that that made this particular holiday stand out. No, it was the catalogue of disastrous events, not caught on camera fortunately, that made this particular holiday so memorable. **A**

Good points

- This response has a clear, lively tone, appropriate for a friend.
- Background information is clear, offering detail: 'the beaches were picture-postcard'.
- It uses a variety of sentences and punctuation.
- It contains wide-ranging vocabulary which immediately engages the reader – 'catalogue of disastrous events'.

Task

Using the same question, write a plan of your own about why a recent holiday was memorable. Now, choose three of the things from your plan, for example: A person I met; Something which made me laugh; Something I learned
For each one, write a short paragraph explaining why that particular aspect was memorable.

Using the language of explanation

- In writing explanations you are presenting **cause and effect** ideas and so you need to use **causal connectives**. Here are some you might include:

As a result of this
This meant that
This is because
As a consequence
Therefore

- Using modal verbs to suggest that there is uncertainty can really improve your explanation writing as it makes your work sound reflective and thoughtful, for example:

It might be
The reason could have been
It may be that
Perhaps
Possibly

REMEMBER

- The writing tasks in Section B may be linked in some way to the reading texts in Section A. Don't worry – the tasks will only ever ask you to write about things that you will be able to do. (You don't have to be an expert on every topic!)

Examiner's tip

It is absolutely fine to 'invent' material – your examiner is not expecting every word you write to be 'true'. For example, you could invent details or statistics about a new mp3 player, but make sure they are believable.

Task

Modern technology is advancing rapidly in the world.
Choose a piece of modern technology, for example a mobile phone or a new mp3 player, and write an article for a gadgets magazine to explain how it has affected your life.

Writing reviews

Key points

- One of the questions in Section B of your examination may ask you to produce a review.

- A review is normally **an account and an evaluation** of an event or experience, giving a clear point of view. Reviews are designed to be read by a **wide audience** rather than one person.

- The **purpose** of a review can be to inform and/or explain, but it can also be to persuade as well, as it normally expresses a point of view.

REMEMBER

Don't give away too much of the story in your review! This means not ruining the story for the reader by telling crucial parts – especially the ending.

Examiner's tip

It is fine to invent an imaginary film or band to review if you cannot think of a real one. The examiner is interested in how you write, not in whether to go and see the film you are recommending!

Review structure

- The first part of a review explains the topic for review in a short summary or synopsis. This usually includes a short description of the holiday, film, book or TV programme.

- The second part goes into more detail giving some examples that provide more information about your topic and why you liked or didn't like it. You might also compare the topic with others: for example, comparing the book you are reviewing with another book of a similar type.

- The final part is where you give your overall recommendation – your view on whether or not your reader will appreciate the film, book or TV programme.

Planning

Here is how one student has sketched out a plan for a review of a film.

Plan

Paragraph 1: summarise the film, early indication of my opinion

Paragraph 2: what was good (story, settings - don't give too much away)

Paragraph 3: what was good (characters, actors, directing)

Paragraph 4: what was bad - what I didn't like and why

Conclusion: final comments, to encourage others go and see it

Give a rating: 4 stars

Tone and point of view

- When you write a review adopt a definite **point of view**. Give an opinion and explain that opinion. Do not be afraid of stating your opinion clearly.

- You want people to read all of your review, so choose your **language** and your **tone** carefully to match your audience.

Look at how this student has responded to the task below. They have used an imaginary film for their review.

> **Write a review of a film you have seen recently for a teenage magazine, persuading your audience either to go or not to go and see it.**

Three Little Pigs Leave Home

The film version of this well-known children's tale works well though it's not for tiny tots as it has a fifteen rating. The use of language is 'modern' to say the least - I don't think I ever expected to hear so much 'effing and cursing' from the mouth of Mr Wolf - thought it was supposed to be 'huffing and puffing'!! 'The three pigs...' is certainly for a broad-minded, probably teenage audience that is familiar with the original story-line. Well, who doesn't know the story-line? The special effects are good, too. Seeing Mr Wolf blown off a chimney top in 3D is both memorable and hilarious.

Clear opening opinion in first sentence

Language appeals to audience – comparing 'effing and cursing' with 'huffing and puffing – with humorous effect too

Specific example of special effects.

What a pity, then, that Claude Sinclair, a clever and single-minded filmmaker, chose such a clumsy, mumbling actor as the eldest pig! Ronald Ross was certainly out of his depth playing such a vital role and for some unfathomable reason spoke his lines in a boring monotone that was difficult to hear and reminiscent of Lincoln Burrows in 'Prison Break.' The quirky Andrew Coles was brilliant as Little Pig and he produced an innovative and dazzling display that saved the film!

The director also excels in his choice of settings with the exotic locations contrasted well with those of the mother pig's sty and the wolf's wood. The camera angles were superb, too - for example, focusing on the wolf's lips and tongue and the dribbles of his saliva when he contemplated eating a pig.

When it comes out, I'll certainly be ordering the DVD, which includes extras - such as extended scenes, outtakes and interviews with the cast. And you should go and see this film - but don't take your granny or your little sister... it might be a bit much for them!!

Star rating: 4

Annotations:

> Clear structure - example of a negative feature of the film starts new paragraph

> Reference out to another film

> Comments on range of technical aspects with example

> Finishes with an evaluation and rating of the film

(A)

Vocabulary

- Use well-chosen descriptive words in reviews to match your opinion. These will engage your reader.

Here are some examples of descriptive words you might include in a review.

Positive	General	Negative
irresistible	plot	bewildering
hilarious	type	disappointing
classic	form	superb
hype	unbelievable	effects
imitation	suspense	mood
captivating	typical	clichéd
impressive	scenes	excessive

- Occasionally, using **adverbial phrases** can be effective in review writing: e.g.

  irresistably delicious   *heartbreakingly attractive*   *unbearably tragic*

  Phrases like these are often a common feature of media writing, in particular reviews and advertisements. You can also use **alliteration** in these phrases to make them even more powerful:

  mesmerisingly menacing   *agonisingly adventurous*

Task

Adapting the plan on page 90 and using some of the vocabulary in the table above, respond to this task:

> **Write a review of either a film or TV programme of your choice to persuade a general audience that it is not worth watching.**

Good points

- The tone and style of this review is appropriate to its audience.
- The response presents both good and bad points giving a sense of balance.
- It comments on a range of aspects, e.g. setting and camera angles.
- It gives an overall evaluation and a rating.

REMEMBER

Structure and organisation are really important in review writing. Make sure that you use each paragraph for a separate purpose but also create links between them.

Writing to advise

Key points

- One of the questions in Section B of your examination may ask you to produce a piece of advice writing.

- Advice writing aims to encourage the **reader** to do **something** or to **behave in a particular way**.

- You will need to **organise** your **ideas**, offer **logical solutions** using **examples** and adopt the right **tone**.

REMEMBER

It is really important to organise your advice well. It is better to offer three pieces of well-structured advice than a random list of nine 'things you could do'.

Types of advice task

- An advice task will give you a specific **audience**, as well as a specific **form** for your writing and these may vary. For example:

   Write an article for your school magazine in which you advise its readers how they could welcome newcomers to the school.

   Write a letter to parents advising them of ways in which they could improve their child's exam performance.

   Write an article for a magazine for teenagers advising readers about how to lead healthier lives.

Presenting your ideas logically

- Your advice will not be convincing unless you are logical. Writing to advise involves clear thinking, and fair and balanced ideas which are well-organised. You could:
   - begin by presenting the subject clearly
   - offer advice which is logical and convincing
   - demonstrate the benefits of following your advice.

Getting the language features and tone right

- Your tone needs to fit your purpose and audience. When writing to advise you are **addressing your reader** directly, so tone is very important.

- You may be asked to write a **formal** response – a letter or an article for a magazine – or you may be asked to write an **informal** response – a letter to a friend.

- Here are some different language features you can use in your writing to vary your tone:
   - **Commands** which tell the reader directly what to do: e.g.

      Make sure you add...   *Don't forget to visit...*

   - **Verbs** like **must** and **should** which encourage the reader to act: e.g.

      You must wash...   *You should exercise...*

   - **Softer verbs** like **can** and **may** or **could** and **might** which give suggestions: e.g.

      You may want to put your planner...   *You could ask your parents...*

   - **'If...(then)...** sentences... shows what would happen if you follow the advice: e.g.

      If you make sure you are well prepared, then you are less likely to worry that you won't perform well...

Look at this extract. from one student's advice writing, which uses some of these techniques:

Command	
Strong verb to enforce advice point	
Further strong verb	
Command	

Don't worry about moving up to our school. You must get to grips with a whole new situation, including the crowds, the size of the school and all the new people. You should take a deep breath and, most importantly, don't panic. You will soon get used to it all.

C

However, this high-level response blends a mixture of commands with a softer approach:

> When you first arrive at our school, the best thing to do is to try not to panic. Everyone has been new at some stage. If you can stay calm, then you will be on the way to coping with your new world. See the long corridors as a challenge; see the complex timetable as a puzzle; and see the students and teachers as future friends. Don't worry if your bag is too heavy or you have no idea what to do next. Think back to how daunting your primary school seemed at first. You soon got used to it and the same will happen here. You may even end up enjoying it!

> **(A)**

| Command is softened by 'try not to' – sounds more like a suggestion |
| If... then sentence shows result of following the advice |
| Command |
| Softer verb – more encouraging than 'should' or must' |
| Command |

Good points

- This response is a good mix of suggestions and commands, making the tone friendly and comforting.
- The commands offer clear advice.
- The detail added to some suggestions makes the advice more convincing.

Offering solutions

- Offering possible solutions to the problem is a key part of writing to advise.

This student has offered a solution to a problem, using an appropriate tone:

> Our school corridors can get very congested at changeover times, meaning it is hard for new people to find the right rooms. However, that need not concern you: discover who is going to your next lesson, then cling on to them for dear life. It might be a rough ride, but you will get through safely and might even have a laugh along the way...

Using examples

- Giving **examples** is a good way of making your writing more convincing and reassuring.

| Positive opening message |
| Humour to lighten the advice |

> If you don't panic and stay positive, you'll have a great experience you will remember. Hopefully, it will be better than Sajid's, when he arrived last year. He seemed to arrive at school late each day and never thought about what might happen next. That was probably why he ended up locked in the toilets! Don't let that happen to you. Ask for help, think ahead, remember it's a happy school and you won't go wrong.

> **(A)**

| Example given |
| Positive ending |

Examiner's tip

A great way of ending your writing is to sum up what the benefits would be if the advice is followed.

Task

Your school is planning its annual foreign exchange trip. Write a short article to be included in the information pack giving advice to students on how to get the most out of this experience. Remember to:

- make your advice points clear and logical
- use the language features of advice text to make sure your tone is right for a student who may have concerns about the trip.

Checking your work

Key points

It is important to **check your writing for errors**, as it is being assessed for several things at the same time:

■ Your **ideas** and whether you can write in the right form for the audience and purpose you have been set, using interesting vocabulary

■ Your skills in **organising** and **structuring** – openings, endings, paragraphing

■ Your use of **sentences**, **punctuation** and **spelling**.

REMEMBER

You need to make sure your handwriting is legible and can be followed by the examiner, but it does not need to be perfect!

Examiner's tip

Don't be afraid to make alterations. As long as your writing is legible, you won't lose marks. However, if the examiner can't make sense of what you have produced, that will let you down.

Spelling and accuracy

• In Section B, **accurate spelling** is expected from higher grade students. So make sure you check your spelling as you read through your work at the end of the exam.

• There are some spelling rules and strategies that can help to make sure that your spelling is as accurate as it can be.

Common spelling patterns

• Where words **follow a set pattern**, learn that pattern so that you can spell other related words, or words affected by the same rule. For example:

– Words ending with **a single vowel and single consonant – double the consonant** if you **add an ending beginning with a vowel**:

sit ➜ si*tter*/si*tting*   ban ➜ ban*ned*/ban*ner*

– **Add 's' to make a plural**:

house ➜ house*s*   pool ➜ pool*s*

but be aware of these **exceptions**:

words ending in –ss, –sh, – ch, -x: add –es	glass*es*, bush*es*, match*es*, fox*es*
words ending in consonant + *y*: change –*y* to –*ies*	lady ➜ lad*ies*, try ➜ tr*ies*
words ending in –*f*: usually change to -*ves*	wolf ➜ wol*ves*, leaf ➜ lea*ves*
some words ending in –*o*: add –*es*	tomato*es*, potato*es*
some plural words don't follow these rules	children, women, mice, sheep

– **Remove the final 'e'** from a verb **before adding 'ing'**:

love ➜ lov*ing*   have ➜ hav*ing*

Knowing the difference

Some words sound the same or very similar but are spelt differently and have different meanings. Learn these common examples and look out for others when checking your work:

your (belonging to you) and **you're** (you are).

their (belonging to them), **they're** (they are) and **there** (any other use.)

where (place), **were** (verb) and **we're** (we are).

too (as well or very), **two** (the number) and **to** (any other use)

whose (belonging to someone) and **who's** (who is)

effect (noun), **affect** (verb)

accept (take), **except** (apart from)

And remember it is:

a lot not **alot**

as well not **aswell**

Spelling strategies

- Make sure you can spell these words which are frequently used and frequently misspelt in writing responses:

argument	conscience	emphasise	metaphorically	professional
atmosphere	definitely	empathise	naïve	psychological
beautiful	develop	environment	necessary	stereotype
beginning	disappear	favourite	occasionally	suspense
business	dynamic	immediately	parallel	symbol
character	embarrassed	independent	prejudice	vicious

- When you are working, either in class or at home, get into the habit of underlining and then checking with a dictionary if you are not sure how to spell a word. (You are not allowed a dictionary in the exam.)

- Try to avoid relying on spell check on the computer. It is often wrong and it can make you a lazy speller.

Spelling tips

- Group words into families, where part of the word is the same, e.g.

  success, successful, succeed, unsuccessful

- Use memory jogging phrases (or mnemonics), e.g.

  'There is *iron* in the *environment* or *a rat* in *separate*.

- Say the word in your mind as it is spelt, e.g.

  Fe*bru*ary, Wed*nes*day, *fri*end

- Chunk or break words down into smaller parts, e.g.

  ex-treme-ly, dis-appear-ed, def-in-ite

Checking and correcting

- Spend five minutes at the end of Section B of the exam **checking** and **improving** your writing.

- Failure to do this can affect your mark considerably, because vocabulary, punctuation and spelling can **all be improved**.

- Ideally, read through your response very slowly, as if reading aloud, and be prepared to **alter** your work whenever necessary.

- With regard to spelling, check for:
  - Words **spelt differently** in different parts of your answer – decide which version is correct.
  - Words which are clearly **spelt incorrectly** – try to apply spelling rules.

REMEMBER

Although you should never copy text from Section A, the text extracts can contain vocabulary that is useful for Section B.

Editing your writing

- If you realise that you have missed out a paragraph break, simply mark it in – either using two diagonal slash marks (//) or with a note in the margin with an asterisk (*) in the appropriate place.

- If you have used evidence, make sure you have put quotation marks around the words you are 'quoting'.

- If you need to move any text around or add a sentence or further information, do so. Your examiner will not mind and it is never too late to pick up a few more marks.

Examiner's tip

There are no marks for neatness. As long as the examiner can read your work, alterations are likely to improve your mark.

Answers

Understanding non-fiction texts

page 11

Extract from a Grade A response

The audience for this report seems to be a general adult audience, given that it is from a national newspaper. The use of language indicates the target audience; the use of vocabulary such as 'sabotaging' and 'appropriateness' are quite high-level vocabulary choices, clearly aimed at a readership with a good level of education.

The headline is rather emotive – it immediately draws the eye not only with its content but the use of punctuation (the exclamation mark) to imply that the idea of 'slang' on the curriculum is ridiculous. This suggests that schools are 'dumbing down' their curriculum. Even though the article itself sounds unbiased in places, the point of view is made clear by this headline and the pull-quote 'studying wigging'. Indeed, even in the first line there is 'sabotaging', which is emotive and sounds serious…

page 15

Grade A*

The writer of 'A clear and present failure' has a definite point of view about the reasons for the amount of disaffected youth. The photograph is a clever device used to engage reader interest and suggest that the article will be critical of today's youth. Furthermore, the first pull quote seems to link directly to the stereotype being prominently displayed in the photo: 'lazy, stupid and worthless' is a strong criticism of this type of teenager and would immediately suggest that this article is going to be another in the long line of critical media reports about teenagers.

However, the second pull quote suggests an alternative point of view: once we, as readers, have done exactly that – 'judged' the youth on display' – we are reminded that it is 'easy to judge'. We have been manipulated as readers into falling into the same trap that the writer is suggesting.

The use of a rhetorical question to open the article presents an honest, if rather negative, view. The whole of that paragraph is critical and brutally honest, describing a very bleak picture of a typical teenage day. However, the short sentence at the end of this paragraph makes

the writer's point of view clear: 'society has failed them' gives a reason rather than blaming.

There is balance in the rest of the article. Using clear topic sentences, the writer sets out the varying viewpoints in the next two paragraphs, considering both sides equally. There then follows a paragraph highlighting the need to offer solutions to the problem rather than condemning and judging.

The final paragraph returns to the idea of 'criticising, blaming and judging' – a rhetorical technique used to highlight exactly what the presentational features directed the reader to do in the first place – before subtly suggesting that the people who 'turn their backs' might equally be the reader.

The writer of this article is not suggesting that there isn't a problem with teenage disaffection. What it is suggesting is that something other than 'blame' might be more productive.

page 17

Extract from a Grade A* response

The way the report has been compiled emphasises the student's dissatisfaction in places: for example, we know that 45% of girls now dislike wearing a blazer, but it does not say that 53% still like wearing one. There are also some significant ambiguities: if only 69% of students complained about the school uniform, why should it be that 96% think it should be abolished all together?

There is, though, an apparent balance in the analysis of the results. Since so many students would be pleased to start school earlier, the fact that they would like a longer lunch break seems more acceptable.

page 18

Extract from a Grade A response

The writer makes no real attempt to appear unbiased in this report. From the first mention of a 'smug grin' on Simon Cowell's face to the final comment from Morello, the writer is on the side of the band against the multi-millionaire.

The strongest quote goes to Tim Morello, as he says they will save the charts from 'this abyss of bland mediocrity'.

It is an emotive phrase which is not countered by anything said by McElderry or Cowell. The metaphor sticks in our mind.

Not only that, whilst McElderry throws darts at Zack de la Rocha, Morello seems pleasanter and more worthy of our respect. He says he likes Cowell and that 'He's a great entertainer'. This wins round the reader, along with the fact that the band is fighting for 'democracy'…

page 19

Extract from a Grade A* response

When it comes to setting out her own viewpoint, the writer is very definite: 'The above view is far from the truth'. This is a simple and absolute sentence. It allows for no disagreement. The view is supported by emotive language ('kicked to death'), and this is highlighted by a contrast – where the incident happened: 'in the quiet Dorset suburb'… Somehow, the juxtaposition of horror and peacefulness adds extra pathos and horror to the event.

When the writer uses inclusive pronouns – 'we' and 'our' – the reader is invited to share blame, and therefore responsibility, for the desperate plight of the homeless. It clearly reinforces this responsibility with the direct 'what we need to do' at the end of the last paragraph, stressing that it is imperative to act immediately.

page 21

Extract from a Grade A* response

The warmth of the colour scheme highlights the sunset, which although rather clichéd in its suggestion of 'happy ending', is nevertheless an enticing promise for a holiday destination.

Since the advertisement sets out to lure us to Devon, it is no surprise that the final detail on the page is a number to ring and a website to contact in order to get additional information about Devon; and the name of the county is balanced in the bottom right-hand corner, solid and red, to link with the colour of the attractions in the heading (where 'Devon' is again prominent). Presumably the name is pointing upwards to take our eyes up, towards the couple, the romance and the beauty…

page 23

Extract from a Grade A response

The swine flu leaflet has been produced for an adult audience so the text is bold and designed to be simply effective. The block capitals scream to the reader that this is important; 'INFORMATION' appears twice, for emphasis, and the telephone number to call is at the top, in a prominent position.

The colours are dark and dismal, because this is an important, dangerous and serious matter. After all, black is the colour of death.

It is clear, though, that the main item which will be noticed is the man and his germs. Using a hand to stop the germs spreading obviously is not working and the spray is unpleasant and certainly threatening. His face, as he sneezes, is crumpled and pained and the idea, therefore, is that flu is not something to be take lightly…

page 25

Extract from a Grade A response

As this is a blog, the style is chatty: 'Hi it's Glen here.' It is clearly informal, because the comma is missed after 'Hi'. Obviously, the intention is to make the readers feel as if they are friends – hence, too the casual 'We're reached…', assuming the readers know who he is talking about. This is all to make the blog more interesting as it makes it seem closer to the readers themselves. The initial details of what is happening are relatively simple and clear ('we camped on the ice very late'). This is in contrast to the more vivid and interesting section later, when the prose becomes more poetic: there is the gasp in the alliteration of 'absolutely astounding', the simile of 'green inverted curtains', which moves the incredible sight into a comparison with domestic normality, and the repetition of 'stunning', as if the writer is simultaneously lost for more varied words…

Scott's writing is more formal and more stoical. Here is a man facing death and setting out exactly what has happened and why. The language is somehow more functional…

page 29

The opening of a Grade A* response

The use of language in these extracts appears to mirror the kinds of people the biographers are writing about. Whereas Jan Marsh uses very expressive, emotive language to describe her subject, an artist, with phrases like 'highly coloured iconic images of loose-haired sirens grace countless items of merchandise', John Wilson's biographer uses a very terse, unemotional style indeed, especially when describing the events leading up to the tragic blinding of the subject: 'One boy present was blinded in one eye. John Wilson was blinded in both.'

The contrast in style is indicative of the contrast in subject; whereas Rossetti inhabited a world of the arts, John Wilson was a Scottish politician – two very different worlds indeed…

Extract from a Grade A response

Orwell uses language to suggest a negative attitude towards his experience: in the first two sentences he uses 'exhausting', 'every quarter' and 'traversed'. He sounds rather unenthusiastic about his experience – 'traversed' suggests he has undergone an arduous expedition, difficult and exhausting. The use of metaphor to describe the 'monstrous' chimneys, coupled with them 'pouring forth smoke', suggests a hellish atmosphere, reinforced with the use of the word 'rosy' – which in other contexts would be a positive word but here merely reinforces the hell-like image with its suggestion of red.

Not only is there a suggestion of hell in the imagery and language used, but Orwell creates a sense of danger. There is a sense that visibility is poor, highlighted through repetition of the mention of 'smoke' and 'misty'. He is periodically surprised by the 'huge jets of flame' which randomly appear out of the chimneys. He ends his description with the powerful metaphor of 'fiery red serpents' which reinforces again the image of hell created in this description of Sheffield. The red is of hell, the serpents are like the devil and the fire seems all-consuming…

The opening of a Grade B response

The Monkey Island review opens with an extended metaphor, using 'set sail', 'journey' and 'come into port' to suggest that the game is in itself an exciting expedition, a great adventure. The first sentence explains the context for the review, before quickly beginning a description of the characters and setting of the game. The writer clearly approves; he or she describes 'amusing twists' which suggests the game will be entertaining. The use of the word 'unconventional' is clearly meant positively in this context also, as if the game offers something new and exciting, breaking with normal expectation. Language is used positively elsewhere with 'engaging' and 'funny' to describe the tone, and 'wacky' to possibly imply that this will please those gamers with an unusual, interesting style themselves.

The final sentence sums up the viewpoint effectively. 'Lengthy' is used here as another positive attribute of the game, as if it offers real value for money. It ties in with

the idea of the game as a 'journey', as if it will be a long but enjoyable one…

Extract from a Grade A* response

The readers of this web page are likely to be people interested in conservation and animal welfare. The internationally recognised logo at the top immediately draws attention to what this web page is about. Then, the use of colour further suggests environmental concerns, earthy greens and browns being the predominant colours. The muted blues and oranges are used to highlight certain features, like information pages available on the site, but are still in earthy, natural colours to suggest that the protection of the earth is important.

This idea is reinforced with a picture of a globe, virtually central to the web page. Using this graphic image reminds the reader of the centrality, the dominant importance, of the work of the organisation…

The opening of a Grade A response

The text is both informing and advising as it tells readers about how to help save the environment. The opening 'Yes, yes…' makes the person offering the advice sound reasonable and as if they are speaking to us directly. Then, once a friendly approach has been established, there is a stream of exclamations and rhetorical questions to tell the reader exactly what is needed and challenge them to become involved.

The list of what we need to do at the start of the second paragraph hammers home the requirements: 'recycle… send…re-use…stop…' The imperatives demand action…

Grade A*

This photograph is used to suggest the overall aims and purpose of this organisation. The slogan 'Fur is Dead' on the tee shirt is suggesting two meanings: firstly that wearing fur is out-moded and out-dated and therefore unfashionable, which is designed to appeal to a fashion-conscious audience. However, the stress used with the colour red of the word 'dead', not only implies it is old-fashioned but also, in a literal sense, that fur as a fashion fabric is created by death – by the slaughter of innocent animals. Using red not only intensifies the effect of this word but also has connotations of blood and violence, suggesting the violent means used to supply fur to the fashion industry.

The tee shirt is depicted as being worn by a live animal, a very friendly-looking domestic dog. Placing the tee shirt in this way creates a sense of sympathy as most people like dogs and many have a dog as a pet of their own. This serves to remind the audience that there is little difference between taking fur from an animal in the wild and taking it from a domestic animal.

So the writer makes Capri so[...] manages to make it seem easy [...] 20 minutes from Sorrento, and th[...] 'short ride' by railway to Capri town.[...]

The advertisement is successful, because[...] of geographical detail, exaggeration and e[...] description to paint a picture of a holiday des[...] that almost anyone would love to enjoy. It 'sells[...] describing it as a place of sights ('the 'gaze' in the[...] and relaxation ('laze').

---

page 45

Grade B

The text is from a holiday magazine, so it is trying to attract people to visit the island of Capri. The audience must be quite intelligent, because the first sentence is very long and the names could be quite confusing ('Sorrento, Positano, Salerno and Amalfi').

The writer uses several linguistic devices to make the idea of a holiday on Capri seem exciting. There are two similes ('mythological statues sit like sentinels' and 'like a satellite') which conjure up powerful pictures in your mind's eye. The town of Anacapri is made to seem special by describing it as a 'Garden of Eden'; this is the paradise garden in the Bible, so we are meant to think of a holiday paradise. Powerful verbs and adjective are used throughout to stir up interest: clouds don't just move but 'flee across the sky', and the alleyways are a 'labyrinth'.

---

page 49

Extract from a Grade A response

The first text is from a blog and uses language in a more imaginative way. There is 'Face it…' to make it seem conversational; and short 'sentences' to make the reader stop short, like the children: 'Frozen. Rabbits caught in the headlights.' Both metaphors make the children seem terrified – frozen stiff – but also sensitive and easily harmed: 'rabbits'.

Of course, the pensioner in the second text is easily harmed too. This text also creates sympathy, through describing Frank as a 'prisoner' and the fact that 'the police don't do anything', which makes him seem vulnerable and helpless in his situation. Perhaps like the bird in the first text. Frank is quoted directly in this report, giving the point of view from his side, allowing the reader to understand things from his perspective and therefore creating even more sympathy…

---

page 51

Assessment objective	Question 1	Question 2	Question 3	Question 4
Read and understand texts	✔	✔	✔	✔
Select material appropriate to purpose	✔	✔	✔	✔
Collate material from different sources				✔
Make comparisons and cross references as appropriate				✔
Explain and evaluate how writers use linguistic and grammatical features to achieve effects and engage and influence the reader				✔
Explain and evaluate how writers use structural and presentational features to achieve effects and engage and influence the reader		✔		
Support comments with detailed textual references	✔	✔	✔	✔

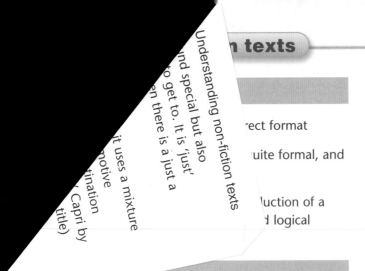

A possible plan might offer:

Introduction:

Why it is important to have interests/hobbies

Part 1:

The kinds of things school offers – music, sport, extra lessons (Science)

Part 2:

- Why it is a good idea
- Free/cheaper cost
- Familiar surroundings
- On-hand expertise

Conclusion:

What you stand to gain and how the school would improve

page 61

Extract from a Grade A* response

Dear Sir,

I am hoping you will undertake a study of how to improve our life in this locality, with particular emphasis on what can be done to improve life for youngsters. It is with considerable regret that I find myself having to write this letter: that a sixteen year old should be outlining to the council the benefits that would arise from the provision of better facilities for young people almost beggars belief, because the positive outcomes which would arise from improved facilities should be obvious.

Of course, currently we are experiencing increased levels of youth crime; and many local residents appear afraid to leave their homes at night. If teenagers had somewhere to go, had role models whose lifestyles they could aspire

to, and had genuine support from a caring council, there is no doubt the situation could be turned around in a matter of months. Their alienation would be gone…

page 65

Possible response:

The day finally came! It was time to put the plans into action. We had been waiting for a long time so everyone was very excited. We had one final meeting; the plans were looked at again, so we could be certain that we hadn't missed anything. We wanted to make sure we had made all our preparations.

page 67

Possible punctuation for paragraph:

The problem with family life today is that people do not spend enough time together. They are all running around, working, playing and leading active lives. Spending time together is not valued any more and that is one reason why times like family holidays can be stressful and difficult.

'It is time to act,' says Mrs Helen Smith from The Family Society. 'It is time to make more effort in supporting families so they can spend more time together and offer them financial support, so that work stops becoming the most important aspect of parents' lives.'

page 69

abundant: plentiful

There was an abundant supply of water once the new well was created.

archaic: very out-of-date, antiquated

She's very old-fashioned in the way she speaks – some of her expressions are archaic.

benevolent: kindly, friendly, with goodwill

My uncle is very benevolent – he always thinks the best of people.

caustic: sarcastic, cutting

That was a very caustic reply to my simple question!

dejected: miserable, despondent

The fans were dejected after being beaten in the Cup.

exuberant: full of high spirits

The children in Mrs Smith's class were exuberant when she told them they could go home early.

exertion: strenuous effort

The exertion proved too much and he had to have a long rest.

fallacious: wrong, misleading

That rumour is fallacious.

gregarious: enjoying the company of other people

I'm very gregarious so I hate being on my own.

jaunty: cheerful and self-confident

When Sam heard he'd got into college, he walked home with a jaunty step.

lackadaisical: lazy, with no sense of purpose

Luke was lackadaisical about doing revision, so his exam results were poor.

myriad: an indefinitely large number

Myriad lights appeared as the plane came down to land.

nostalgic: longing for home or for things to be as they were

Many older people seem nostalgic for their youth.

proverbial: famous, notorious

She ran home like the proverbial wind.

reminiscent: reminding one of something

That music is reminiscent of an old song we used to sing.

stationary: still, not moving

Luckily I was stationary at the traffic lights when the child ran into the road.

verdant: green

After all the rain, the hills were verdant with the new vegetation.

wrench: a sudden twist or pull

She had to give a wrench to get the door open.

---

page 71

Grade A*

Violence towards women should never be tolerated. To some people, it seems acceptable for women to be beaten, abused or degraded – but it is time for the world in general to say 'Enough is enough'. We should never again have to turn on our televisions and see women in tears or begging for a better life. Everyone should be equal and the days of female torment should be ended.

---

page 72

Possibilities:

The one thing I didn't want was a bruise on my arm.

I will simply look ugly with that lump on my neck.

Could there be anything more cowardly than beating up a defenceless 98-year-old pensioner?

---

page 73

A Grade A* conclusion

You yourself would benefit from all this, of course. Out walking with your young children and beautiful wife at the weekends, you would be so much safer – as would we all. No more leaping into local hedges to avoid the screeching wheels of a baseball-capped ex-sixth-former… No, tranquillity would once more stroll along, hand in hand with your daughter, nodding at passers-by and advanced young drivers alike.

The school is the place to start the transformation and our school needs to move into the modern era and help students develop the skills which will really benefit them in life. What is more useful: an hour's driving instruction or a typical RE lesson? There really is no contest…

---

page 77

Extract from a Grade A response

17 Brunswick Mount
Barthinsham
Gloucestershire
JL4 5KB

16 June 2011

The Environmental Health Officer
Barthinsham Council Offices
Nubb Road
Barthinsham
JL7 1AA

Dear Sir

As you are aware, we spoke on the telephone yesterday about the problems I have been having with my neighbours, who recently moved in to 19 Brunswick Mount. You asked me to set out my complaints in writing, and I hope this letter will clarify my main concerns.

Firstly, we are suffering because of the amount of noise coming from next door. Throughout the day, their dogs bark in the yard and no one makes any effort to quieten them. Both are tied to a stake in the centre of the grassed area. We also have music coming through the walls at all hours of the day and night. It is 'heavy metal' and allows us no peace at all. Since our neighbours never seem to sleep during the hours of darkness, the bedlam continues all night.

Secondly, we are concerned about their general behaviour…

page 79

Extract from a Grade B response

The school play was a tremendous experience and I will remember it all my life. For three nights, the school hall was full and 'Our Day Out' went down a storm.

The main interest for a lot of people who came to watch was the fact that the teachers in the play were played by our own staff. The horrible Mr Briggs was the really lovely and warm Mr Sellers (Can I have a top grade for my next controlled assessment, sir?) and Mrs Kay, who all the kids loved, was Miss Farriday. She was made up to look really quite old and carried off the role with real conviction.

The staging was imaginative. For a start, the bus that the children travelled on whilst on their day out was just a set of chairs that seemed to come and go almost magically…

page 80

Grade A*

I passionately believe that tackling bullying and letting students come to school to learn and be happy is vital. Until you have suffered at the hands of stronger, bigger or uncaring people, you cannot understand the pain that it causes. I have had friends who have regularly cried themselves to sleep at night; I myself have had to have medical treatment because of the abuse to which I was subjected and the effect it had. Such situations cannot be allowed to continue.

To sum up: it is vital that our school and other schools in this area take the problem seriously and work together on an anti-bullying charter that would form the basis of concerted action to eradicate the curse of the bully in our community. Individuals can then be counselled and

everyone can be happier. It would be for the good of all, not for the good of the few and if we are genuine in our desire to improve things, we can succeed.

page 81

Grade A*

Steppington: just the place to be!

It might not be Paris – but it just might be better
Maria Hills is convinced you could do much worse
than visit

For some of you seasoned travellers, you might think of Steppington as the last place on earth that you would choose to spend some quality time. However, there are some real bonuses to living here, especially if you are, like me, a teenager.

One of the great things about this town is the wide mixture of people who live here. And there's something for everyone! My gran, who is in her seventies, has a better social life than I do – she's forever popping off to the day centre to take advantage of the huge range of stuff they offer to senior citizens including, would you believe, line dancing! The Community Centre is a thriving place for little ones as well, offering all kinds of classes and lessons during day time and evening hours.

Because the public transport system is so efficient, it's only a short hop on the bus or train to get Gran, and the rest of us, to the massive shopping centre or the sports centre. During the holidays, most of us spend a lot of time at the sports centre; the range of facilities is fantastic and you can really take advantage of the expertise on offer. In fact our basketball coach is in charge of the national team, so there's really some high-level training provided there.

The local shops are fine – not 5th Avenue by any means but that's no bad thing. They are friendly, family-run in the main, offering everything you need on a daily basis: butcher, grocer, newsagent and Post Office. The local bakers are famous in our area and people do in fact come for miles to get their fancy pastries and buns. And the Coach and Horses pub has just been given a national award for the quality of its lunches – you haven't lived until you've tried their famous toad in the hole!

Our area is what it is – a local community – friendly, safe and fun. It's not a tourist resort, it's a home to a lot of lovely people, and we teenagers love living here. Visitors always have a pleasant surprise and usually come back again!

page 83

Extract from a Grade A* response

Dear Editor,

I felt I had to write to make clear to so many of your readers that the internet is not some agent of Satan and about to bring the world to an end. It is, actually, a tool that will improve the lives of mankind, just as the wheel did, and the plough; and it will help the education of our young people and the development of ideas and teachings throughout the world. Has there ever been a most universally accessible tool for the advancement of mankind?

Of course, we have all heard about the pornography that is available and the fostering of terrorist links via the internet, but that is far from being a balanced picture. Anything in life can be used or abused – just think about the axe or any piece of sharpened steel – but the benefits must always be taken into account as well as the problems…

page 85

Extract from a Grade B response

Dear Mrs Dagnall,

You asked for our thoughts on the School Learning Area (SLA), so I felt I should set out in writing how unhappy we all are with the facility as it stands. Everyone knows it is very rarely used, but before this there has never really been a chance for us to say why – so here goes.

It is essential that it is regularly staffed if the best is to be got out of it. Students want to go in to learn but it is often not possible to find what we need and there is no one there to help us. If we had the staffing in there that is required, our work would improve and, after all, that is what the school is wanting, isn't it?

Only last week I needed to find some facts about Zoroastrianism for an RE project and I got absolutely nowhere. The encyclopaedias are old and battered and not one of the PCs was functioning. It was impossible to get the information I required…

page 87

Grade A*

To our new students

Hello and welcome!! I'm delighted to have the opportunity to say a few words to you, our new students, on behalf of the Year 11 Student Council. Do you know, it feels like only yesterday that I was where you are now; coming to the end of Year 6, feeling a huge mixture of excitement and anxiety about what the coming year at a new school was going to bring with it.

You should have received your Welcome Pack by now, and visited the school at least once. I'm sure it all feels very confusing and overwhelming, but please don't worry. Your form tutor, who you met at Welcome Evening, will go through everything you need to know and keep a close eye on you for the first few weeks until you find your feet. Also, I'm sure you know that each form has 'Peer Mentors' attached to it – students from Year 10 who are carefully selected from the crème de la crème of those students queuing up to offer their help and support. You see, the school is full of people ready and willing to help make the transition as easy as possible. Trust me, within a couple of weeks you'll feel like you've always been here!

It's always a big concern for new students: are the teachers really that strict, will I get bullied, what do I do about equipment, what if I get lost… but don't worry, it really isn't that bad. You'll get a map on your first day, and the Peer Mentors will guide you around until you get the hang of the building. You need to make sure you listen to your Form Tutor carefully, as they'll run through everything with you. If I were you, I'd check those lists in your Welcome Pack about standard dress and equipment though – you don't want to be worried that you've missed or forgotten something.

One thing I found very useful was the homework diary – I used to write absolutely everything down in that, because I was so terrified I'd forget something! You'll get a lot of information in your first week or so, and it can seem a bit like a minefield of information, so just make a note of everything you might forget. And remember the homework diary has got a map of the school in it as well, which is another reason to hang on to it.

I'm sure you'll be fine and will really enjoy coming up to secondary school. We're waiting to welcome you, and please remember – if you don't know something, just ask! The teachers are all great (well, most of them!) and the students are much, much more friendly than you might think they look, from the outside…

We are all looking forward to seeing you in September.

page 89

Extract from a Grade A* response

… The result of buying this wonderful new device is that I can navigate anywhere, stay in touch via the airways or the internet, play more games than I ever imagined I would need, listen to the radio and my downloaded tracks and still have a hand free to hold the hand of my girlfriend as we wander into the park.

My mum has, only recently, grudgingly admitted that one of the benefits of modern technology has been the mobile phone. They can be annoying, granted, but they can also really help to keep us safe. So now that battle's won, I'm on to my next one – the iPod touch 64 Gb. I just need an angle to persuade her that it's going to save the world – or at least save my little brother from a burning building – which is apparently what it's going to take!

page 91

Grade A*

(Terrible) Tales of Terror

I sat down last night, armed with not only the obligatory bucket of popcorn but also this time my choice of shield – cushion and cat – prepared to be deliciously terrified by Channel 4's much-hyped new season of ghost stories (10 pm, Channel 4). But oh dear.

The cast list is impressive. Not only some old favourites but some real rising stars, including Mary Fawcett, recent BAFTA award winner. The writing credits promised quality scripting (Paul Morello of 'The Chaser' fame, no less). However, despite the hype, neither the impressive cast nor quality writing pedigrees were going to save this Christmas turkey from being a huge, crushing disappointment.

There were a couple of decent storylines, but unfortunately the plots and atmosphere were spoiled so early in the tale by horrendously overblown performances that I couldn't have cared less whether anyone discovered who'd been haunting the turret, who'd 'opened the window' (you'll have to watch it if you want to know the significance of this) and by 10.20 I'd already picked up the remote to flick over to the other side.

A shame – I looked forward to this but wouldn't recommend it. Don't waste your time.

page 93

Grade A

For all those participating in the Foreign Exchange Trip...

Having a foreign visitor can be a great experience – but if you know what you are doing, everything is likely to go much more smoothly. So, here are a few hints which might just make the visit easier and much more fun...

To begin: when you first meet your visitor, make sure you smile and look friendly! There's nothing worse for their morale than looking disappointed with your visitor. They will be tired from their journey and just as worried as you, so it is your job to reassure them. Please try to at least greet them in their own language – remember, that is the point of this exchange visit after all, and it will also make your visitor feel welcome. Even if you are not very confident about your accent, give it a try; your guest will thank you for it and it will help to break the ice.

At home, hopefully your guest will be given their own room. Even if they are sharing a room, make sure they know where to put their things. It's a good idea to leave them alone for a little while so they can get used to their own surroundings. Make sure you show them where the bathroom is, how the stereo or mp3 dock works and so on – and then, give them a bit of peace.

When introducing them to your family, say each person's name really clearly. This will be appreciated by your guest, who will be worried that they will make a mistake with someone's name. And if you have the kind of relatives that I do, please warn them in advance that shouting slowly in English is not the best way of speaking to someone in a foreign language!

Above all, we want this exchange trip to be the great success that it always is. If you are friendly, polite and try hard to put yourself into your visitor's shoes, you can ensure that they will have a lovely time and you will have made a friend for life.

Collins Revision

New GCSE English

✔ **For GCSE English from 2010**

Higher

Exam Practice Workbook

Written by Keith Brindle

How to use this workbook

How this workbook is organised

This exam practice workbook is designed to help you develop your exam skills and test how well you are doing. Hopefully, it will show you are working 'on the right lines' as well as allowing you to spot some areas in which you might be able to improve.

It deals with the exam only because your controlled assessments will be prepared with the help of your teacher.

Its coverage links closely to the AQA English and English Language exams which are assessed like this:

	English	English Language
Examination paper (Reading and Writing)	2 hours Section A: 1 hour Reading non-fiction texts 20% of final marks Section B: 1 hour Writing two responses – one shorter, one longer 20% of final marks	2 hours Section A: 1 hour Reading non-fiction texts 20% of final marks Section B: 1 hour Writing two responses – one shorter, one longer 20% of final marks
Speaking and listening	3 assessments • Presentation • Discussing and listening • Adopting a role 20% of final marks	3 assessments • Presentation • Discussing and listening • Adopting a role 20% of final marks
Controlled assessments (Reading and Writing)	2 assessments Literary Reading 20% of final marks Producing Creative Texts 20% of final marks	3 assessments Extended Reading 15% of final marks Creative Writing 15% of final marks Spoken Language Study 10% of final marks

There are two major sections in this exam practice workbook:

Examination reading:

Understanding non-fiction texts   (pages 108–155)

Examination writing:

Producing non-fiction texts   (pages 156–197)

As you work through the book, you can check how well you have done by referring to the Answers section that follows.

How to use this workbook

Work through the tasks provided in these two sections and then mark your own work, to see how well you have done. This will test your ability to respond to the requirements of the exam.

You can also consider what else you might have done, which would have brought you higher marks.

Exam Section A: Understanding non-fiction texts

First, you will have the opportunity to examine different kinds of media and non-fiction texts and answer questions on them. These will be the kinds of questions which you will meet in the exam.

Then, you will work though sections focusing on the sorts of questions you will be asked, one sort at a time. The same skills are tested each year, so you will know exactly what to expect in the exam.

Finally, you will tackle a complete practice Section A.

Exam Section B: Producing non-fiction texts

First, you can work through practice sections which focus on the skills you will require for the writing section of the exam.

Next, you will be guided through fundamental requirements for the writing tasks, for example: planning, writing in varied sentences, using punctuation and paragraphs appropriately.

Then, there are opportunities for you to practise the different kinds of writing you might have to face: for example, persuasion and argument.

As you move through these important sections, there are extra writing tasks, so that you can practise writing at length.

Exam Section A: Understanding non-fiction texts

Responding to the questions

Section A of the exam should take you one hour to complete. It is important that you manage to finish in the time, because the tasks in Section B are still to come. The exam paper will contain three texts. On the Higher Tier paper, there will be four questions; on the Foundation Tier paper, there will be five questions.

The questions will be based on the following assessment objectives, which expect candidates to:

- Read and understand texts, selecting material appropriate to purpose, collating from different sources and making comparisons and cross-references as appropriate.
- Develop and sustain interpretations of writers' ideas and perspectives.
- Explain and evaluate how writers use linguistic, grammatical, structural and presentational features to achieve effects and engage and influence the reader.

These may seem difficult or confusing, but when you respond to texts in the exam, you will be asked to:

- find information
- explain what writers are saying and suggesting
- say how language has been used
- compare presentational features of texts, like pictures and heading

The way the marks are awarded is predictable, so you will know in advance how long to spend on each question according to how many marks are awarded for the answer.

The key to success is to:

- read the texts carefully, so you know exactly what they are saying and so that you can find the material necessary for the answers
- read the questions carefully, so that you include the detail and interpretation for which you can be rewarded. You will not gain marks for writing about the wrong things. Consider underlining the important words in any question, so that you focus on them when responding
- respond in appropriate detail and in the right amount of time, so that you answer all the questions but still have enough time to complete Section B without having to panic
- support what you say with evidence from the texts. Usually, the best technique is to offer point/evidence/ explanation or analysis.

What the questions involve

The Reading section of the exam is slightly different for each tier.

For the **Higher Tier exam**, you will have to:

- read three quite detailed texts
- answer four questions, testing your ability to
  - find information (this is information retrieval)   8 marks
  - write about presentation   8 marks
  - analyse what is being suggested or inferred   8 marks
  - compare how language is used in texts.   16 marks

  Total 40 marks

For the **Foundation Tier exam**, you will have to:

- read three texts

- answer five questions, testing your ability to
  - find information (this is information retrieval)   4 marks
  - write about what is being suggested or inferred   4 marks
  - find evidence and say what it is suggesting   8 marks
  - write about language   12 marks
  - compare the presentational features used in texts.   12 marks

  Total 40 marks

Section A questions will look like this:

Paper has two sections: only Section A is given here

Higher Tier

Section A: Reading

Answer all questions in this section.

You are advised to spend about one hour on this section.

You need to allow a few minutes to read through the texts before answering the questions

You will be given three 'unseen' texts in the exam

Read **Source 1**, the newspaper article headed *Can this be true?*, by Steven Gale.

1 What do you learn from Steven Gale's newspaper article about the strange sightings over Kennilworth?

(8 marks)

This is a retrieval question, so you just need to find relevant information

Now read **Source 2**, the letter and the picture that goes with it, called *What I saw – and it's not fiction!* by Ailsa McMurray.

2 How do the headline and picture add to the effectiveness of the text?

(8 marks)

This question is asking you to analyse the presentational features of the text and comment on their overall effect

Now read **Source 3**, *My other life*, which is an extract from an autobiography.

3 What are some of the thoughts and feelings Zac has during his adventure?

(8 marks)

This is an inference question, asking you to look beyond what is said to what is being suggested and to support your comments with evidence from the text

Now you need to refer to **Source 3**, *My other life*, and either **Source 1** or **Source 2**. You are going to compare two texts, one of which you have chosen.

4 Compare the ways in which language is used for effect in the two texts. Give examples and explain what effect they have.

(16 marks)

This question carries the highest mark and demands a detailed comparison of how language is used and with what effect

Remind yourself of the number of marks given to each question and allocate your time accordingly

Why are purpose and audience important?

The terms 'purpose and audience' are often a vital starting point when you are answering the exam questions, because everything in the text is likely to be targeted at a particular purpose and audience. For example, the purpose and audience are the reasons why the writer chooses particular language and presentational features.

Focus on the **purpose** of this text.

We'll be there in a minute – teenagers fly on school run

Some children moan about having to get a bus to school. A small group of teenagers on a remote Scottish island, however, have the rather more exciting prospect of going to school by plane on what is believed to be the world's shortest commercial flight.

The journey from Papa Westray to Westray in the Orkney Islands takes 96 seconds, covering a distance of just over a mile. With a tail wind, it can take as little as 47 seconds. Normally the teenagers go by ferry but when the vessel was taken out of service for refurbishment, Loganair stepped in and offered to fly them to Westray Junior High. It has changed its schedule to ensure the children get to school on time.

Willie McEwen, acting head teacher at Westray Junior High, said: "We're delighted that Loganair has come forward with this solution. Our children will enjoy the flying especially as, at this time of year, it can be quite rough on the boat."

Guinness World Records said that it did not recognise the world's shortest scheduled domestic flight. "The category is currently under research," a spokesman said.

The Times, 06.11.09

1 Why has the writer written this text? Try to support what you say with evidence from the text.

_____

_____

_____

_____

_____

_____

_____

_____

(4 marks)

2 For each extract in the grid opposite, say:
- who you think they were written for – the audience
- why you have come to that decision.

Extract	Audience	Reason for decision	Marks
My husband snores all night. Why not do something about it..?			2
Stop throwing things away. Householders need to be more environmentally aware.			4
After centuries, nurses are starting to get some credit for all they do.			2

(8 marks)

Focus on the **purpose** and **audience** of this text.

3 What is the purpose and audience for this text and how does it appeal to its audience?

Support everything you say with evidence from the text.

_____

_____

_____

_____

_____

_____

_____

_____

_____

_____

_____

_____

Continue on lined paper if necessary.

(8 marks)

In the exam, you are tested on your ability to find exactly the right details to answer questions correctly.

Read this newspaper item.

Get your votes in for heroes

THE nominations are in – and now the voting can begin for the Your Heroes Award for 2009.

The response we received was staggering, with more than 100 individuals and organisations being put forward.

As previously stated, the competition now separates into a voting and judged section.

This is because we felt some categories required further careful consideration before winners and runners-up were chosen.

In other categories, we felt it was fairest to let the community decide who should take the plaudits.

And in this week's *Express* there will be another chance for you, our readers, to cast your votes in the categories for Health Service hero, Teenage Hero Award, Top Teacher and Police Community Support Officer Award.

All the nominations are featured on our websites www.wakefield express.co.uk, www.pontefractand castlefordexpress.co.uk and www. hemsworthandsouthelmsallexpress. co.uk to help you make an informed choice before casting your vote.

In true X-Factor style you can vote as many times as you like but each vote must be on an original coupon. No photocopies will be accepted.

The coupon will be printed in this week's *Express*. The judges will be examining the nominations in the other categories during the next few weeks.

Once all the choices have been made, we will be left with a top three in each category and they will be invited to the final event, which takes place at Wakefield Town Hall on November 30.

Compere for the night will be Ian Clayton, and also represented will be the competition's sponsors, Wakefield Council and NHS Wakefield District.

Wakefield Express, 28.10.09

1 Find two details in the text which show that the competition is popular.

_____

_____

_____

(2 marks)

2 How can the public be involved in selecting the winners? List four things they can do.

_____

_____

_____

_____

_____

_____

(4 marks)

Read these letters to a newspaper carefully.

Booking agents bleeding us dry...

Thanks for your article last week. It is disgraceful that we are faced with extortionate booking fees for concert and theatre tickets. If a ticket 'costs' £30 but you are forced to pay £4.50 on top, it should be advertised at £34.50. The booking agents are guilty of deception and the law should do something about it. Why doesn't someone use the Trades Descriptions Act to sort them out?
Steve Forbing, Hackney

I wanted to go to see my favourite band recently, but the booking agent had added a huge 40% booking fee to the price of the ticket. If something isn't done soon, the artists will suffer because fans will simply refuse to pay.
Janice Barrell, NW7

Last year, I went to see Leonard Cohen in concert at the Albert Hall. I paid £90 plus a booking fee of £3.50. I saw my hero 20 years ago in the same place and I paid £12.50 and no booking fee. Is it me, or is this appalling?
Danny Southern, Bromsgrove

3 Find four details in these letters which indicate that people have a right to complain about booking fees.

_____

_____

_____

_____

(4 marks)

4 Write down four words or phrases from the text which are critical of the current pricing policy.

_____

_____

_____

_____

(4 marks)

Will there be a report in the exam?

It is likely that there will be a newspaper report in the exam, which you will be expected to analyse. You might, for example, be asked to look at the language or the presentational features or at what the report says or is suggesting.

Read this newspaper report.

BOOTY & BEAST

Blonde bruiser kicks up storm

by RICHARD PEPPIATT

HEAD CASE: Elizabeth pulls ponytail

FOOTBALL babe Elizabeth Lambert is facing a life ban for sticking the boot in.

The blonde bruiser, 20, has been branded the dirtiest player in the women's game after a series of violent fouls in one match.

She yanked a player to the ground by her ponytail, punched another in the back and lunged into knee-high tackles. And it was all caught on camera.

Face

Midfielder Lambert was finally booked for booting the ball into the face of an attacker who was flat out on the ground. The vicious incidents came as her University of New Mexico team lost 1-0 to Brigham Young University in America. Her university has suspended her and she could now be banned from all football.

Coach Kit Vela said: "She clearly crossed the line of fair play."

But Lambert said: "I am deeply regretful. My actions were uncalled for. I let my emotions get the best of me in a heated situation."

TAKE THAT: She boots ball into girl's face

Star, 11.11.09

1 What are the purposes of this text? Explain your ideas.

_____

_____

_____

_____

(2 marks)

2 How does the report try to attract the attention of the reader?

_____

_____

_____

_____

(4 marks)

3 What is the effect of the headline, sub-heading and captions?

_____

_____

_____

_____

_____

(6 marks)

4 What impression of Elizabeth Lambert is created in the main section of text? (Do not comment on headings, captions, etc. in this answer.)

_____

_____

_____

_____

_____

_____

_____

(8 marks)

Next read this newspaper report.

Gales, floods and chaos on the roads... it's Friday 13th

By **John Ingham**

BRITAIN is on alert for a Friday 13th storm with violent gales of up to 70mph and half a month's rainfall in a few hours.

Forecasters yesterday issued an early severe weather warning ahead of the first major storm of the autumn tearing in from the Atlantic overnight into Saturday.

The West, North-west and Wales face the worst pummeling although no-one is expected to escape.

Much of the nation is on high alert for flooding and treacherous driving conditions. Motorists have been told to expect severe delays with power lines and trees likely to be brought down.

Intense downpours of more than two inches (60mm) – half the average for November – threaten towns such as Bocastle in Cornwall, devastated by flash floods in August 2004.

A Met Office spokesman said: "The West and North-west will be worst affected. In the South there'll be gale force winds gusting to 50mph and 60mph with the potential for storm force winds gusting to 70mph in the north of Scotland."

Daily Express, 11.11.09

5 What is the purpose and audience for this text, and how successful is it? Explain.

_____

_____

_____

_____

_____

Continue on lined paper if necessary.

(8 marks)

Aren't articles the same as reports?

Articles take a more considered view of events, including opinions and sometimes referring to related issues. Reports are more immediate and are usually about what has just happened.

Read this article carefully.

Sporting value
Heroes leading on from the front

STRIDING OUT: Sir Ian Botham, with leukaemia sufferers, launches Beefy's Great Forget Me Not Walk in London

ON and off the cricket pitch, Sir Ian Botham has always been a larger than life character. His barnstorming performances inspired a nation, and his relentless charity walks, in aid of Leukaemia research, have added to the aura and invincibility of the former all-rounder who lives in North Yorkshire.

Typically, he was not going to allow the 25th anniversary of his first walk from John O'Groats to Land's End, to pass unmarked as he looks to build upon the incredible £10m that he has already raised for the charity. His latest marathon effort deserves the fullest possible support.

But, just as importantly, Sir Ian, and former Olympic champion Sebastian Coe, who was revisiting his Sheffield childhood roots yesterday, continue to show that the impact of sports stars is not consigned to the field of play. What they do, away from the sporting arena, counts just as much, if not more so.

Thirty years after they captured the public's imagination, Lord Coe hopes the 2012 Olympics will inspire a grassroots sporting revolution, while Sir Ian believes that his fundraising can save lives. Typically, he has pledged to continue his charity walks until childhood Leukaemia is beaten. Without such determination, Britain would be a much poorer place.

Yorkshire Post, 11.11.09

1 What is the purpose and audience for this text? Explain.

_____

_____

_____

_____

(4 marks)

2 Find four words or phrases which are intended to show Ian Botham as a hero.

_____

_____

_____

_____

(4 marks)

Next read this article.

Facebook generation knits with the WI for a rest

Will Pavia

Sometimes it's hard to be a young woman. City life is relentless: there are work pressures, home pressures and the worry of constantly updating one's Facebook profile.

The answer, according to thousands of young people in cities across the country? Join the Women's Institute.

In the upstairs rooms of pubs in New Cross and Borough, South London, they gather to knit. In lofts in Shoreditch and Islington, London, they cross-stitch. In universities up and down the country, they learn crafts their grandmothers knew all drawn by a modern cry: modern life is stressful, let's make some chutney!

The phenomenon of the urban Women's Institute was first noted in 2005, when a group of young ladies in Fulham, West London, began meeting every month. The next year there was a group in Islington called N1WI. The Shoreditch sisters formed in 2007, sparking copycat WIs in Leeds and Manchester. A network of university WIs is now forming, with branches at Goldsmiths College and King's College London, and in Newcastle upon Tyne, Sheffield, Birmingham and Reading.

An investigation into what drives the new urban WIs suggests that it is the jam-making, crocheting and even darning that draws members. The very crafts that WIs have taught since 1897 are suddenly attractive.

At this week's meeting of the King's College WI, 20 women sat at tables learning how to make jewellery and spoke of the joys of meeting each other in actual physical locations.

Holly Thompson, 21, a theology student, said: "You're

Just as it was: women learning crafts

on your BlackBerry or iPhone the whole time. If there is an opportunity to talk to people in real life, that's appealing." Jenny Parker, 18, an English student from South London, said: "People don't go to youth clubs any more – there is nothing like this around."

A few said that their parents were worried. One feared that

her daughter would become a Young Conservative.

At the end of the evening, Jade Landers, 19, a medical student from southeast London, put on her home-made bracelets and went to leave. "I'm going to the Black Eyed Peas after a party at the Ministry of Sound," she said. "It's a pretty random evening."

The Times, 06.11.09

3 How does the writer use language to interest the reader?

_____

_____

_____

_____

_____

_____

(8 marks)

4 How does the writer want us to react to:
- the first three paragraphs
- the last three paragraphs?

_____

_____

_____

_____

_____

Continue on lined paper if necessary.

(8 marks)

Advertisements

You are most likely to be asked about how an advertisement uses language and presentational features, or what it is suggesting to the reader, and to relate these to its purpose and audience.

Read this advertisement.

Specialist Foster Carers Required

The National Fostering Agency wants to recruit highly motivated individuals to become specialist foster carers for 12-17 year olds.

In return you will receive:
• A generous retainer based package with a 'top up' care allowance
• Specialist training and 24 hour support

If you believe you have the skills to make a difference to a young person's life and want to be part of a professional team, then contact us on

0845 200 4040

www.nfa.ws

nfa national fostering agency

1 What impression of fostering is presented by this picture?
Use detail to support your ideas.

_____

_____

_____

_____

(4 marks)

2 How does the language used try to persuade the reader to become involved?

_____

_____

_____

_____

_____

_____

_____

_____

_____

(8 marks)

Next look at this advertisement.

3 How does the advertisement try to capture the reader's imagination in the following extracts?

Extract	How is the imagination captured?
Not exactly an ordinary desk job	
How many arms smugglers pop up in your inbox?	
Being in the front line of the fight against terrorism...	
...you're looking for something more suited to your extraordinary talents	

(8 marks)

4 What effect is created by the picture and other presentational features?

_____

_____

_____

_____

_____

_____

Continue on lined paper if necessary

(8 marks)

Some leaflets can be very long. Won't writing about them be difficult?

Some leaflets can sometimes stretch to four or six pages, sometimes folded, but you are likely to be asked to focus on just the front of a leaflet and perhaps one other page.

Read the front of this leaflet.

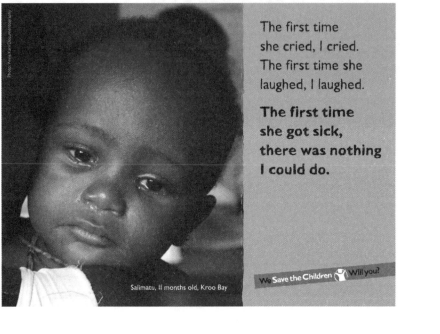

The first time she cried, I cried. The first time she laughed, I laughed.

The first time she got sick, there was nothing I could do.

Salimatu, 11 months old, Kroo Bay

We Save the Children Will you?

1 How does the picture attempt to make an immediate impact?

_____

_____

_____

_____

(4 marks)

2 How are we supposed to react when we read the words? Give evidence to support what you say.

_____

_____

_____

_____

_____

_____

_____

_____

(4 marks)

Now read the second part of the same leaflet.

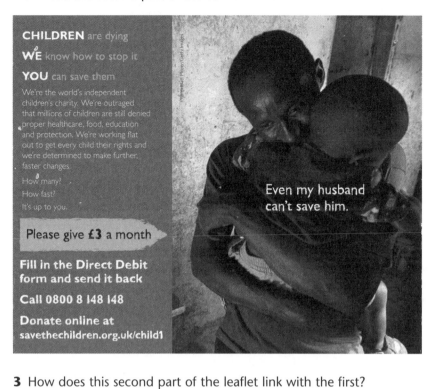

CHILDREN are dying
WE know how to stop it
YOU can save them

We're the world's independent children's charity. We're outraged that millions of children are still denied proper healthcare, food, education and protection. We're working flat out to get every child their rights and we're determined to make further, faster changes.

How many?
How fast?
It's up to you.

Please give **£3** a month

Fill in the Direct Debit form and send it back

Call 0800 8 148 148

Donate online at
savethechildren.org.uk/child1

Even my husband can't save him.

3 How does this second part of the leaflet link with the first?

_____
_____
_____
_____
_____
_____

(4 marks)

4 What is the effect of the short sentences?

_____
_____
_____
_____

(4 marks)

5 What is the purpose of this leaflet? Do you think it would be successful? Give reasons.

_____
_____
_____
_____
_____
_____
_____

(4 marks)

You might be asked write about *any* form of media or non-fiction text. It is best to be prepared. Be aware that letters can be very formal and functional or they can offer more personal views.

Read this letter from a regional newspaper.

Colourful local language that is disappearing

From: W Michael Waite, Carr Lane, Sutton on the Forest, North Yorkshire

I FIND the letters regarding our dialect fascinating, as they evoke many happy memories for this old Leeds loiner.

Regarding the use of the word "whisht", my old landlord in Edinburgh, a Scot born and bred, used to say "hod your whisht" meaning stop talking.

There are many other words which I recall as a child but no longer hear, such as my mother telling me to stop moidering her when she was busy and I wanted attention.

In the midlands, the word mithering was used with the same meaning. We used to have our bins emptied by the midden men, and road gulleys were fever grates, harking back to the days when disease was thought to be caused by bad smells.

Mother used to use scouring stone to edge the doorstep while I sat on the causer edge watching her. When I was older, I went apple kipping, and occasionally took a bit of tusky (rhubarb).

When playing taws, a cardinal sin was gibbing, or jibbing, when the forearm was used to supplement the impulse given by the thumb. My father-in-law, who came from Sheffield, used terms such as broddling your lug, meaning a vigorous poking of the ear, and taldering meaning tuneless singing.

It is sad that our colourful dialect is being replaced by sloppy television-derived speech from American sit-coms and rap. I know language is continually evolving, but I'm like, no way man.

Yorkshire Post, 11.11.09

1 What is the writer's main point? How does he attempt to convince the reader?

_____

_____

_____

(4 marks)

2 Find four examples to support his viewpoint.

_____

_____

_____

(4 marks)

3 How does he use language in the final sentence? Compare it with the language used in the first sentence.

_____

_____

_____

_____

_____

_____

(4 marks)

Diaries usually give a personal angle on what has happened.

This extract is taken from a teacher's diary.

> The whole day was dreadful again. I am sick and tired of standing in front of kids who don't want to learn anything and, worse still, seem determined to stop anyone else learning. First it was Year 7s: they look like little cherubs if you see them on their own, but put them together and they turn into a pack of deranged hounds. Uncontrollable at times. Then it was Year 9s, then 11s, then 10s but none of them were any better. They just get bigger and even more confident. It's shocking, it's demoralising and it's a daily occurrence. I can't help thinking that if an inspector walked in on any ordinary day, she would wonder where the senior members of staff are and why the ordinary teachers are just left to flounder. My previous school was so different...

4 Comment on the following language. What does it make the reader think?

Language	What the reader thinks
they look like little cherubs	
they turn into a pack of deranged hounds	
Uncontrollable at times	
It's shocking, it's demoralising and it's a daily occurrence	

(4 marks)

5 Why does the fact that this is written in the first person make it more effective for the reader?

_____

_____

_____

(2 marks)

6 Who does the teacher hold responsible for what is happening and how does she make this point?

_____

_____

_____

_____

_____

(4 marks)

Biographical writing

What sorts of writing does 'biographical' include?

The term biography refers to the story of someone's life. In the exam, you could be presented with a biographical extract, an autobiographical extract (where someone tells their own story), or even a piece about someone's adventures when travelling.

This is an extract from a biography of Florence Nightingale, who, with her nurses, introduced cleanliness into the care of injured soldiers during the Crimean War (1853–56). She had not been allowed to help much, but then there was a rush of casualties.

> It was Miss Nightingales's opportunity – at last the doctors turned to her. In this urgent work she met no opposition. Just as it was no one's business to clean the lavatories, so it was no one's business to clean the wards. She ordered two hundred hard scrubbing brushes and sacking for washing the floors. Her next step was to try to wash the men's clothes. The men said they preferred their own lice to other people's and refused to part with their shirts, stuffing them, filthy and vermin-ridden, under their blankets. The total amount of washing satisfactorily accomplished for the vast hospital was seven shirts. Miss Nightingale made arrangements to rent a house outside the barracks and have the washing done by soldiers' wives. She said she wished to have boilers put in by the Engineers Corps. The boilers were installed and paid for.

1 Find two improvements Florence Nightingale made.

_____

_____

(2 marks)

2 Whose fault was it that the conditions were so dirty? Offer evidence for your ideas.

_____

_____

_____

_____

_____

_____

(4 marks)

3 What sort of woman does 'Miss Nightingale' appear to be in this extract? Explain.

_____

_____

_____

_____

_____

_____

(4 marks)

This extract is taken from the autobiography of a nurse in the First World War. She is writing about one of her patients who tried to commit suicide rather than fight.

> When he could stand it no longer, he fired a revolver up through the roof of his mouth, but he made a mess of it. The ball tore out his left eye, and then lodged somewhere under his skull, so they bundled him into an ambulance and carried him, cursing and screaming, to the nearest field hospital. The journey was made in double-quick time, over rough Belgian roads. To save his life, he must reach the hospital without delay, and if he was bounced to death jolting along at breakneck speed, it did not matter. That was understood. He was a deserter, and discipline must be maintained. Since he had failed in the job, his life must be saved, he must be nursed back to health, until he was well enough to be stood up against a wall and shot. This is War. Things like this also happen in peace time, but not so obviously.

4 How does the nurse want us to feel about this man? Support your ideas with close reference to the text.

_____

_____

_____

_____

_____

_____

_____

_____

_____

_____

_____

(8 marks)

5 How is language used to make this incident particularly shocking?

_____

_____

_____

_____

_____

_____

_____

_____

_____

_____

_____

(8 marks)

Will we be expected to write about internet texts?

You can regard the web page as just another form of text. Any question(s) about it will be of the same kind you might be asked about an article or an advertisement. (You will not be asked about the function of any buttons or navigational tools shown on a web page, for example.)

Look carefully at this web page.

This page is sponsored by Fastrax and Complete Runner, Ilkley and Nelson - click the logos above to visit their sites

- Home
- New On Site
- Contact Me
- Race Calendars
- Results Index
- York RRL
- Entry Forms
- Search site
- Links
- Other Pages
- Login

Site Map
Register as an Organ Donor and save a life
UKResults supports the following organisations:
Lewa Wildlife Conservancy (Kenya)
Tusk Trust (UK)

Associate sites:
VLA Events
Sport Systems

In partnership with

St John Ambulance

St John Ambulance for all your event's First Aid Cover

Welcome to UKResults - Skype *ukresults* or *ukresults.ontheroad*

For friendly advice and assistance relating to your event, please contact me. My associates **VLA Events (Ramsbottom, Bury)** and **Sport Systems** are also available to lend their expertise to your event. Contact me for availability. *If you're thinking about chip timing, please contact me to discuss availability and suitability for your event.*

Are you a charity? Do you have places available in races which you want to advertise to runners? Use my NEW FREE service - Click here to register your places. If you are a runner looking for a charity place, maybe this would be a good place to start (once details start to come in of course!!).

Aches and pains due to a sports injury? Want to find a massage gel which can help both before and after training? Visit the Albmaleaf page. Albmaleaf is now available to be ordered online via this site.

ENTER ONLINE **Thinking of online entries for your event?** Race Organisers, you can now accept your **online entries** inexpensively (or for free!) and flexibly via *ukresults* - contact me to discuss your requirements. I can also accommodate your event's requirements with regard to **full entry management** (postal or online entries, database compilation and submission to you, posting race packs etc.)

Runners - postage costs and envelope sizes causing you a headache with your race entries? Use my service and beat the Mail - postage charges went up again in April 2009!! Always use C5 envelopes - 1st class stamp is now 39p and a large letter stamp (for those bigger envelopes) is 61p - as you will need 2 of these, it makes more sense to enter online!! *Click here for information about using Online forms and registration of your details at UKResults* **ALL ONLINE ENTRIES ON THIS SITE ARE GENERALLY CHEAPER THAN RUNNERS' WORLD, ACTIVE EUROPE ETC. The problems which have recently affected Runners' World entries don't affect my site all your entries are handled personally by a real person so I can deal with any problems which might crop up! None of your email addresses and other information will be released to anyone other than the race organiser without your consent.**

Click here to see the full list of Online Entry Forms available on this site

Freckleton Half Marathon 2010 - online entry now open exclusively on UKResults - no postal entries for 2010!

Online entry for some races in November will close on Monday evening, 2nd November, as I will not be able to fully manage entries for the next couple of weeks. Sorry if this causes you any inconvenience. PRESTON 10 AND EAVES WOOD ENTRIES ARE BEING PROCESSED AS NORMAL THOUGH! THE AUTOMATED REPLY YOU GET IS A GENERIC ONE SO DON'T PANIC THAT YOUR ENTRY WILL NOT BE INCLUDED IF YOU HAVE MADE A COMPLETED PAYMENT.

Now Accepting

Payl

Noch=x
Online Payment Services

Payments by Nochex Merchant Account

UCanLearn

Want to learn to drive? Around Accrington, Blackburn or Darwen? Contact UCanLearn2Drive.c

Albmaleaf

Visit Tulloh Books

Which way did they go?

1 Find four services the webmaster is offering.

1_____

2_____

3_____

4_____

(4 marks)

2 How effective is the layout of this web page? Give reasons for your views.

_____

_____

_____

_____

_____

_____

_____

_____

_____

_____

_____

_____

_____

_____

(8 marks)

3 How persuasive is the language used?
Find four examples and comment on them.

_____

_____

_____

_____

_____

_____

_____

_____

_____

_____

_____

_____

_____

_____

(8 marks)

If there is a review in the exam, is it likely to be a review of a book?

If you are asked to read a review – or write one in Section B of the exam paper – it could be a review of anything: a trip, a CD, a concert...

Read this book review.

The Beacon
Susan Hill
Vintage £6.99

Best known for her ghost stories, Susan Hill tackles a different kind of spectre in this gripping tale. The Prime children – Colin, May, Frank and Berenice – have an uneventful childhood living in a secluded farmhouse called the Beacon. May goes off to university, but she experiences terrible hallucinations and returns home. Frank, the mysterious one, distances himself, moving to London and becoming a journalist. Then he writes a memoir, detailing the horrific abuse he suffered as a child at the hands of his parents and siblings. The book's publication changes all of their lives forever, raising questions about truth and memory. Short and spare it might be, but Hill's novel is expertly structured, her beautifully written prose as haunting as the best ghost story. **SOPHIE MISSING**

Observer, 01.11.09

1 Find four examples of language linked to a sense of ghostliness and haunting.

1_____

2_____

3_____

4_____

(4 marks)

2 Are we supposed to think *The Beacon* is a good book or not? Find information to support your ideas and explain your views.

_____

_____

_____

_____

_____

_____

_____

_____

(8 marks)

3 Why are the opening and ending sentences particularly effective?

_____

_____

_____

_____

_____

(4 marks)

This is a review of a television programme.

When A Mother's Love Is Not Enough, Rosa Monckton's film aboput the pressures that bear down on the parents of disabled children, was deeply moving and sometimes uncomfortable viewing. Having children of any kind has its tough moments, but recalling one's own grumbles about fatigue and mess and tantrums in the light of the ordeals faced by some of these parents was a shaming business. Monckton spoke from personal experience as the mother of a Down's syndrome daughter, and was bravely candid about the points at which fatigue and grief overwhelms you. She'd also captured a very touching moment when David Cameron struggled with his emotions on recalling the challenges of living with his disabled son. But it was hard not to feel that something had been left out in her calls for better support for such parents. "What is missing from the state is the help," she concluded, "What is missing is the compassion and the common sense." Surely what is missing is the money that would render state compassion effective?

Independent, 11.11.09

4 What is the writer's opinion of parents who care for disabled children? Support your ideas with details from the text.

_____

_____

_____

_____

_____

_____

_____

_____

(8 marks)

5 What conclusion does the writer come to after watching this television programme? Give supporting evidence in your answer.

_____

_____

_____

_____

_____

_____

_____

_____

(8 marks)

How do we analyse?

In the exam, this means looking beyond one straightforward meaning and giving an extended, detailed explanation instead. If you show you understand layers of meaning in the text, you will get more marks.

Read this sports article.

Murray's down and out in Paris

A LONG season and a short night took their toll on Andy Murray with a 1-6, 6-3, 6-4 defeat to Czech Radek Stepanek in the Paris Masters third round. The world No.4, who battled for over two hours to beat James Blake on Wednesday night, finishing well into the early hours, started well, relying on his strong serve, but then collapsed after too many unforced errors. The 22 year old Scot, seeded fourth, joined Roger Federer on the indoor event's casualty list. 'Obviously, I was not at my best but I was not expecting to [be],' Murray said. 'It was four o'clock by the time I got to bed and that's not the ideal preparation.'

Metro, 13.11.09

1 What impression of Murray's performance do we get from the following words? Offer more than one simple explanation.

• 'battled'

_____

_____

_____

• 'collapsed'

_____

_____

_____

(4 marks)

2 Look at the picture. What does it make us think about Andy Murray?

1_____

_____

2_____

_____

(4 marks)

Read this text from a school newsletter.

> On Thursday 26 November 2009, Ossett School is organizing a Careers Information Event for all students, and their parents, in Years 10, 11, 12 and 13. The world of work and Higher Education is becoming more complicated and competitive. It is essential that your child attends so that they have a chance to explore the many opportunities available to them. With higher levels of skills and knowledge being needed by all workers in the future, it is important for your child to have the chance to learn more about their future options so they can make the right choice for their future.
>
> I would like to stress the importance of this event to members of the Sixth Form – it is a valuable opportunity to meet people from local universities and national gap year providers. For Year 12 it is crucial that they start their planning for after Year 13 early, as Higher Education is becoming much more competitive. Visiting the universities in the sixth form centre will give them an insight into what they need to be doing and what is available. For students in Years 12 and 13 who are looking to go into work and training our exhibitors in Kendal Hall have a wealth of opportunities aimed at students leaving sixth form. Finally, I would recommend that students sign up for talks so that they can find out more about a specific career or learning opportunity.

3 Analyse the ways in which this school is trying to stress the importance of the evening. Select four pieces of language and comment on them, making more than one comment on each.

_____

_____

_____

_____

_____

_____

_____

_____

_____

_____

_____

_____

_____

(8 marks)

4 What is the effect of this phrase: 'our exhibitors… have a wealth of opportunities aimed at students leaving sixth form'?

_____

_____

_____

_____

(2 marks)

131

What does 'extending analysis' mean?

If the exam question encourages you to develop your ideas, do this, perhaps by linking different parts of the text, and you will be rewarded.

Look carefully at this text from a newspaper.

Ronnie steps in...

Ronnie Corbett stepped into Bruce Forsyth's shoes on BBC1's *Strictly Come Dancing* last night after a bout of 'flu kept the veteran host in bed. "If anyone can help out at short notice, it's me," joked the 5'1" comedian, who was towered over by his co-host, Tess Daly. After *EastEnders* actor Ricky Groves and Phil Tufnell were left in last night's dance-off, it was the former England cricketer who lost out in a close judges' vote.

Observer, 15.11.09

1 What do you think about the presenters when you look at the picture?

_____

_____

_____

_____

_____

_____

(4 marks)

2 How is your initial impression developed or confirmed when you read the text?

_____

_____

_____

_____

_____

_____

(4 marks)

This is the opening of an article about Smart cars.

Squeezy living

You can fit 14 cheerleaders into the new Smart – or two adults. Martin Love stretches out in style

SMART FOR TWO £7,748
MILES PER GALLON: 85.6
CO2 PER KM: 88 GRAMS
GOOD FOR: CONURBATIONS
BAD FOR: CONTORTIONS

What's the first thing you think about when you see a very, very small car? Safety, probably. Or fuel consumption, or maybe its ability to sniff out a parking space in the most uncompromising cul-de-sac… But if you are an Ascension Eagle cheerleader your mind will turn to car cramming. Four years ago they set the world record and squeezed 14 into a Smart. Clearly only two wore seat belts, and there was no room for their pom-poms. Six months ago a party of girl guides in Germany had a crack – they must have been bigger as they only managed 13. But they were quicker, all 13 managed to get into the car in under 20 seconds. Inspired by these girls, I had a go at car cramming myself. I fancied my chances. The new Smart is 3cm longer, after all, and I was using a group of under 8s. We called it quits at seven, plus me as the driver…

Small car, big heart: the Smart is the most efficient production car on the road, doing over 80mpg

The Observer Magazine, 15.11.09

3 How does the writer use humour to interest the reader?

_____

_____

_____

_____

_____

_____

_____

_____

_____

_____

(8 marks)

Both the Foundation Tier and the Higher Tier papers will expect you to look at inference in a text or texts. This means deciding what is being suggested, perhaps by the images, presentational features or by the language. You do not just write about 'what is there' but also about 'what the thoughts are *behind* what is there.'

Read this newspaper article.

Beat stress 'with daily chocolate'

By Jo Steele

THE train was late. Your umbrella collapsed in the rain. The boss has been giving you a hard time. You can't think straight and the steam is beginning to come out of your ears.

What do you do?

You take five and nibble some chocolate. That's what you do.

Stressed people have long known that a little bit of chocolate is much like getting a hug but new research claims ten squares of dark chocolate a day for two weeks can cure stress.

A regular helping of the treat rebalances chemicals in the body during times of high anxiety, according to a study by Dutch and Swiss scientists published by the American Chemical Society.

Dark chocolate is being described as the latest superfood because of its anti-oxidants and health-boosting compounds called flavinoids.

These reduce the risks of heart disease and lower blood pressure. People with high levels of stress hormones, such as cortisol, also have lower levels of other 'markers' which are meant to correct stress.

The dark chocolate brought these back into balance, said researchers.

'The study shows that a daily consumption of 40 grams over two weeks can modify the metabolism,' said Nestlé researcher Sunil Kochhar.

Next they'll be telling us it can help you lose weight and clean your teeth…

Metro, 13.11.09

1 Read the opening, down to 'That's what you do'. What is the tone of the writer? Does she sound serious or jokey? Give evidence for your opinions.

_____

_____

_____

_____

_____

_____

(4 marks)

2 How might we react to the penultimate paragraph, which begins 'The study shows…'? Explain why.

_____

_____

_____

_____

(4 marks)

3 What is being suggested in the final paragraph?

_____

_____

_____

_____

(2 marks)

These pictures of Barack Obama appeared in an article about him.

Picture 1

Picture 2

Picture 3

4 What impression of the President do we gain from each picture? In each case support your ideas with detail.

Picture 1

_____

_____

_____

_____

(4 marks)

Picture 2

_____

_____

_____

_____

(4 marks)

Picture 3

_____

_____

_____

_____

(4 marks)

Dealing further with inference

Why is there more practice on inference?

Dealing with inference is a skill that needs to be practised and so in this further section, you will be finding the details yourself which you need to write about, rather than having them identified for you. This is likely to be what you are asked to do in one question in the exam.

Read this advertisement.

Throw away your kettle! There's a revolution in kitchens! 100°C boiling water is now on tap - from the unique Quooker. Ultra-convenient, ultrasafe with a built-in child-proof safety mechanism and brilliantly energy-efficient, Quooker's unique compact under-sink tank still leaves ample space for a waste disposal and ancillary storage. The Quooker also offers a wide range of height and handing adjustable tap designs for contemporary and traditional kitchens. The stainless steel tank has revolutionary vacuum insulation and thermos technology, making it highly efficient to run, cool to the touch and allowing delivery of boiling water at 100 degrees unlike any other hot water system in the world today. Uses for the Quooker don't stop at hot drinks. Its filtered boiling water blanches vegetables, prepares instant soups, sterilises baby bottles and food containers and fulfills a myriad of cooking uses once catered for, slowly, by the space and energy-greedy kettle.

Find true boiling water on demand at www.quooker.co.uk, call +44 (0)207 9233355 or mail info@quooker.co.uk

Quooker®
THE BOILING WATER TAP

1 Find four 'selling points' for the Quooker and explain their appeal.

_____

_____

_____

_____

_____

_____

_____

_____

_____

_____

_____

_____

_____

(8 marks)

This is an extract written by a young Sudanese girl. She has been left alone to keep birds off the newly-sewn seed.

Suddenly I saw a movement amongst the trees, and out stepped a wild dog. I watched transfixed. I knew the rest of the pack would be somewhere nearby. I was scared that if I made a move he would hear me and come after me. But I also knew that if I stayed where I was, he would eventually smell me out. Finally, terror forced me to run for the big tree in the middle of the field.

I jumped up into the lowest branches and quickly climbed to the top. I could feel my legs shaking uncontrollably: I was still scared that the dogs had heard me or seen me. Although I knew they couldn't climb trees, I imagined them waiting for me to fall out when I dropped asleep.

I turned and caught sight of the wild dog stalking slowly across the field towards me, its belly to the ground. Then, when it was quite close, it suddenly pounced. I heard a bird making a sickening, squawking sound, as the wild dog sank its teeth into its neck, holding it down with its paws. It was a big forest chicken. Then the wild dog ran off, jumped the fence and disappeared into the forest with the bird in its mouth. That could have been me, I thought.

2 How is the girl's fear presented?

_____

_____

_____

_____

_____

_____

_____

_____

_____

_____

_____

_____

_____

_____

_____

_____

_____

_____

_____

_____

_____

_____

_____

_____

(8 marks)

Will we always have to examine language?

There will always be a question in the exam that focuses on the language used in texts and its effects.

Read this news report.

It's catupuncture..

▲ **TO THE POINT** Therapist assess the sick feline

▶ **FELINE PRICKLY** Kiki bristles as needles are in place

NEEDLES give most people paws for thought but Kiki the cat seems to be enjoying her acupuncture session.

The 11-year old has suffered asthma and a cough for three years.

Traditional medicine did not help, so owner Virginia Sanders of Western Cape, South Africa, tried the alternative therapy – and three sessions later Kiki was feline much better.

It has been used on animals for thousands of years in China and India, so it's a furly old remedy…

Daily Mirror, 17.12.08

1 What is the effect of the headline and the captions?
'It's catupuncture'

_____

_____

_____

(2 marks)

'TO THE POINT Therapist assesses the sick feline'

_____

_____

_____

(2 marks)

'FELINE PRICKLY Kiki bristles as needles are in place'

_____

_____

(2 marks)

2 How are the following sentences intended to appeal to the reader?

'Needles give most people paws for thought…'

_____

_____

_____

(2 marks)

'It has been used on animals for thousands of years in China, so it's a furly old remedy.'

_____

_____

_____

(2 marks)

Look at this advertisement.

advertisement

Dear **Esther**

"Should I claim for my injury?"

Dear Esther, I was a passenger in a taxi when we stopped to give way and a van drove into the back of us. I have been suffering with severe neck and back pain ever since. Do you think I could claim?

■**ESTHER SAYS: I'm sorry to hear about your accident.**
If the accident wasn't your fault then you should claim. It is very easy to do, phone **0800 740 8313** and speak to an experienced advisor at Accident Advice Helpline.
Their expert panel of Solicitors specialise in getting you maximum compensation and work on a **NO WIN NO FEE** basis, the process is fast and hassle-free.
It should only take around five minutes to find out if you can make a claim.

Esther Rantzen

Thank You! I made a quick call and within minutes I discovered that I could claim substantial cash compensation for my injuries. The advisor was very knowledgeable and assured me I had nothing to lose as the claim was on a 100% No-Win No-Fee basis. I'd advise anyone to make that call today.

Cornelius, London

Claimed £4,625

If you'd like to find out more about making a claim with Accident Advice Helpline

0800 740 8313

or visit: **www.starclaims.com**

3 Why is the following language used?

'an experienced advisor'

_____

_____

(2 marks)

'maximum compensation'

_____

_____

(2 marks)

'fast and hassle-free'

_____

_____

(2 marks)

4 What effect are Cornelius' words intended to have? Analyse what he says and how he says it.

_____

_____

_____

_____

_____

_____

_____

_____

(8 marks)

Read this news article.

If there were a device that could measure toughness – an adrenalin radar scanning the planet for nutters in harnesses – hardcore hotspots would probably include the Himalayas and the Alps. But the sick-ometer (as in "dude, that was like the sickest jump ever") is at risk of blowing up over a grey corner of northern England later this month when some of the world's greatest daredevils gather for the Kendal Mountain Festival.

If you like mountains, or films about mountains, or doing dangerous things on mountains on film, then Kendal is your Cannes. Just swap red carpets for cobbles, and canapés for mint cake. "It's a tribal gathering for mountain lovers," says the festival's director, Clive Allen. "We get at least 7,000 people over the weekend and put on screenings and exhibitions and family events. It's a big deal for a small town."

Independent Life, 11.11.09

5 How does the language used in the first paragraph aim to interest the reader?

_____

_____

_____

_____

_____

_____

_____

(8 marks)

6 What is the reader's reaction when she/he reads the following? Explain the effect of the language.
'If you like mountains, or films about mountains, or doing dangerous things on mountains on film...'

_____

_____

_____

_____

_____

(4 marks)

'swap red carpets for cobbles and canapés for mint cake'

_____

_____

_____

(4 marks)

'it's a tribal gathering for mountain lovers'

_____

_____

_____

(4 marks)

This is an extract from an autobiography by the actor, David Niven. His father sent him away to a boarding school run by an old navy Commander.

> He and his thin-lipped, blue-veined, tweedy, terribly 'refained' wife added to his meagre pension and indulged their mutual passion for pink gin by taking in a dozen or so boarders.
>
> We were treated like young criminals and soon began to feel that we might as well behave like them. The house was a three-storeyed rabbit warren and terribly over-populated, but oh! it was clean. We scrubbed and re-scrubbed every inch of it daily. Oil lamps had to be spotless too – there was no electric light – and an ill-trimmed wick was evil-smelling evidence of highly punishable inefficiency. We did not sleep in hammocks but on wooden shelves, four to a room. The Commander and his wife prowled around at night in stockinged feet hoping to catch us talking.

7 What impression is given of the Commander's wife and how is the impression created?

_____

_____

_____

_____

(4 marks)

8 Why are the following phrases used?
'like young criminals'

_____

_____

(2 marks)

'three-storeyed rabbit warren'

_____

_____

(2 marks)

'prowled around'

_____

_____

(2 marks)

Why are 'presentational features' important?

You will be asked to examine the **visual features** of at least one text – perhaps the pictures or illustrations, headings, text boxes, colours and so on. You could also be asked about the general **layout** – how the text and features have been arranged on the page.

Look carefully at this advertisement.

1 How are the pictures used in this advertisement?

_____

_____

_____

_____

_____

_____

_____

(8 marks)

2 What other presentational features are used and how effective are they?

_____

_____

_____

_____

_____

_____

(8 marks)

Read this short text from
a magazine.

Time for tea?

If you're increasing your number of
tea breaks in the hope it might reduce
your risk of diabetes, you may be
wasting your time – despite recent
reports telling us tea can cut our risk
by 42 per cent. "So far, the evidence
that it can cut your risk of developing
type 2 diabetes is inconclusive," says
Dr Iain Frame, research director at
Diabetes UK. "We all want to find a
way to stop the epidemic, but until
solid scientific eveidence proves
otherwise, the best way to prevent the
condition remains keeping active and
eating a healthy, balanced diet that is
low in fat, salt and sugar, and with
plenty of fruit and vegetables."

Best, 06.10.09

3 Who are the presentational features designed to attract here, and how?

_____

_____

_____

_____

(4 marks)

4 Decide what different effect this text would have if:
  • the background were green and the girl's top beige

_____

_____

_____

(2 marks)

  • the background were pink and the girl's top orange.

_____

_____

_____

(2 marks)

5 Imagine you were given the task of re-designing the 'Time for tea' text.
Say what presentational features you would use and why.

_____

_____

_____

_____

_____

(4 marks)

Read this newspaper article.

MAIN ATTRACTION: WHY ENCOUNTER IS NOT WHAT IT SEEMS

THEY may have a lion on their bonnet, but the occupants of this jeep can see the funny side. They are enjoying an optical illusion on a vist to the Werribee Open Range Zoo in Victoria, Australia, where their "broken-down" truck is one of the main attractions of the lion enclosure. Its bonnet is on one side with the big cats, while the visitors sit on the other side, protected by a wall of glass in front of the dashboard. No wonder they can afford to roar with laughter.

Evening Standard, 06.11.09

6 How does the headline link with the picture?

_____

_____

_____

_____

(4 marks)

7 Why has this picture been used? Explain.

_____

_____

_____

_____

(4 marks)

8 What effect do we get from the expressions on the people's faces? Use precise detail in your answer.

_____

_____

_____

(4 marks)

Look carefully at this magazine cover.

Best, 08.09.09

9 How is the magazine cover trying to appeal to the reader?

_____

_____

_____

_____

_____

_____

_____

_____

(8 marks)

10 How has the designer prioritised the stories and how effective is this layout?
(Which story comes across as most important, which is next important, etc? Would the reader respond positively to the way the cover is set out?)

_____

_____

_____

_____

_____

_____

_____

_____

(8 marks)

Why is this section targeted specifically at Foundation Tier?

The final question in Section A of the Foundation Tier paper will ask you to compare the presentational features in two texts. This type of comparison will not be required for the Higher Tier.

Look carefully at the following two adverts.

Compare how the advertisers use presentational features to try to sell their shoes in these adverts.

Write about:

- the target audiences
- how the Ethletic shoes are presented
- the methods Brantano use to draw the consumers' attention
- the essential differences in the advertisements.

Tread Softly

in the Worlds first Fairtrade certified footwear

ETHLETIC shoes may look like an iconic American brand but the **ETHLETIC** logo tells a very different story. These Organic canvas sneakers will be the first shoes in the world to carry the official Fairtrade label under new Fairtrade composite rules that allow products containing Fairtrade certified cotton to bear the famous Fairtrade mark. They also have rubber soles that carry the logo of the Forest Stewardship Council meaning almost every every material part of the sneakers is Fairtrade or ecologically certified. Even the final construction of **ETHLETIC** sneakers is covered by a fair trade project that supports workers and their families in Pakistan, making these perhaps the world most ethical shoes.

They come in a range of great colours and are available in both low and high cut style models. The arch supports make for a cushioned and comfortable sneaker that rivals the major brands for shear wearability and with prices starting from £36.50 positive minded shoppers can convert to Fairtrade and Organic without hitting their pocket.

www.fairdealtrading.com
Enquiries to
contact@fairdealtrading.com
or call **0845 094 4746**

Ethical Manufacture · 100% Vegan · 0% Plastic · Organic Cotton Canvas · Fairtrade Certified Cotton · Arch Supports · FSC Certified Rubber Soles · Fairly Traded Rubber

THE ETHICAL ALTERNATIVE

Write your response to the question below.

_____

_____

_____

_____

_____

_____

_____

_____

_____

_____

_____

_____

_____

_____

_____

_____

_____

_____

_____

_____

_____

_____

_____

_____

_____

Continue on lined paper if necessary.

(12 marks)

Why is this section targeted at Higher Tier?

Foundation students will just write about language in one text; for the final question in Section A, Higher Tier students will be required to compare the language used in two texts.

This film review is from *Sky Movies Magazine*:

TAKEN 18

DIRECTOR PIERRE MOREL **STARRING** LIAM NEESON, MAGGIE GRACE, LELAND ORSER

A muscular action thriller that packs a political punch, *Taken* sees Liam Neeson cut up rough as a retired CIA operative out to rescue his daughter from evil Arabs. It's Bourne in middle age: a straightforward shoot-em-up given a little heart by the regret and redemption of a hard-working professional trying to re-connect with his alienated sprog.

There's also the dubious but undeniable pleasure of watching bone-crunching scraps involving an Oscar nominated actor soon to play Abraham Lincoln in Spielberg's biopic of the revered American president. Neeson makes for a surprisingly credible action hero, adding brawn to his usual brooding gravitas, delivering well-practised beat-downs and stone-faced ultimatums.

The story's as simple as it sounds. After a half hour of scene-setting – Neeson's a deadbeat dad who has put his country before his family; his ex-wife (Famke Janssen) doesn't understand; his daughter (Grace) is spoilt but, y'know, adorable – we're off to Paris, where Grace is half-inched. So Neeson decides to get her back... by killing everybody.

Then we're into a string of set-pieces of varying degrees of brutality, as Neeson storms through the French capital on his bloody, one-man revenge mission. Visually, Pierre Morel – director of *District 13* and cinematographer on Louis Leterrier's *Unleashed* – opts for fast-cut camera work and relentless energy to keep you going once your disbelief hasn't so much been suspended as hung, drawn and quartered.

Daniel Webb

10.09

This is the start of a review from the London *Evening Standard*.

Now that's poetry

Jane Campion's biopic of John Keats is a love story that achieves the rare feat of making verse captivating on screen

Andrew O'Hagan
Film of the Week
Bright Star
Cert PG, 119 mins
★★★★☆

Films about poets are under a lot of strain to prove themselves poetical. Jane Campion's *Bright Star* manages to avoid this in some old-fashioned ways: first, by being full of confidence about its artistic vision and second, by being genuinely poetic. Anybody who thinks 'poetic' should mean limp, airy, or flouncy is either not reading enough good poetry or is reading good poetry badly.

Bright Star is poetic, but that is because it is tough, replenishing, beautiful and true – a film about John Keats that conjures the strange spirit of the man.

Based on Andrew Moon's brilliant biography, the movie seeks to express itself by a series of fine discriminations. We first meet the young Fanny Brawne (Abby Cornish), Keats' first love, in 1819, when he was 24 and she is 19.

The Keats who begins his love affair with Fanny is different from the mythical one. Living in Brawne's house, he is given to laughter and to boyish excesses of both laziness and torment, though Keats (Ben Wilshaw) conveys such gentle thoughtfulness at all times that you never doubt the poet is a special soul.

The film is an artist's work about an artist – which the best biopics and biographies always are...

6.11.09

Compare the language used in the two texts.

Comment on:

- how it is appropriate for the audiences
- the effect of words and phrases
- the differences in the style of the two texts.

_____
_____
_____
_____
_____
_____
_____
_____
_____
_____
_____
_____
_____
_____
_____
_____
_____
_____
_____
_____
_____
_____
_____
_____
_____
_____
_____

Continue on lined paper if necessary. _(16 marks)_

Should I treat this as practice for this part of the exam?

This section contains texts of the kind you might well be faced with in the Higher Tier exam itself. These are followed by exam-style questions for Higher Tier. Ideally, you should take an hour to read the texts and respond to the questions. This will offer you an opportunity to answer typical questions in the time you will be allowed when you sit 'the real thing'.

Higher Tier texts

Source 1: an advert for a holiday

AMERICA

Enjoy the award-winning escorted tour of your life in 2010

Expert Tour Managers • Quality hotels • Select Excursions Included

Wherever you want to travel, there is one operator that stands head and shoulders above the rest - Titan HiTours. Nowhere is this more true than to the USA, whose delightful highways and byways and stunning sights we've been revealing to clients for over thirty years. Having been voted many times best tour operator by newspaper readers as well as topping leading consumer surveys, we know that travellers continue to expect the best organisation, service and quality from us. Our philosophy is that your holidays are among the most important investments you make in your life. Our job is to make them perfect and with Titan HiTours' unique VIP Home Departure Service® included on every date from every address in mainland England and Wales, your escorted holiday begins and ends at your front door. So try us and experience the difference for yourself. Call us now for your FREE copy of our new Worldwide 2010/11 brochure featuring 34 unbeatable itineraries to America including those shown below.

California and the Golden West - 16 days from £1295
The Awe-inspiring National Parks - 17 days from £1895
Las Vegas - 7 days from £995 (Dec 2009)
Southern Sights and Sounds - 14 days from £1695
Eastern Extravaganza - 15 days from £1695
Heart of New England and Niagara Falls - 10 days from £1295
USA Coast to Coast - Classic Rail Journey - 21 days from £2795

including the unique **Titan HiTours VIP Home Departure Service®**
from every home in mainland England & Wales. Or take advantage of complimentary
regional flights, now with FREE private transfers from many postcodes*

PAY IN FULL AND SAVE UP TO 5% - CALL US FREE

0800 988 5816

Our Service Makes a World of Difference!®

BOOK ONLINE www.titanhitours.co.uk

ABTA V4585 • ATOL 2850

*Calls free from BT landlines, mobiles may vary. *Conditions apply.* **NOW OPEN ON SUNDAYS 10am-4pm**   DMUSA

Source 2: a travel article from a newspaper

THE TRUE PERU

From soaring condors to plunging gorges, the little known Colca Canyon will take your breath away

by Chris Leadbeater

THE ROAD from Arequipa to Chivay leaves you breathless. Literally. As the bus carrying my tour group inches up this highway in the southern Peruvian Andes, I can feel the air thinning with each mile.

By the time we hit the hamlet of Canahuas, 4,000 metres above sea level, I am having to focus on the simple ins and outs of breathing.

This is just the start. An hour later we break the 5,000 metre barrier – higher than Mont Blanc, the roof of Europe – and the world changes. The landscape has gone lunar, a plain of rocks and dust. And the oxygen seems to have gone entirely. I tilt my head back, open my mouth as wide as possible, and suck at the meager atmosphere. Happily, there is good reason for this madness – as becomes clear as the road dips towards the relative sanity of 3,000 metres. In the valley below, the town of Chivay, all white walls and low houses, glints in the sunlight. Beyond is the geological scar that has lured us to this distant corner of South America.

Highlight: Peru is packed with mountainous beauty

Thirty-five miles long and 3,269 metres deep at its most vertigo-inducing point, Colca Canyon is undoubtedly worth a flirtation with the side effects of altitude.

Even at first glance, it is a marvel. Snow-capped peaks rise on either side. Agricultural terraces that pre-date the Incas cling to its sloping flanks. Pale churches, evidence of Spanish conquest, act as centerpieces to tiny villages that hover near the edge.

It is proof that there is more to Peru than its poster image – Machu Picchu.

Every year, half a million visit this 'lost city' and no other Peruvian site can compete on fame or publicity.

Little known outside Peru, Colca Canyon certainly cannot. But any doubts I'd had that it could compare as a spectacle are banished when we reach 'Condor Cross'. At this point, the canyon is 1,207 metres deep, its wall plunging to shadow.

Yet the main attraction here is not the drop. It is the birds of prey that soar overhead, searching for carrion.

Daily Mail, 05.09.09

Source 3: an account of visiting Rome from a travel book by Bill Bryson

On my final morning I called at the Capuchin monks' mausoleum in the church of Santa Maria della Concezione on the busy Piazza Barberini. This I cannot recommend highly enough. In the sixteenth century some monk had the inspired idea of taking the bones of his fellow monks when they died and using them to decorate the place. Is that rich enough for you? Half a dozen gloomy chambers along one side of the church were filled with such attractions as an altar made of rib cages, shrines meticulously concocted from skulls and leg bones, ceilings trimmed with forearms, wall rosettes fashioned from vertebrae, chandeliers made from the bones of hands and feet. In the odd corner there stood a complete skeleton of a Capuchin monk dressed like the grim reaper in his hooded robe, and ranged along the other wall were signs in six languages with such cheery sentiments as WE WERE LIKE YOU. YOU WILL BE LIKE US, and a long poem engagingly called 'My Mother Killed Me!!'. These guys must have been a barrel of laughs to be around. You can imagine every time you got the flu some guy coming along with a tape measure and a thoughtful expression.

Four thousand monks contributed to the display between 1528 and 1870 when the practice was stopped for being just too tacky for words. No one knows quite why or by whom the designs were made, but the inescapable impression you are left with is that the Capuchins once harboured in their midst a half-mad monk with time on his hands and a certain passion for tidiness. It is certainly a nice little money spinner for the church. A constant stream of tourists came in, happy to pay over a stack of lire for the morbid thrill of it all. My only regret, predictably, was that they didn't have a gift shop where you could purchase a boxed set of vertebrae napkin rings, say, or back scratchers made from real arms and hands, but it was becoming obvious that in this respect I was to be thwarted at every turn in Rome.

Questions: Higher Tier

Section A: Reading

Answer **all** questions in this section.

You are advised to spend about one hour on this section.

Read **Source 1**, the advertisement headed *America*.

1 According to the advertisement, what would make Titan HiTours a good choice if you wished to visit the United States?

(8 marks)

Read **Source 2**, the travel article entitled *The True Peru*.

2 How do the presentational features add to the effectiveness of the text?

(8 marks)

Read **Source 3**, the extract about visiting Rome from a travel book by Bill Bryson.

3 What thoughts and feelings does Bryson have when he visits the Capuchin monks' mausoleum?

(8 marks)

Now you need to refer to **Source 2**, *The True Peru*, and **either** Source 1 **or** Source 3. You are going to compare two texts, one of which you have chosen.

4 Compare the ways in which language is used to interest the reader in the two texts. Give some examples and explain how they are used to interest the reader.

(16 marks)

Total: 40 marks

Should I treat this as practice for this part of the exam?

This section contains texts of the kind you might well be faced with in the Foundation Tier exam itself. These are followed by exam-style questions for Foundation Tier. Ideally, you should take an hour to read the texts and respond to the questions. This will offer you an opportunity to answer typical questions in the time you will be allowed when you sit 'the real thing'.

Foundation Tier texts

Source 1: an advertisement for a holiday to America

Discover America's Golden West

12 days from £999

On this great value tour you will visit the famous sights of **Las Vegas, Los Angeles and San Francisco** accompanied by a friendly and experienced Tour Manager. They will ensure you see all the sights of America's West Coast plus you'll get plenty of free time to relax or make your own discoveries.

Highlights:

- ✓ Grand Canyon
- ✓ Hollywood
- ✓ Las Vegas
- ✓ Stunning Pacific Coast
- ✓ Palm Springs
- ✓ San Francisco

Fly from your local airport - Flights available from Heathrow, Gatwick, Birmingham, Bristol, Glasgow and Manchester

Our holidays include all this:

- ✓ Services of a Travelsphere Tour Manager
- ✓ Sight-seeing tours of Las Vegas, Los Angeles and San Francisco
- ✓ Return scheduled flights & transfers
- ✓ Ten nights room only accommodation

Add on:

- ✓ Extend your stay in **San Francisco** from **only £48 pp** per night
- ✓ Add-on 6 nights in **Hawaii** from **only £699**

Please speak to a Holiday Advisor for further details

Departures throughout 2010

To book or to speak to a friendly Holiday Advisor call:

0800 987 5011

or visit **travelsphere.co.uk** for our full holiday range.   quoting ref: **VWC**

We're open 7 days a week: Mon - Fri 9am - 8pm / Sat 9am - 4pm / Sun 10am - 3pm

 ABTA ABTA No. V5874

Source 2: an article from a weekend newspaper supplement

Holiday Disaster

Turkey is for Christmas, not for holidays, writes David Donald

 My wife loves cats. Cats in general, but not Turkish ones. She has good reason. We visited Turkey, once.

She and I were enjoying a tasty lamb meal in a restaurant in Datca, away from the usual tourist routes, when she laughed suddenly and swept her arm from her side to her mouth, and a cat beside her chair bit her. Its teeth dug deep.

Next morning, the hand was swollen. We went to the local doctor, who sent us to the hospital. The rooms there had blood on the walls, used syringes just lying around, and flies everywhere. My wife was examined and the doctor, who spoke next to no English, said she might have 'rubies'. 'Rabies?' I asked. 'Yes – rabies,' he said.

My wife panicked but we had to face the treatment. She was braver than me. I was sick outside the room because the doctor had told me what was to come: 'Injection … umbilical,' said the doctor. We went to the chemist's and got syringes, then returned to the hospital. My wife lay on a table and had an injection into her stomach. Two days later, she had another. Then another. Six injections over eleven days. Her stomach was bruised and swollen. Apparently, the

needle going in was painful: the serum going in was worse. A male orderly stroked her hair; the nurse who gave the injections was efficient, but the flies buzzed all the time and no one spoke English to make it all any better.

On our last visit, the orderly got out his guitar and sang and the nurse offered us food. All we wanted to do was escape.

The individuals there were lovely and the waiters from the restaurant where it all started even came onto our coach when we were leaving and gave my wife flowers. Even so, we will not be returning to Turkey …

Source 3: an account of visiting Paris from a travel book by Bill Bryson

This is what happens: you arrive at a square to find all the traffic has stopped, but the pedestrian light is red and you know that if you venture so much as a foot off the kerb all the cars will surge forward and turn you into a gooey crêpe. So you wait. After a minute, a blind person comes along and crosses the great cobbled plain without hesitating. Then a ninety-year-old lady in a motorized wheelchair trundles past and wobbles across the cobbles to the other side of the square a quarter of a mile away.

You are uncomfortably aware that all the drivers within 150 yards are sitting with moistened lips watching you expectantly, so you pretend that you don't really want to cross the street at all, that actually you've come over here to look at this interesting fin-de-siècle lamppost. After another minute 150 pre-school children are herded across by their teachers, and then the blind man returns from the other direction with two bags of shopping. Finally, the pedestrian light turns green and you step off the kerb and all the cars come charging at you. And I don't care how paranoid and irrational this sounds, but I know for a fact that the people of Paris want me dead.

Questions: Foundation Tier

Section A: Reading

Answer **all** questions in this section.

You are advised to spend about one hour on this section.

Read **Source 1**, the advertisement headed *Discover America's Golden West*.

1 What are the attractions offered on this holiday package?

(4 marks)

2 Why might the reader imagine this is a good value holiday package?

(4 marks)

Now read **Source 2**, the article from the weekend magazine headed
Holiday Disaster.

3 What is the writer suggesting about Turkish health care?
  Write about:
  • the hospital
  • the people.

(8 marks)

Now read **Source 3**, an account of a visit to Paris by Bill Bryson.

4 How does Bill Bryson use language to make his story clear and
  interesting for the reader?

(12 marks)

Now look again at all three **Sources**. They have each been presented to
attract the interest of the reader.

5 You are going to compare the presentational features of two of the texts.
  Choose two of the **Sources** and compare them, using these headings:
  • pictures
  • headings and any other presentational features

(12 marks)

Total: 40 marks

Exam Section B: Producing non-fiction texts

What questions will I face in Section B?

Whilst Section A of the exam tests your Reading skills, Section B tests your Writing skills.

You could be asked to write in almost any form, so you need to be prepared for all eventualities.

You will have 60 minutes to complete two writing tasks.

The **first writing task** will be shorter and should take you about 25 minutes.

It is worth up to 16 marks.

You will be expected to write 1–1½ sides of A4.

You could, for example, be asked to write a letter or an e-mail.

You might have to write to inform or explain.

It is likely to be a more 'functional' task, such as writing to apply for a job or telling new students how to behave in your school.

The **second writing task** should take you about 35 minutes.

It is worth up to 24 marks.

You are likely to write 1½–2 sides of A4.

In this case, you will have a little more time to develop ideas.

You might have to write to argue or persuade.

For example, this might be an article for a newspaper or magazine, encouraging readers to support a charity or arguing that we should or should not bring back the death penalty.

If no particular audience is prescribed, you will be writing for the examiner. However, if you are asked to produce a text form which is more specific, such as a letter or an article, your audience will also be provided. For example: 'Write an article for a local newspaper in which you argue that…' or 'Write a letter to a relative living abroad to explain…'.

For both tasks you will be expected to write appropriately to:
- meet the purpose you have been given
- appeal to your particular audience
- produce any form that has been specified.

Will both my written responses be marked in the same way?

Essentially, both pieces of writing will be marked in the same way. In each case, you will receive one mark for Organisation and Communication and another for Accuracy. However, because the first one has to be written more quickly and is likely to be shorter, there are more marks for the second piece.

Organisation and Communication

This mark will be awarded for:

- how well you deal with purpose and audience
- how well you communicate your ideas
- how interesting your ideas and your expression are
- how well you use paragraphs and structure your writing.

Accuracy

This mark will be awarded for:

- how well you vary your sentences
- the accuracy of your spelling
- your ability to write in standard English.

If you do well on one set of skills, it can compensate for any slight weakness elsewhere. So, for example, if you use good expression but fail to use paragraphs properly, the examiner will decide on a mark that balances both aspects; and if your punctuation is good but your spelling is less secure, both abilities will be considered so that a fair mark is awarded.

Isn't writing in the examination just like any other essay you write in school?

Writing skills are transferable, and you use them in different situations. In fact, you will use them for the rest of your life. However, to be successful in the exam, you need to know exactly what is required so that you can respond appropriately.

Timing

The time constraints are a vital consideration when performing in the exam. You need to be able to produce:

- the right material
- in the time available.

This means being able to write a **shorter response** in just **25 minutes** that reveals your abilities and the skills that the examiner expects to see; and to write a more detailed, **longer response** in **35 minutes**.

Practice is the key to success: the more time you invest in practising the skills that will be rewarded and the more opportunities you can find to write for just 25 minutes and 35 minutes, the better your final grade is likely to be.

A routine for writing

If you adopt a regular routine for writing, then you will learn techniques to support you in the exam itself.

Consider spending:

- 5 minutes planning a response
- 16–17 minutes writing (shorter response) or 25 minutes writing (longer response)
- the remaining time checking and improving what you have produced.

Planning

Aim to produce a detailed plan, because that will make the writing much easier. Planning is not just a case of collecting some random ideas, because that does not necessarily result in the best structure for your response. It helps if you can put the ideas into a numbered order, so you have something like a route map which you can follow as you write. Each numbered section can even be the basis for a paragraph, when that is appropriate to the form you are writing in.

Here is one possible planning approach.

1 Underline the significant words in the task title, so you produce exactly what is required.

For example:

Write an <u>article</u> for a <u>local newspaper</u> in which you <u>argue</u> that <u>local transport needs improving</u>.

2 Produce a spider diagram of ideas.

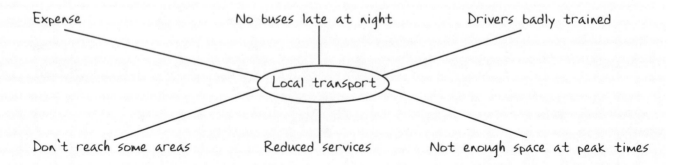

3 Put those ideas into the order you will use them: but leave a couple of empty lines beneath each idea or sub-heading.

Put extra thoughts into the spaces you have left: these will become the detail you will use in that section. For example:

> <u>3 Drivers badly trained</u>
>
> not just prices/ some drivers have no manners/ drive erratically/ no consideration
> for public (grandma actually fell off when bus started suddenly)/ treat teenagers
> as if they are all hooligans

4 List words and phrases you know you are likely to use – such as connectives (however, nevertheless, on the other hand, etc).

When you are writing, you can then use these to join ideas, expand your thoughts and so on, but choose a different one to use each time to offer variety.

Writing

As you write, remember:
- your response must be in the form specified by the task (for example, letter, article…)
- you must argue or persuade or do whatever is requested
- your ideas must come in a structured, logical order
- your responses should be in paragraphs
- you need to demonstrate a range of punctuation
- your language should be varied and appropriate for the audience
- your spelling should be as accurate as possible
- you are aiming to keep the examiner interested in what you have to say.

Checking

Checking your work is vital, so that you can correct and improve it. Alterations are a sign that a candidate has made every effort to do his or her best. Importantly, there are no marks for neatness: so long as the examiner can read what is there, there is no problem.

Do we have to plan our written responses?

It is not compulsory, but you are advised to plan your writing. Plotting your essay's development makes its structure more logical. Without planning, ideas tend to be presented in a random order, and it is be easy repeat yourself, omit vital ideas or use paragraphing less effectively.

Write a newspaper article in which you argue **either** for **or** against the idea that students should set the rules in school.

1 Identify the most important ideas in the title.

Purpose _____

Audience _____

Form _____

2 Produce a spider diagram of your ideas, using the outline below.

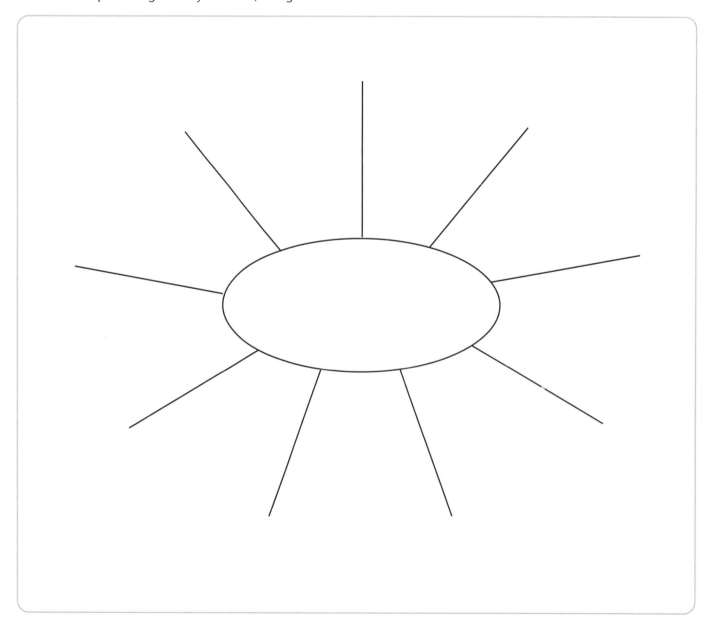

3 Put your ideas in order, adding detailed notes under each idea or sub-heading.
Remember to include an introduction and a conclusion.

_____

_____

_____

_____

_____

_____

_____

_____

_____

_____

_____

_____

_____

_____

_____

_____

_____

_____

_____

_____

4 Write down some of the words and phrases you might need for this response, for example, connectives.

_____

_____

_____

_____

_____

_____

Further practice

Plan a response to this task:

Write an essay in which you try to convince the reader that love is – or is not – the most important thing in life.

Paragraphing

Are paragraphs really important?

Paragraphs are very important when examiners are deciding what mark to give you for Organisation and Communication. If you can use topic sentences but then vary your paragraph length, you can add extra impact and meaning to your writing. This will help you achieve a higher grade.

1 Write a section of a response in which you review a recent book you have read or programme you have seen. Try to write logically linked paragraphs in this order:

- a paragraph of about 8-10 lines explaining what the book or programme was about
- a longer, descriptive paragraph about the main character or presenter
- a short, punchy paragraph giving your opinion on how successful the book or programme and its main character or presenter was.

Continue on lined paper if necessary.

(16 marks)

2 Write the opening of a response in which you explain what is wrong with the world today.
Produce:
- an introduction of 8–10 lines, in which you set out your ideas
- a short paragraph in which you identify one as particularly important
- a longer paragraph in which you give much more detail about that idea.

(16 marks)

Sentences

Why are sentences so important to my writing?

Since sentences carry our meaning, it is essential that they work effectively. In addition, varied sentence structures offer more interest to the reader and can add extra meaning to what you say.

1 Combine the following short sentences to create complex sentences – sentences with a main clause and sub-clauses:

> You should move out of the house. Your mother is treating you in an unacceptable way. You are a teenager now, not a child. You don't have to accept what is happening. Find another place to live and leave before it is too late. Your mother is like a brutal jailor.

_____

_____

_____

_____

_____

_____

(2 marks)

2 Complete this paragraph with a short, effective sentence:

> With unemployment so high in this area, it is tragic that the government and the local authority can find no extra funding to support the people out of work. When you walk though the estates right across the town, you see men leaning on walls, you hear women complaining to their neighbours about how they can't afford even simple treats for their children and the children themselves seem to be just running wild.

_____

_____

(1 mark)

3 Using an ellipsis (…) leaves a sentence unfinished and allows the reader to imagine what might have come next. This can add humour or mystery, for example, and can engage the reader more fully in the ideas or the situation.

* Add an unfinished sentence here to add humour:

> He had a head that was big, in more ways than one.

_____

_____

(1 mark)

* Add an unfinished sentence here to make the reader wonder what might come next:

> His reputation spread widely, so that he was recognised wherever he went.

_____

_____

(1 mark)

- Add an unfinished sentence here, so that the reader will not immediately know which side you are on:

    The newspapers would have us believe that he is the most over-rated player to ever set foot on a pitch; his manager claims to have rate him more highly than any other member of the team and says his skills go largely unnoticed.

_____

_____

(1 mark)

4 Very short sentences can add impact to your writing if used occasionally. They can also be used show emotion.

- Add a short 'sentence' (perhaps of just one word) or two short 'sentences' to the following paragraph – to show an emotional response to what has happened:

    The posters were all taken down within hours and the graffiti was removed and it was as if there had never been a protest or a baying crowd of people complaining at what was being proposed. It was a heartbreaking end to a day that had begun with hopes high and resolution strong.

_____

_____

(1 mark)

Further practice

You have been asked to describe the most important event in your life so far.

Write a paragraph in which you include:

- at least two complex sentences
- at least one short sentence
- an ellipsis.

_____

_____

_____

_____

_____

_____

_____

_____

_____

_____

_____

_____

_____

_____

_____

_____

(6 marks)

Punctuation

When we are writing, isn't it just a matter of punctuating accurately?

Since your punctuation will be assessed, you do need to be as accurate as possible. However, varied punctuation helps create more interesting sentences; and, as the examiner does not know how good your punctuation is, it will help if you can demonstrate all your punctuation skills when completing your responses.

1 Add the commas, question marks and an exclamation mark into this opening paragraph.

> Why is it that some schools have some teachers that are far from perfect. Why is it that some students do not as a consequence reach the grades of which they should be capable. It simply is not fair. In my own case the teachers in my school most of whom have been here for many years seem excellent. How lucky am I. What a relief it is to be here.

(8 marks)

2 Re-write this extract, adding correct speech marks and commas.

> As soon as I walked into the classroom Mrs Reynolds saw me. Just the young man I was looking for she said. I would like a word with you. I immediately feared the worst. I don't think I said that I have done anything wrong yet today. No. I just want some information she said smiling like a rattlesnake.

_____

_____

_____

_____

_____

_____

_____

(10 marks)

3 A colon can be used, following a general statement, to introduce a list.
A semi-colon can be used to separate the parts of a complicated list with lengthy items.
Re-write this extract, making the punctuation more adventurous.

> Each of the schools in this area has been improved massively in the past few years. There are new buildings with state of the art computer facilities. Two schools now have their own swimming pools. And in every school the libraries have been completely replaced.

_____

_____

_____

_____

_____

(4 marks)

4 Colons can also be used to introduce quotations; and semi-colons can be used to connect closely-related ideas, replacing a full-stop.

Complete each sentence below, adding colons or semi-colons and additional ideas as appropriate.

The headteacher was clear about what he expected _____

_____

I had to tell the truth about what happened _____

_____

My friend was excluded _____

_____

It shows that you cannot just behave any way you want _____

_____

(4 marks)

5 Add apostrophes of possession and of omission to this short extract.

The schools security measures werent perfect, thats for sure. Some of the boys lockers were ransacked and one girls bag was stolen.

(5 marks)

Further practice

Write a paragraph which informs the reader about what is best about your school. Include:

- commas
- at least one question mark and an exclamation mark
- apostrophes
- speech marks
- a colon and semi-colons.

_____

_____

_____

_____

_____

_____

_____

_____

_____

_____

_____

_____

(6 marks)

The use of language

What affects my choice of language?

It is essential that you use language that is appropriate for your audience in your written responses. In some cases the language you use might also be affected by the purpose of the writing.

1 Re-write this chatty extract so that it is suitable for a newspaper audience.

> Kids these days! They've no idea what's happening in the world – nor how it's got to where it is. Something for nothing, that's all they're after. Whether it's right or not, they don't know and don't care. Tragic, isn't it? No values, no sense of right and wrong and knowing nothing about our tradition of duty and fair play and fighting for what's right. Get 'em in the army. That'd sort them out…

_____

_____

_____

_____

_____

_____

_____

_____

_____

_____

_____

(6 marks)

2 Find more interesting words or phrases to replace the casual ones in italics.

Original	Replacement word or phrase	
	Alternative 1	Alternative 2
It was a *good* night out.		
We started in a *lovely* restaurant		
which had the *best* waiters		
I have ever *had*		
and the food was *great*.		
It was *fantastic*.		

(12 marks)

3 Re-write this set of instructions for new employees in a hotel complex so that they form an effective paragraph in a health and safety manual for hotel workers.

Make sure your paragraph:

- is suitably organised
- uses appropriate language
- includes effective connectives.

1 When by the pool, stay alert.

2 Make sure all children are accompanied by an adult.

3 No diving is permitted: if necessary, warn guests of the dangers.

4 Stop any silly behaviour, to prevent serious accidents.

5 No one under the influence of alcohol is allowed to use the pool.

6 Remove any dangerous objects, such as glass bottles.

7 Tell anyone who is not behaving appropriately to leave the pool area.

8 If you are in need of any assistance, contact the site manager.

_____

_____

_____

_____

_____

_____

_____

_____

_____

_____

(6 marks)

4 Write the opening of a speech to a group of MPs, in which you argue in favour of free bus travel for the young.

Make sure you use:

- language which avoids slang and casual expressions
- vocabulary to impress the listeners.

_____

_____

_____

_____

_____

_____

_____

_____

(6 marks)

Rhetoric and humour

Do we have to include rhetoric and humour?

Rhetorical questions challenge the reader and usually involve them more in what you are saying. Humour, if used appropriately, will enliven your writing. If you can make the examiner stop and think or if you can bring a smile to his or her lips, it is usually a good sign.

1 Write the opening paragraph of an article for a local newspaper, to persuade the readers to support your plan to raise money for a new skate park. Begin with one or two rhetorical questions (e.g. Surely, anyone can see that a skate park would mean fewer teenagers on the streets causing trouble?).

_____

_____

_____

_____

_____

_____

_____

_____

_____

(6 marks)

2 Write the concluding paragraph of a letter in reply to the newspaper article from an angry local resident, arguing that there is no suitable area available and no real need for a skate park.
Conclude with two rhetorical questions.

_____

_____

_____

_____

_____

_____

_____

_____

(6 marks)

3 Exclamations are another feature of rhetoric: language used for particular effect.
Write a paragraph from a blog in which you react to news that new drivers will not be able to take their test until they reach the age of 21.
Use two exclamations in your response.

_____

_____

_____

_____

_____

_____

_____

(6 marks)

4 Complete this paragraph, describing a package holiday to Spain, continuing its sarcasm.

What a wonderful hotel we had booked! It had been beautifully decorated in the primitive style which excites us so much when we go to see cave paintings produced thousands of years ago. The pool area

_____

_____

As for the staff they _____

_____

_____

Breakfasts were a treat too _____

_____

_____

(6 marks)

5 Use a funny anecdote to illustrate how dreadful conditions were on the beach during the holiday to Spain. An anecdote is a brief story which adds detail and creates interest.

_____

_____

_____

_____

_____

_____

_____

_____

(6 marks)

6 Try to make the reader smile by using exaggeration to say how pleased you were to arrive home from Spain.

_____

_____

_____

_____

_____

_____

_____

_____

(6 marks)

Similes and metaphors

Should we only use similes and metaphors when we are writing to describe?

Using similes and metaphors will help make any response more interesting, for example, even if you are reviewing or arguing.

Similes make a comparison using 'like' or 'as'. **Metaphors** say things which are not literally true. For example: 'he was all alone in the world'.

1 Explain why we should consider giving money to 'Children in Need'. Consider three original similes you might use to complete this opening:

It is tragic when you see people living in real poverty. Those living on the street are like…

1 _____

2 _____

3 _____

(3 marks)

2 Add similes to this extract, to show clearly why these people are in need of help.

When you visit some homes in the inner cities, you understand how desperate they are for some

kind of assistance. Living rooms can be like _____

_____ ;

and often the cramped sleeping area is like _____

_____

(2 marks)

3 Here, a student has decided to include similes, but has only managed to use well-worn examples he has come across before. Change the similes, offering more original ideas.

I needed this new problem like <u>a hole in the head</u> _____

_____

I didn't know what to do, and I felt like <u>an idiot</u> _____

_____

(2 marks)

4 Write a paragraph from a letter in which you try to persuade your headteacher to make the lunchtime break longer. Include two original similes.

_____

_____

_____

_____

_____

_____

(6 marks)

5 Write the opening section from a report on a sporting or musical performance. Include three metaphors.

_____

_____

_____

_____

_____

_____

_____

_____

_____

(6 marks)

Further practice

Continue your report on the sporting or musical performance by writing:

• a paragraph describing one of those involved and how they performed

• another paragraph describing the crowd.

Use at least three similes and three metaphors in your answer.

_____

_____

_____

_____

_____

_____

_____

_____

_____

_____

_____

_____

_____

_____

_____

_____

_____

_____

(10 marks)

Using evidence and quotations

Don't we only use evidence in the Reading section of the exam?

Any response you produce is likely to be more convincing if you include evidence, an anecdote or quotation. Supporting your points will help you argue, persuade, explain or inform more successfully. In the exam, you are free to invent any evidence you need, because you do not have books or search engines to help you.

1 If you had to support these points, what evidence would you use?

Statement	Evidence
I live in a country I can be proud of.	
There are some things in this country that need to be improved.	
My friends value some aspects of life here that I don't.	
My mother/father/carer gets excited about some elements of life that I find very unimpressive.	

(4 marks)

2 In a letter, you are informing your pen friend about the things in daily life that can make you angry. Write a paragraph about one of these things. Include some evidence to show why it annoys you. (Consider using statistics, facts or relevant examples.)

_____

_____

_____

_____

_____

_____

_____

_____

(6 marks)

3 Write another paragraph, using an anecdote to show, in contrast, what appeals to you or makes you happy in life.

_____

_____

_____

_____

_____

_____

_____

_____

_____

(6 marks)

4 Add a name and quotation to support this statement and conclude your letter.
(Remember: you can invent this quotation but try to make it sound convincing.)

I have to say that, overall, I am pleased to be living in this country.

As _____ once said: '_____

_____

_____ '

(2 marks)

Further practice

Write a short response (three or four paragraphs long) to argue that young people work quite hard enough in school: more should not be expected of them and homework should be banned.
Use evidence to support your views.

_____

_____

_____

_____

_____

_____

_____

_____

_____

_____

_____

_____

Continue on lined paper if necessary. *(16 marks)*

Emotive language

What, exactly, is emotive language?

Emotive language affects us emotionally. It is designed to make us feel sympathy, inspire us to act or make us feel happy, angry, guilty, etc. For example: 'Imagine the pain: bleeding feet, burnt skin and a stomach which has been empty for many days…'

1 You have been asked to explain the attractions of the most amazing place you have ever visited. Write a general description of the place, using emotive language where appropriate. For example: 'It was so beautiful, I could have cried with joy…'

_____

_____

_____

_____

_____

_____

_____

_____

_____

_____

_____

(6 marks)

2 Explain what stands out most about the place. Try to blend facts with some emotive language.

_____

_____

_____

_____

_____

_____

_____

_____

_____

_____

(6 marks)

3 Write a paragraph about something that has happened to you there which was not totally positive. Include emotive detail.

_____

_____

_____

_____

_____

_____

_____

_____

(6 marks)

Further practice

Write the text of a letter informing the Prime Minister about three key things the government should concentrate on improving.

In no more than 25 minutes, write three paragraphs and use some emotive language in each.

_____

_____

_____

_____

_____

_____

_____

_____

_____

_____

_____

_____

_____

_____

_____

_____

_____

_____

_____

_____

Continue on lined paper if necessary.   *(16 marks)*

Openings and endings

Why are openings and endings particularly important?

The opening is the first thing the examiner reads – it presents an immediate impression of your writing abilities. The ending is the last thing the examiner reads before putting a mark on your work: it makes a final and probably lasting impression.

1 Your cousin is about to move abroad. Write the first paragraph of a letter to advise them about what their first few weeks might be like and what they should do to settle in.
Remember the high-quality writing features you have been practising (pages 162–177) and try to include some that are appropriate.

_____

_____

_____

_____

_____

_____

_____

_____

_____

_____

(6 marks)

2 Write the ending of the letter. You might wish to explain why they are especially lucky and wish them all the best as they settle in.
Use some high-quality writing features you did not use in the introduction, to further impress the examiner. Also make sure that you link your ending with your opening – often a quality found in excellent responses.

_____

_____

_____

_____

_____

_____

_____

_____

_____

_____

(6 marks)

3 Write the opening paragraph for a broadsheet newspaper, in which you argue that we must act immediately to save the environment.

_____

_____

_____

_____

_____

_____

_____

_____

(6 marks)

4 Write an opening paragraph on the same topic for a magazine aimed at young teenagers. Adapt your content and tone to match this different form and audience.

_____

_____

_____

_____

_____

_____

_____

_____

_____

_____

(6 marks)

5 Write the concluding paragraph to either of the openings. Link it back to what you said in your opening.

_____

_____

_____

_____

_____

_____

_____

_____

_____

_____

(6 marks)

Writing letters

Aren't letters basically the same as emails?

Letters and emails can be very different. Letters need to be set out more formally and generally have a more formal structure throughout; emails can be more in note form – though in the exam if you are asked to write an email, you will certainly be expected to include a good deal of detail, paragraphing and effective structure.

1 Write a letter to an elderly relative, persuading them to install security equipment around their home.
Make sure you:
- set out the letter correctly
- adopt an appropriate tone
- include detail
- end the letter correctly.

_____

_____

_____

_____

_____

_____

_____

_____

_____

_____

_____

_____

_____

_____

_____

_____

_____

_____

_____

_____

_____

_____

_____

_____

_____

_____

Continue on lined paper if necessary.   *(16 marks)*

2 Write a short letter to a security firm, asking them to install security equipment for your elderly relative and informing them of what he or she will require.

Use the conventions and layout of a formal letter, as shown below. Take no more than 25 minutes.

your address

_____

_____

_____

_____

date _____

Name and address: person and firm

_____

_____

_____

_____

_____

Dear _____

_____

_____

_____

_____

_____

_____

_____

_____

_____

_____

_____

_____

_____

Yours _____

_____

(16 marks)

REMEMBER
- 'Dear Sir/Madam' ends 'Yours faithfully'.
- 'Dear Mr/Mrs/Ms…' ends 'Yours sincerely'.

181

Writing news reports

Isn't writing a news report just the same as telling a story?

A report will tell the story, but give it emphasis and structure, so the focus is on the central point(s). The basic events are presented in the opening, then detailed later; the story will be filtered so that only the important people are named; and the ending will sum up the situation or, sometimes, predict what might happen next.

1 You have been asked to write a report for a school magazine about:
- a trip you have been on
- a match or competition or
- an unusual event that has happened.

Write your opening paragraph in three or four sentences summing up what happened.

_____

_____

_____

_____

_____

_____

_____

_____

(6 marks)

2 Write a paragraph explaining what happened at the start of the event.

_____

_____

_____

_____

_____

_____

_____

_____

(6 marks)

3 Move on to write about the main person or persons involved in what happened.

_____

_____

_____

_____

_____

_____

_____

(6 marks)

4 Develop your explanation of what happened, remembering not to confuse the reader with too much detail.

_____

_____

_____

_____

_____

_____

_____

_____

(6 marks)

5 Write about the climax of the event.

_____

_____

_____

_____

_____

_____

_____

(6 marks)

6 End your report in a memorable way: summarising what happened or hinting at what was to come.
If appropriate, comment on the effect it had on the individual(s) involved.

_____

_____

_____

_____

_____

_____

_____

(6 marks)

Writing to argue

What is it most important to remember when writing to argue?

Your argument needs to be convincing. It is usually easier to put together a line of argument if you have something to argue against, so it helps to include the opposite viewpoint. The two sides do not have to be equally matched – you might just mention the alternative viewpoint in passing as a way of introducing or balancing your arguments.

You are going to write an article to argue that the death penalty **should** or **should not** be re-introduced for the most serious crimes.

1 Make a list of points for and against the re-introduction of the death penalty.

For	Against

(4 marks)

2 Read this opening paragraph then re-write it, maintaining the viewpoint but including:
- a topic sentence
- variety in the expression
- additional or different detail as appropriate
- at least one feature to attract the reader's interest.

There are too many murderers walking the streets. Other people should be arrested and executed too if they do terrible crimes. My brother got beaten up only a couple of weeks ago. Old people aren't safe in their beds at night. The world would be a better place if we got rid of all the bad people. Hanging might be too good for them.

(6 marks)

3 Write a paragraph in which you run through your points for and against the death penalty, but end by choosing which view to support.

_____

_____

_____

_____

_____

_____

_____

_____

_____

(6 marks)

4 Write a paragraph supporting your own viewpoint, in which you provide evidence (either quotation, example, anecdote and/or statistics).

_____

_____

_____

_____

_____

_____

_____

_____

_____

_____

(6 marks)

5 Write a concluding paragraph which is linked to the previous one but finishes off your argument convincingly.

_____

_____

_____

_____

_____

_____

_____

_____

_____

_____

(6 marks)

Practice essay title

Write the text of a speech in which you argue that 'There is no place like home': either because it is the best place or, perhaps, just because there could not be another place like it.

(24 marks)

Writing to persuade

What are the differences between arguing and persuading?

Sometimes we persuade by arguing effectively. However, often we persuade by putting forward just one point of view. We can use a range of techniques to support our ideas, such as emotive language, convincing examples and appropriate anecdotes.

You are going to write a letter to your local council to persuade them to provide a good range of leisure facilities for young people.

1 List at least five facilities you would like to see provided, reasons why they are needed and how they would improve life in your area.

Facility	Why needed	How life would improve

(5 marks)

2 Begin your letter, setting it out appropriately and including a persuasive opening paragraph.
(For a reminder about letter layout, see page 181.)

_____

_____

_____

_____

_____

_____

_____

_____

_____

Continue on lined paper if necessary.   *(8 marks)*

3 Write a second paragraph, outlining one or two of your suggested facilities. Use some emotive language, which touches the reader's emotions.

_____

_____

_____

_____

_____

_____

_____

_____

(6 marks)

4 Write a third paragraph about another facility. Try to win round the reader by using humour, exaggeration or an anecdote.

_____

_____

_____

_____

_____

_____

_____

_____

_____

_____

(6 marks)

5 Sum up your reasons for wanting these changes in a conclusion. End with an effective point or a final plea – perhaps using a rhetorical question.

_____

_____

_____

_____

_____

_____

(6 marks)

Practice essay title

Write an article for a national newspaper, persuading the readers to watch less television and, instead, to do things which are more productive or creative.

(24 marks)

Writing to inform

Isn't it easy to write to inform?

Presenting information can be straightforward, but in the examination, the marker will be looking for detail and relevance and will be expecting the information to be well-structured. Of course, what you write will also need to be suitable for the purpose and audience.

You are going to write a section of a guide book for your local area to inform visitors about what it has to offer.

1 List the local features you intend to include. Try to offer a range that would appeal to different sorts of people.

_____

_____

_____

_____

_____

_____

(3 marks)

2 Write the opening paragraph. Indicate the range of attractions and aim to engage the reader.

_____

_____

_____

_____

_____

_____

_____

_____

_____

(6 marks)

3 Write the next paragraph, including details such as facts or statistics and a quotation. (Remember: you can invent details like this but try to make them sound convincing.)

_____

_____

_____

_____

_____

_____

_____

(6 marks)

4 Write the final two or three paragraphs, including a touch of humour if possible and any other features to interest your audience.

Make you ending memorable if you can.

_____

_____

_____

_____

_____

_____

_____

_____

_____

_____

_____

_____

_____

_____

_____

_____

_____

_____

_____

_____

_____

_____

_____

_____

_____

_____

(12 marks)

Practice essay title

An older couple you like and know well have recently moved abroad – it could be your grandparents. Write a letter to inform them about what has been happening locally since they moved away.

Aim to include information which will interest them and write in a way that will entertain them.

(24 marks)

189

Writing to explain

What is the difference between informing and explaining?

When you inform, you give facts and interpretations of them; when you explain, you are saying why something happens or how a situation arose. You move beyond the obvious to give reasons or causes for things.

You are going to write an article in which you explain how to lead a healthy life.

1 Produce a spider diagram of ideas for your article.

Now, structure your ideas into a logical sequence.

Idea for a healthy lifestyle	How this will make you healthy
Example: run regularly	Explanation: improves fitness, strengthens lungs
1	
2	
3	
4	
5	
6	

(6 marks)

2 Write a first paragraph, to introduce the readers to your ideas for a healthy lifestyle.

_____

_____

_____

_____

_____

_____

_____

_____

(6 marks)

3 Write a second paragraph, linked to the first but explaining one or two of your ideas in more detail. Try to introduce some facts and figures. It may be appropriate to use some emotive language to reinforce your reasons.

_____

_____

_____

_____

_____

_____

_____

_____

_____

_____

(6 marks)

4 Omit the rest of the central section of your response which might take up several more paragraphs. Write the conclusion for your article.

_____

_____

_____

_____

_____

_____

Continue on lined paper if necessary.   *(6 marks)*

Practice essay title

Write an article for a teenage magazine, explaining how to be fashionable. You can choose to write about clothes, music or lifestyle.

(24 marks)

Writing to review

What is special about review writing?

In a review, you are likely to give your opinion of whatever you are reviewing, describe important elements of it, probably judge some of the people involved and try to entertain the reader.

Write a review of your least favourite television programme.

1 As an introduction, describe an incident from the programme and what was wrong with it.

_____

_____

_____

_____

_____

_____

_____

_____

(6 marks)

2 Move on to a second paragraph in which you offer your opinion of the programme as a whole but also give more objective details about it.

_____

_____

_____

_____

_____

_____

_____

_____

(6 marks)

3 Choose an individual or individuals from the programme and write about how good or bad they are and why.

_____

_____

_____

_____

_____

_____

_____

_____

(6 marks)

4 Analyse the storyline, filming or staging – whatever is appropriate to the type of programme. Give precise details but also a personal interpretation of what happens, saying why it is disappointing/repetitive/how it could be improved, etc.

_____

_____

_____

_____

_____

_____

_____

_____

(6 marks)

5 Comment on others' opinions of the programme. Consider using one or more quotations.

_____

_____

_____

_____

_____

_____

_____

_____

(6 marks)

6 Conclude with your summary of the programme, offering some final opinions in an entertaining way.

_____

_____

_____

_____

_____

_____

(6 marks)

Practice essay title

Write a review of the most memorable holiday you have had. Summarise the main events and give your opinions on any high and low points.

(24 marks)

Writing to advise

What is the key to successful advice?

You need to convince the reader to take your advice. To do that, you need to present a logical response, using effective detail and supported opinion. You might choose to include anecdote, rhetoric, emotive language or other high-quality writing features to persuade the reader that your advice is sound.

You are an agony aunt for a national newspaper. A reader has written asking you for advice on how to make sure her teenage son or daughter does not get into any trouble. They seem to be mixing with the 'wrong sort' of friends…

1 Complete this planning grid, listing the problems of getting in with the wrong group of friends and how to avoid each one.

Problem	Advice

(6 marks)

2 Write an opening paragraph of your 'reply', addressing the reader who has written in. Show that you are well aware of the problems and that you have possible solutions to offer.

(6 marks)

3 Choose one of the problems and offer advice. Use an anecdote to support your ideas.

_____

_____

_____

_____

_____

_____

_____

(6 marks)

4 Deal with a second problem. This time, use emotive language to convince the reader.

_____

_____

_____

_____

_____

_____

(6 marks)

5 Choose another problem. Use humour or rhetoric or both in your advice.

_____

_____

_____

_____

_____

_____

(6 marks)

6 Write a concluding paragraph, addressing the same reader directly and demonstrating confidence in
your opinions.

_____

_____

_____

_____

_____

_____

(6 marks)

Practice essay title

Write an article for your local newspaper, advising readers how to cope if they lose their job: how
to make money go further; how to find another job; or how to use any spare time they might have.   *(24 marks)*

Checking your writing

Is checking what we have written really important?

There are no marks in the exam for neatness. What matters is the quality of what you produce. So, as long as the examiner can read your work, the number of alterations does not matter. This means that you can change as much as you like without fear of losing marks: and every correction you make might well help to improve your final grade.

1 Improve the punctuation in this extract.

did'nt

I did not know where to turn. I had bills to pay, the car had broken down,and my sister said its no

good we will have to leave here. The rent is too high; What an awful day that was.

(3 marks)

2 Correct the incorrect spellings in the following paragraph.

Unfortunaty, the rise in global temprature is likely to continue. Siting in Britain, it's easy to forget

that unpresedented numbers of people are being made homeless as sea levels rise and storms

decamate frajile comunities. It will take a huge effort from govenments and a change in lifestiles

before we can even begin to think that there might be a future for the world as we now it.

(10 marks)

3 Re-write this extract from a teenager's email, to make it suitable for older people.

I hate school and nothing will change that. A lot of the other kids are minging and the lessons are just *****. I used to be in a better school. I'd still have been better lying in bed with my ipod but I had some OK times and a couple of teachers there were well fit. Mind, even there I got stuck with some chavs in music and they were like, 'This is banging' but it wasn't. They didn't know nothing.

_____

_____

_____

_____

_____

_____

(6 marks)

4 Read this response and make changes to improve it.
- Decide where paragraphs might go.
- Correct the spelling/grammar/punctuation.
- Improve the vocabulary/sentences/phrasing whenever necessary.

My next door neghbour is the most boring person I have ever met for a start he loves basketball

and I hate it but he spends hours hamering a ball against the wall of his house and we get the

noise in our's. When hes not bounceing the ball around hes talking about basketball or watching

basketball or dreaming about basketball I guess When he first moved in I though he could be

a good mate and I tried to be friendly with him but he didn't want to know 'Yeah we can go out'

he said. There's a basketball game on Sunday at the leisure centre we could go there and that was

that. I could just see him sat there eating a burger or something and drinking coke like it were a

proper meal or something and then jumping up and spilling chips or fries as that's probably what

they are at a basketball match all over the place. I just don't get it at all. I never went and you

wouldn't of either would you. His sister must lead a terrible life cos she has to be around him like

all day long she seems nice but what a sad life, eh? It's not nice being next door so it must be

very not nice in the same house. His parents never seem to come out at all. I don't know what

they look like. They probably look like him really tall with a baseball cap on all the time and a

basketball in their hand all the time and there might be pictures of basketball players on all the

walls and framed ones on top of the telly. Like a museum, sort of. I just don't get it. How boring

can you get?

(10 marks)

Revision advice

Working through the sections in this book will have helped you to focus on the important elements in each part of the exam.

You can extend your revision and preparation in various ways.

Section A

Spend five minutes every day reading and analysing a text. For example, read newspaper articles, reports, or advertisements.

Try to look at a different type of text each day. Read anything and everything, from broadsheet newspapers to the back of cornflake boxes.

You could follow this kind of routine.

Day 1: purpose and audience – what form is the writing in, is there a specific audience and how do you know?

Day 2: presentational features – what effect do these have on the reader and how does this fit with the purpose of the text

Day 3: language features – what stands out about the language and what is its effect?

Day 4: the writer's main message and how the parts of the argument or story fits together – how is the writing structured?

Day 5: what the writer wants the reader to think and how that effect is created – which presentational or language features are chosen to achieve this?

And then begin again.

Section B

The more you practise the vital skills, the better you are likely to perform in the exam.

Consider:

* setting your own titles and producing detailed plans
* writing openings and endings or central sections of responses
* using high-quality features like rhetoric, anecdotes, humour, similes and so on
* writing whole responses in 25 minutes and 35 minutes, to become familiar with the exam timings
* checking your work for errors and making appropriate improvements.

Students who invest time like this preparing for the exam paper generally make the greatest improvements.

It is also true that in English exams students usually get what they deserve. This means that your hard work will be rewarded!

Index

Answers

Understanding non-fiction texts

Most of the answers that follow are not 'the correct answers' but should help you to see the sort of answer you need to write in order to get a Grade C.

As a reminder, here is an outline of the skills you need to show at different GCSE grades. You should refer back to this, and use the grids provided with some answers, when working out your mark and grade for a question.

Grade	Skills demonstrated
A*/A	• has thorough understanding of the text and able to apply it fully to the question • engages with the text showing perception throughout • selects and uses apt quotations to support detailed understanding • makes perceptive and analytical comments
B/C	• has a clear and focused understanding of the text and is able to handle the question with confidence • engages with the text and is able to interpret it clearly • uses relevant quotations to support understanding • makes clear and relevant comments
D/E	• has some understanding of the text and attempts to respond to the question appropriately • attempts to engage with the text • uses quotations to support understanding • some focus on what is required
F/G	• shows limited understanding of the text with random comments in response to the question • is aware of the text, but unable to respond in detail • may copy sections • offers little relevant material
U	• offers nothing relevant

Answers Understanding non-fiction texts

pages 110–111

1 Some likely responses:

- to interest the general reader
- to inform about the situation
- because it is such an unusual occurrence
- possibly to publicise the efforts of Loganair

A/A*:	4 marks – likely to offer three or more reasons, with detailed support
B/C:	3 marks – likely to offer two or three reasons, with convincing support
D/E:	2 marks – likely to offer two or three reasons, with some convincing support
F/G:	1 mark: – likely to give one or two reasons and offer general comment

2 Likely answers:

Extract 1: advice column, perhaps from newspaper (1) – clearly a response to the first statement (1)

Extract 2: perhaps article on conservation (2) or advice column again (2) or anything appropriate (2) – it is telling the reader what to do (using imperative) (1) and sounding superior/ knowledgeable (1)

Extract 3: an article (1) or speech (1) or textbook (1) or anything suitable (1) – offering an opinion on nurses and how they are seen by the public (1)

A/A*:	8 marks
B/C:	6–7 marks
D/E:	4–5 marks
F/G:	1–3 marks

3 Likely responses:

Audience: older people who need cash or have debts;

How: picture suggests the deal will make people happy, 'FREE' to attract people, idea you will then 'enjoy life; language like 'unique', 'up to 100% of the value', 'absolute discretion', 'all costs will be covered'

A/A*:	7–8 marks
B/C:	5–6 marks
D/E:	3–4 marks
F/G:	1–2 marks

pages 112–113

1 'response was staggering' (1); more than 100 individuals and organisations put forward (1)

2 Any four from:

- can vote in different categories (1)
- categories named (1)
- can go on line to vote (1)

- can read details and make informed choice (1)
- can vote as many times as you like (1)

3 Any four from:

- a £30 ticket really costs £34.50 (1)
- the 'hidden charge' is a kind of deception (1)
- booking fee added 40% to the ticket price (1)
- the price of a Leonard Cohen ticket has rocketed (1)
- you used to be able to get Leonard Cohen tickets without paying a booking fee (1)

4 Possible words and phrases:

- extortionate (1)
- this kind of deception (1)
- corporate avarice (1)
- eye-wateringly pricey (1)

A/A*:	14 marks
B/C:	11–13 marks
D/E:	7–10 marks
F/G:	below 7 marks

pages 114–115

1 Any two from:

- to report on what happened (1)
- to interest a tabloid newspaper reader (1)
- to highlight Lambert's foul play (1)
- to surprise readers because she is not like a typical female stereotype (1)

C/A*:	two purposes, with explanations
D/F:	two purposes, perhaps with attempted explanation
G:	one purpose

2 Any four from these details likely to be mentioned:

- pictures (1)
- headings (1)
- alliteration (1)
- dramatic opening (1)
- vocabulary like 'dirtiest', 'violent', vicious', etc (1)
- list of Lambert's fouls (1)

A/A*:	4 marks
B-C/A:	3 marks
E/F:	2 marks
F/G:	1 mark

3 Likely comments, with explanations of effects:

headline – play on 'Beauty and the Beast'; alliteration

2

sub-heading – alliteration continued; focus on 'blonde', to link with 'beauty'; metaphor ('kicks up storm') to link with 'Booty'

captions – 1. 'Head case' double meaning; alliteration 2. 'Take that' as if from comic; 'boots' repeated

A/A*:	6 marks
B/C:	4–5 marks
D/E:	2–3 marks
F/G:	1 mark

4 Possible points of focus:

'football babe', 'sticking the boot in', 'blonde bruiser', 'dirtiest player in women's game', 'violent', 'yanked, punched, lunged', 'knee-high tackles', 'booting the ball into the face…', 'vicious', 'suspended' and 'banned', 'deeply regretful'

Better answers will include mention of her remorse at the end.

A/A*:	7–8 marks
B/C:	5–6 marks
D/E:	3–4 marks
F/G:	1–2 marks

5 Extract from a Grade A* response

The writer clearly sets out to make Lambert seem as violent as a footballer can be. She is accused of 'sticking the boot in' (although a cliché, this action sounds intentional as if she has chosen the action), she is a 'bruiser', with the implication she is like a boxer or street fighter, and 'the dirtiest player in the women's game' – which makes her the worst there is. The fact that she has been 'branded' makes her appear a criminal – or an animal. The vocabulary chosen to describe her is consistently rough: she 'yanked a player by her ponytail' (the other player sounds pretty and young because of the 'pony' connection, and perhaps just playful, unlike Lambert); and she 'punched' and 'lunged into knee-high tackles'…

pages 116–117

1 Two marks for purpose(s):

Answers might include: Botham presented as hero/shows sports stars can do more than just perform in sports/show what is good about Britain, etc.

Two marks for audience:

Answers might include: newspaper readers/those attracted by headings and pictures/fans of Botham, etc.

A/A*:	purposes and audience(s) with detailed explanation – 4 marks
B/C:	purpose(s) and audience(s) with clear explanation – 3 marks
D/E:	purpose and audience explained – 2 marks
F/G:	attempt to identify purpose and/or audience – 1 mark

2 Any four from:

- 'Heroes leading from the front' (1)
- 'His … performances inspired a nation' (1)
- 'relentless charity walks' (1)
- 'the aura and invincibility' (1)
- 'looks to build on the £10m that he has already raised for charity' (1)
- 'his latest marathon effort' (1)
- 'such determination' (1)

C/A*:	4 details – 4 marks
D/E:	3 details – 3 marks
F:	2 details – 2 marks
G:	1 detail – 1 mark

3 Possible language to be commented on:

'Facebook generation'; repeat of 'pressures' and phrasing ('in lofts', 'in universities', etc); question and answer; humour – 'they gather to knit'; the unexpected - 'modern life is stressful, let's make chutney'; lists ('jam-making, crocheting and even…'); quotations from people involved, etc.

A/A*:	7–8 marks
B/C:	5–6 marks
D/E:	3–4 marks
F/G:	1–2 marks

4 Possible points:

Opening: apparently 'everyday' first sentence, then the sarcasm (updating the Facebook profile); introduction of the unexpected (the Women's Institute as a solution); repetition of phrasing in third paragraph to make it sound as if it is happening everywhere; and the joke to end the paragraph, poking fun at the women.

Ending: quotations to make it more real; ridiculous idea that these groups have to exist so people talk to each other; novelty stressed; 'Young Conservative' – joke, poking fun at the women and their old-fashioned pursuits; final paragraph perhaps showing that normal young women are involved in these activities.

A/A*:	7–8 marks
B/C:	5–6 marks
D/E:	3–4 marks
F/G:	1–2 marks

Extract from a Grade A* response

At the start, the writer pokes fun at the concept of young women going to the WI. He says 'it's hard to be a young woman', echoing the old song 'Sometimes it's hard to be a woman…' However, he does not say this is because of just those tasks traditionally associated with females: he picks out work pressures and home pressures but climaxes the list of three with mention of 'updating one's Facebook page. He wants us to smile at the ridiculous nature of modern life. He then introduces the unexpected – the idea that the problems of young women can be solved by joining the WI. When he says they are knitting in upstairs rooms and lofts, they sound hidden away, almost like secret agents. The situation sounds absurd, so we see them as eccentric. The repetition of 'in lofts… in universities… in bedrooms…' reinforces this effect…

---

pages 118–119

1 Possible points:

Fostered children will be 'fun' (face and action); they will be attractive; they will be fit and healthy, so good to have around; you will make them jump for joy; she is in the sky, so could be like a god-send…

A/A*:	4 marks
B/C:	3 marks
D/E:	2 marks
F/G:	1 mark

Extract from a Grade A* response

Obviously, the advertisement does not show a carer, but the girl is presumably being fostered, and seems to be having a wonderful time. She looks young and happy and is intended to attract adults to become involved. It suggests that looking after someone like this is a joy: she is smiling and almost flying – she is set amongst the clouds, inspiring us to reach for the sky, and is cheering and waving. It appeals to a sense of fulfilment in us all…

2 Possible language for comment:

'Specialist' – making carers seem valuable; 'highly motivated individuals' – anyone who becomes a carer should feel good about themselves; financially rewarding – 'generous retainer' with 'top-up'; sounds like a profession – 'specialist training', 'part of a professional team; '24 hour support'; appealing for people with 'skills' – makes people feel positive about themselves if they apply; 'make a difference' – emotive appeal

A/A*:	7–8 marks
B/C:	5–6 marks
D/E:	3–4 marks
F/G:	1–2 marks

3 Two marks for each explanation. Answers might include:

1 sense of something different; links to picture and war scenario

2 rhetorical question; metaphor; sense of dealing with dangerous situations; comparison with normal boring life

3 to appeal to people wanting to make a difference/wanting excitement; sense that you will be facing danger; use of cliché

4 making reader think they are special; implies we are all looking for something more exciting

A/A*:	2 detailed explanations of each (7–8 marks)
B/C:	2 clear explanations of 2–3 of them and one clear explanation of the other(s) (5–6 marks)
D/E:	explanations showing some understanding (3–4 marks)
F/G:	comments, some of which are valid (1–2 marks)

4 Possible comments:

Picture: desk in middle of a war zone; linking of desk job and job of soldier; sense of danger and risk; someone has left the chair to..?; sense of desk job being modern (PC etc) and important – it is in the foreground…

Other features: 'Not exactly…' – in larger font to emphasise it; white on black (goodness coming out of darkness?); upper case stresses importance

'Careers in British intelligence' and 'Cheltenham' put it into context

GCHQ logo and details top left give it credibility and status

A/A*:	7–8 marks
B/C:	5–6 marks
D/E:	3–4 marks
F/G:	1–2 marks

---

pages 120–121

1 Possible comments:

emotive appeal; pretty but sad baby girl; wet nose for sympathy or suggesting sickness; forlorn look in eyes; no sense of parent; face fills picture, giving importance

A/A*:	4 marks
B/C:	3 marks
D/E:	2 marks
F/G:	1 mark

2 Possible comments:

Stressing togetherness of parent and child to begin ('cried…cried', 'laughed… laughed');

Repetition of 'The first time' to show newness; contrast of 'normality' of parental reactions in the opening with 'The first time she got sick…'

Intended to shock, reveal hopelessness of parent's situation; intended to motivate reader to react and help

Bottom banner: request for support – joining others who care. Simple appeal: 'Will you?'

A/A*:   4 marks
B/C: 3 marks
D/E: marks
F/G: 1 mark

3 Likely points:

picture link, this time focusing on parent/child bond; 'Even my husband' connection; 'we/you' again; questioning reader again; the picture shows a wider view of what is happening in this second text.

A/A*:   4 marks
B/C: 3 marks
D/E: 2 marks
F/G: 1 mark

Extract from a A* Grade response

The second part of the leaflet builds on the first in various ways. The sick child is now held (desperately, it seems), by the father – and focus is on his sorrow, rather than on the tragic picture of the child in the first picture. Interestingly, too, there is a change of tense: whereas the mother says 'There was nothing I could do', we now have 'Even my husband can't save him'. This is in the present, so the death is happening right now, which makes it more immediate and more moving. The reader is addressed directly in both instances, so we are targeted, but in the second part we are told exactly what is required: a regular monthly donation…

4 Some possible points:

First page: 'The first time', etc – almost like a song or a lament

Second page: situation simply stated, simple solution, simple appeal; 'We're… We're…' – confident statements; 'How many/fast/up to you' – all made to sound straightforward. Also, brevity makes it easily accessible to any reader.

A/A*:   4 marks
B/C: 3 marks
D/E: 2 marks
F/G: 1 mark

5 Purpose: to raise donations

Success: likely to focus on effectiveness of pictures, presentational features and perhaps layout; and on text and general appeal.

A/A*:   4 marks
B/C: 3 marks
D/E: 2 marks
F/G: 1 mark

pages 122–123

1 Point: the old language was more varied and interesting

How: giving examples from around the country; probably trying to amuse or confuse the reader; making clear comparison with Americanisms; using touch of humour at the end, as a clear contrast in language styles.

A/A*:   4 marks
B/C: 3 marks
D/E: 2 marks
F/G: 1 mark

Extract from a Grade A* response

The writer thinks that the ways people used to speak were much more interesting (there was 'colourful dialect', which sounds varied and attractive); whereas nowadays we have to cope with language that is much less precise ('sloppy') and comes from the pervasive influence of the television, from 'American sit-coms and rap'. He is an older writer – clearly, because of how he looks back – and so he can reflect on what used to be around, setting out a list of all the language that was heard then and which, in fact, he prefers…

2 Any four from:

'hod your whisht', 'moidering', 'mithering', 'midden men', 'fever grates', 'scouring stone', 'causer edge', 'apple kipping', 'tusky', 'taws', 'gibbing', 'broddling your lug', 'taldering'

C/A*:   4 examples
D/F: 3 examples
G: fewer than 3 examples

3 Final sentence: colloquial style; first half formal but second half Americanised and less correct, as young people might speak (2)

First sentence: formal throughout; vocabulary unlikely to be used in Americanised context, like 'fascinating' and 'evoke'; use of (presumably) local term 'Leeds Loiner' (2)

A/A*:   4 marks
B/C: 3 marks
D/E: 2 marks
F/G: 1 mark

4

1 'cherubs': simile, suggesting they look like angels; possibly 'they look' suggests this is an incorrect impression

2 'deranged hounds': metaphor, suggesting they work together ('pack') are mad and unpredictable ('deranged') and like animals ('hounds')

3 'Uncontrollable': at start of sentence gives it emphasis; sense of wildness

4 'It's shocking': 3 for emphasis, stressing 'shocking' and 'demoralising' as powerful effects on teacher; 'daily' comes as an unpleasant surprise

A/A*: four detailed analyses – 4 marks
B/C: two or more clear explanations with some analysis and remaining language explained in less depth – 3 marks
D/E: all four explained, with some understanding – 2 marks
F/G: two or more brief comments

5 Any two points from:

we hear the writer's 'speaking voice' / we understand exactly how the writer is feeling / we get exactly what she is thinking and not necessarily in processed sentences, e.g. 'Uncontrollable at times'

C/A*: 2 points
G/C: 1 point

6 Possible points:

• The students (1)

• Students and senior members of staff (2)

• Students with examples, e.g. 'deranged hounds', etc; and senior members of staff (because ordinary teachers are 'left to flounder') (3)

• Above points with explanations (4)

B/A*: 3 points, with valid explanation
C: 3 points, with some explanation
D/E: 2 or 3 points, with attempted explanation
F/G: 1 or 2 points

---

pages 124–125

---

1 Any two from:

• Getting the floors washed (1)

• Getting the men's clothes clean (1)

• Suggestion she got the toilets cleaned (1)

E/A*: 2 points
F/G: 1 point

2 Likely points:

Men would not allow their shirts to be washed. Suggestion at start that the doctors had not insisted on important cleanliness. No one took responsibility

A/A*: 4 marks
B/C: 3 marks
D/E: 2 marks
F/G: 1 mark

3 Possible points:

Wants things cleaned / dynamic enough to order what was needed / puts necessary system in place to get shirts clean / natural organiser, leader

A/A*: 4 marks
B/C: 3 marks
D/E: 2 marks
F/G: 1 mark

4 Either of:

Sees him as a deserter, so his suffering is all he deserves / she seems cold in her description, right from the start

Writes about how he is treated with sarcasm, as if it should not be happening like this / the initial description is to show his desperation and the horror of his situation

So, 'This is War' could be interpreted as agreeing that men must die in this way or as showing how terrible war is.

A/A*: 7–8 marks
B/C: 5–6 marks
D/E: 3–4 marks
F/G: 1–2 marks

Extract from a Grade A* response

The cold but vivid details given by the nurse to begin, makes us feel that she cares little for the man. He is treated like something inhuman ('bundled') and described without sympathy, even as he is 'cursing and screaming'. The nurse does not protest that this is unacceptable, even after his eye has just been shot out. There is also the apparently heartless comment that 'if he was bounced to death… it did not matter.' She could just be describing what the authorities think, but states simply: 'He was a deserter and discipline must be maintained'…

5 Some possible points:

clinical description ('The ball tore out his left eye'); uncaring nature of ambulance men ('bundled'); his pain ('cursing and screaming'); 'if he were bounced to death' and 'breakneck speed' (with play on 'break' 'neck') sounds careless; simple grim reality ('discipline must be maintained') etc.

A/A*: 7–8 marks
B/C: 5–6 marks
D/E: 3–4 marks
F/G: 1–2 marks

pages 126–127

1 Any four services from:

help with events / chip timing / help for charities / help with sports injuries / cheap or free online race entries / entry management for races / online entry for runners / cheaper online entry / list of online entry forms / confidentiality with details / exclusive entry to Freckleton Half Marathon

C/A*:   4 services
D/F: 3 services
G/U: fewer than 3 services

2 Likely points:

dense, small, hard to read / full of detail / lacks clarity in side-bars etc / short of visual elements / lacks clear heading, sub-heads, etc / useful side-bar with items to click on

A/A*:   7–8 marks
B/C: 5–6 marks
D/E: 3–4 marks
F/G: 1–2 marks

Extract from a Grade A* response

It does not seem likely that the reader would be helped by the layout, because all of it seems so muddled and confusing. Even the bold font (e.g. 'Aches and pains due to…?') fails to stand out from the rest. The headings and subheadings are few and the text is closely written: it is hard to find any particular information without reading the whole page. For example, even 'Online Entry Forms' cannot be easily found, and they would seem very important for a site about races. The side bar on the left offers some support for web surfers, offering 'Race Calendars' and so on, but the pictures are uninspiring and small…

3 Any four from:

Possible language: 'Welcome' and 'friendly' / 'expertise' / 'please' / enticing questions / 'Free' / 'click here' / first person approach, etc.

A/A*:   7–8 marks
B/C: 5–6 marks
D/E: 3–4 marks
F/G: 1–2 marks

pages 128–129

1 Any four from:

'spectre'/ 'secluded' / 'terrible hallucinations' / 'the mysterious one' / 'haunting'

C/A*:   4 examples
D/E: 3 examples

F: 2 examples
G: 1 example

2 Answers are likely to consider details in the story: characters and story-line. Also likely to consider final sentence: 'short and spare' – which sounds critical; 'expertly structured', 'beautifully written prose' both offering praise; style of writing memorable – 'as haunting as the best ghost story'.

A/A*:   7–8 marks
B/C: 5–6 marks
D/E: 3–4 marks
F/G: 1–2 marks

Extract from a Grade A* response

The reviewer indicates that the book has attractive elements. It is described as 'gripping', which implies it is the sort of book you would read from start to finish, and which holds your attention. It is 'expertly structured' and 'beautifully written', both of which are clearly positive comments. It is also described as 'short and spare' which, of course, could suggest criticism…

3 Opening: likely to focus on emphasis on ghostly vocabulary ('ghost stories', 'spectre') and on attraction ('gripping tale').

Ending: returns to idea of ghost stories; and on language as in previous question; and repetition of 'best'

A/A*:   4 marks
B/C: 3 marks
D/E: 2 marks
F/G: 1 mark

4 Likely to mention: 'pressures', 'ordeals', 'fatigue and grief', 'challenges'; and 'touching moment', 'struggled with emotion'… It is a sympathetic picture, recognising the difficulties for parents and how they have to cope with their situation and how they need more support.

A/A*:   7–8 marks
B/C: 5–6 marks
D/E: 3–4 marks
F/G: 1–2 marks

5 Answers likely to mention how she feels sympathy for parents, how they need support, 'compassion' and more 'common sense' from the state. Finally, more money needs to be invested.

A/A*:   7–8 marks
B/C: 5–6 marks
D/E: 3–4 marks
F/G: 1–2 marks

1 'battled': Two from: a fighter/ he found it a struggle/ maybe heroic / or anything sensible

'collapsed': Two from: broke down / could not cope with pressure / maybe has a medical problem / not equal to the task / or anything sensible

2 Two marks for each idea plus analysis, e.g.

1 look on face / eyes closed (1): exhausted / devastated / can't believe what has happened / in pain…(1)

2 black background (1): sense of darkness / doom; as if he has fallen into darkness and disappointment / nothing else matters – just his pain…(1)

3 Some possible answers:

- **'The world of work and Higher Education is becoming more complicated and competitive'**: alliteration builds effect / 4-syllable words stress complexity …

- **'It is essential… to explore…'**: no apparent alternative/ inducement of 'exploration'…

- **'opportunities'/'wealth of opportunities'**: opening up the future / sounds exciting, full of possibilities / value…

- **'important'/'importance'**: repeated/ stresses how vital it is…

- **'valuable'/'crucial'**: building up effect / balance between reward and desperate need…

A/A*:   7–8 marks
B/C: 5–6 marks
D/E: 3–4 marks
F/G: 1–2 marks

Extract from a Grade A* response

The school is trying to make the evening a valuable and fascinating event. For instance, those who attend will be able to 'explore the many opportunities available to them'. This is clearly enticing. The concept of 'exploring' makes the evening sound exciting and like a voyage of discovery; and it will be a 'valuable opportunity', so if students do not attend, they will miss the range of information which is, presumably, on offer…

4

C/A*:   Analytical comment on 'wealth of opportunities' for: 'wealth' (value) and range of chances ('opportunities'); and perhaps on 'aimed' – precisely targeted, like a trained marksman (2)

D/G: one comment on the phrase or paraphrase of statement (1)

1 Possible comments, with support:

strange looking funny man, with elegant woman; she is glamorous and embarrassed by his behaviour; 'frequent' TV technique – attractive young woman and older less attractive man; fashionable woman and old-fashioned man

C/A*:   2 points with clear support from text (4 marks)
D: 2 points with some support (3 marks)
E/F: 2 points (2 marks)
G: 1 point (1 mark)

Extract from a Grade A* response

The picture indicates immediately that this is not a serious programme. There is the usual situation, where a glamorous young woman, presumably selected for her good looks, hosts the show with an ageing comedian – and in this case, seems to be almost carrying him! His trousers look like a golfer's cast-offs and he could well be wearing a smoking jacket – like they used to do many years ago. Even his glasses look like something from an age gone by…

2 Detail will depend on points made. However, likely to select the joke ('short'); Corbett's height; 'towered over'.

A/A*:   4 marks
B/C: 3 marks
D/E: 2 marks
F/G: 1 mark

3 Possible points:

'Squeezy living'; concept of 14 cheerleaders; 'stretches out'; 'sniff out'; 'only two wore seat belts'; 'no room for the pom-poms'; 'must have been bigger'; speed of getting into car; group of under 8s…

A/A*:   7–8 marks
B/C: 5–6 marks
D/E: 3–4 marks
F/G: 1–2 marks

1 Likely details:

umbrella collapsed, steam coming out of ears, list of disasters, 'take five and nibble chocolate'. Answers might see this as serious or jokey, but should be supported with evidence and explained.

A/A*:   4 marks
B/C: 3 marks
D/E: 2 marks
F/G: 1 mark

2 Might say this is offering evidence, which convinces; might focus on apparently scientific interpretation of evidence. Better answers likely to question whether the interpretation can be believed when given by employee of a chocolate company.

A/A*:   4 marks
B/C: 3 marks
D/E: 2 marks
F/G: 1 mark

Extract from a Grade A* response

At first glance, the paragraph offers definite proof that chocolate can do us good. The quotation uses suitably 'scientific' vocabulary – 'consumption' and 'metabolism' – and apparently comes from someone who has researched the matter. It is also extremely precise in its information ('40 grams over two weeks'). However, the perceptive reader will be sceptical when he sees the researcher is from Nestle, which is a company manufacturing chocolate, and with an interest in seeing sales increase. This might not be the most unbiased study ever…

3 Suggestion that the theory is nonsense; ideas ridicule the idea; ellipsis implies we should consider how foolish this is – or that the final list could go on indefinitely.

C/A*:   idea that this is ridiculous with convincing explanation of why (2 marks)
D/F: attempt to explain what is being suggested (1 mark)
G: paraphrase of the ideas (0 marks)

4 The priority is to justify ideas with reference to details in the pictures.

Picture 1: likely to focus on family man, laughing and happy with children, casual away from work, sitting on doorstep like ordinary person…

Picture 2: happily married man, enjoying life with his wife, loving, what he's like when behind curtains and out of sight of public…

Picture 3: focus on seal of office, how his wife is beside him on grand occasions, contrast with earlier personal shots, wearing clothes which befit his position, striding out as national leader…

For each picture:
A/A*:   4 marks
B/C: 3 marks
D/E: 2 marks
F/G: 1 mark

pages 136–137

1 Any four from:

'free installation'; don't need kettle; saves time etc; 'unique'; 'ultra-convenient, ultrasafe'; 'built-in childproof safety mechanism'; 'brilliantly energy-efficient'; leaves ample space for other things; 'wide range of height and handling adjustable tap designs'

A/A*:   7–8 marks (4 points, explained fully)
B/C: 5–6 marks (4 points, explained clearly)
D/E: 3–4 marks (3-4 points, with some attempted explanation)
F/G: 1–2 marks (2–3 points, with little convincing explanation)

2 Answers likely to comment on effect of:

'transfixed', rest of pack nearby, scared to move, 'terror forced me to run for…', 'legs shaking uncontrollably', 'still scared', effect of imagination, description of dog – how she sees it and describes it, details of dog killing bird, with knowledge it could happen to her

A/A*:   7–8 marks
B/C: 5–6 marks
D/E: 3–4 marks
F/G: 1–2 marks

Extract from a Grade A* response

… the girl is trapped in what seems an impossible situation. To stand 'transfixed' will lead to the dog finding her, whilst to run will probably make the animal spot her and attack. She says 'Finally, terror forced me to run…' and we empathise with her plight, because 'terror' is such an extreme emotion. When she says that her legs were 'shaking uncontrollably', we can understand why – and we are reminded of the fact that she is only a child, as evidenced by the fact that she also has to cope with the horrors brought on by her imagination: 'I imagined them waiting for me to fall out…'…

pages 138–141

1 Possible points:

'It's catupuncture': play on words (acupuncture); stresses text is about a cat; links to idea of sticking in needles

'To the point: Therapist assesses the sick feline': 'To the point' link to needles; 'therapist' and 'feline' trying to make it sound medical/serious, despite nature of content

'Feline prickly: Kiki bristles as needles are in place': plays on words ('feline' and feeling); linking of 'prickly', 'bristles' and 'needles'; needles stick out like bristles

In each case:
C/A*:   1–2 points explained in detail
D/E: 1–2 points with attempted explanation
F/G: 1 point with little understanding

2 Possible points:

'Needles give most people paws for thought': to make us think about what it feels like to have needles put in; to make us laugh because of pun ('paws' / pause)

'It has been used on animals for thousands of years in China, so it's a furly old remedy': to give sense of the history; to mock the idea by using the pun ('furly' / fairly)

In each case:
C/A*:   1–2 points explained in detail
D/E: 1–2 points with attempted explanation
F/G: 1 point with little understanding

3 Possible points:

'an experienced advisor': to give confidence; sense that the advisor will know everything

'specialise': firm can be trusted; people will get full attention; firm knows all about these cases

'maximum compensation': can be trusted to get all their clients deserve – nothing will be charged from that; will get as much as it is possible to get; will get as much as anyone could

'fast and hassle-free': will be a speedy and painless process; sounds as if this is all anyone could hope for; possible comment on 'fast' and 'hassle-free' in more detail

In each case:
C/A*:   2–3 points explained in detail
D/E: 1–2 points with attempted explanation
F/G: 1 point with little understanding

4 Likely points:

Focus on 'quick call' and 'within minutes'; 'substantial cash compensation'; very knowledgeable advisor; 100% no win no fee basis; 'I'd advise anyone...': all intended to encourage readers to use Accident Advice Helpline.

A/A*:   7–8 marks
B/C: 5–6 marks
D/E: 3–4 marks
F/G: 1–2 marks

5 Answers likely to focus on complex vocabulary; 'nutters in harnesses'; alliteration of 'hardcore hotspots'; modern vocabulary ('sick-ometer' and 'dude...'); 'some of the world's greatest daredevils'; and the fact that it is all one long, meant-to-sound-exciting sentence.

A/A*:   7–8 marks
B/C: 5–6 marks
D/E: 3–4 marks
F/G: 1–2 marks

Extract from a Grade A* response

The first paragraph uses two long sentences and polysyllabic words to stress the arduous nature of what is happening in Kendal. The vocabulary includes 'toughness' and 'daredevils', which lays emphasis on the brave nature of the participants – but there is also humour, as in 'an adrenalin radar scanning the planet for nutters'. In this case, the colloquial 'nutters' hints that these people might have mental problems, and contrasts with the formality and complex nature of the language generally, as well as linking with the jokey Americanism: 'dude, that was like...'. The reader is being challenged by the complexity but also amused by the sarcasm...

6 Possible points:

'If you like mountains, or films about mountains, or doing things on mountains in film...'

Comments likely to be on: repetition ('mountains') to get readers to focus on that aspect; list to make it seem there are many aspects; 'If...or...or...' widening the appeal; building through to 'danger' to maximise appeal at the end

'swap red carpets for cobbles and canapés for mint cake'

Comments likely to be on: alliteration ('carpets for cobbles... canapés'); contrasts in words/ideas

'it's a tribal gathering for mountain lovers'

Comment likely to be on: metaphor and/or implications of 'mountain lovers'

In each case:
A/A*:   2 points explained in precise detail
          (4 marks)
B/C: 1–2 points explained in detail (3 marks)
D/E: 1–2 points with attempted explanation
          (2 marks)
F/G: 1 point with little understanding (1 mark)

7 Likely examples:

'thin-lipped' – image of strictness; 'blue-veined' – colour suggests old age and coldness; 'terribly 'refained'' – suggests this is how she spoke, pretending to be posh; 'prowled' – image of stalking lioness; 'in stockinged feet' – sneakily

A/A*:   4 marks
B/C: 3 marks
D/E: 2 marks
F/G: 1 mark

8 Possible points:

'like young criminals': simile gives impression of how they were regarded

'three-storeyed rabbit warren': metaphor makes it sound large and possibly not clean and where there might be places to hide

'evil-smelling evidence of highly punishable inefficiency': sounds legal, stress on the evil leading to punishment, and the impression this creates of their lives

In each case:

C/A*:	1–2 points explained in detail (2 marks)
D/E:	1–2 points with attempted explanation (1 mark)
F/G:	1 attempted point with little understanding (0 marks)

---

pages 142–145

1 Possible presentational points:

cat: to attract cat-lovers; looks 'cuddly' and beautiful, implying beautiful casts love Gourmet; plate of food looks full and rich, suggesting it is attractive; tins of food show some variety, and presented so they will be easily identified by cat-loving shoppers

A/A*:	7–8 marks
B/C:	5–6 marks
D/E:	3–4 marks
F/G:	1–2 marks

Extract from a Grade A* response

The advertisement is trying to sell Gourmet cat food, and the main picture is appropriate for that purpose. The big fluffy cat is intended to look well-groomed – almost affluent, aristocratic. It looks as if it would need the best, gourmet, food. It also strikes the reader as soft and healthy (perhaps because of the food?), and there is focus on the eyes peering out of the beautiful white fur: they are appealing and attractive. The reader is lured to the product…

2 Comments likely to centre on how 'GOURMET' logo is presented twice, and the use of capitals – where and why; quotation: why it is used; 'The Perfect Breakfast' – capitals plus sounds like food for humans; 'Purina', logo for the firm, at the bottom; the offer 'Try delicious GOURMET Gold on me'

A/A*:	7–8 marks
B/C:	5–6 marks
D/E:	3–4 marks
F/G:	1–2 marks

3 Possible points:

'Time for tea?' – tea lovers – stands out – big question mark to grab attention and challenge the reader; young woman: younger people as well as old, because she is clearly young, and

anyone attracted by prettiness; her hair 'breaks out' of the box so we notice her particularly

A/A*:	4 marks
B/C:	3 marks
D/E:	2 marks
F/G:	1 mark

4 Likely points:

if the background were green and the girl's top beige

less attractive – background might suggest sickness and she might appear bland (or background could appear natural and she might blend in with it)

if the background were pink and the girl's top orange

might seem very modern and attractive to young people; specifically aimed at girls (pink) and suggesting it will make them brighter, maybe more exciting (orange)

In each case:

C/A*:	1–2 points explained in detail (2 marks)
D/E:	1–2 points with attempted explanation (1 mark)
F/G:	one point with little understanding (0 marks)

5

A/A*-A:	3–4 sensible ideas, explained in detail with justifications (4 marks)
B/C:	2–3 sensible ideas with some justification (3 marks)
D/E:	2 ideas with attempted justification (2 marks)
F/G:	1 idea with a little comment (1 mark)

6 'Mane' of lion (main attraction pun); 'encounter' – because the people seem to be faced by the lion; 'not what it seems' – otherwise they would not be smiling

A/A*:	4 marks
B/C:	3 marks
D/E:	2 marks
F/G:	1 mark

7 Purpose is to attract readers; to shock / surprise; to demonstrate what the text is talking about; to show size of lion; to show how visitors are excited / shocked / delighted by the experience

A/A*:	4 marks
B/C:	3 marks
D/E:	2 marks
F/G:	1 mark

8 Woman on left at back looks shocked – realise how realistic this must be; person beside them registers no apparent surprise, suggesting…; couple at front laughing, clearly indicating they are enjoying their visit and that they are not afraid

A/A*:   4 marks
B/C: 3 marks
D/E: 2 marks
F/G: 1 mark

9 Likely to comment on:

'ruined' faces of celebrities and dramatic 'Sun damage'; more glamorous picture of Lynda Bellingham plus mention of 'Strictly'; dramatic headlines at top ('I live free…' and 'Gill lost 7 stone'); smiling women at top to suggest feel-good stories; heartwarming heading and picture about baby at bottom; 'best' name plus presumably implies these are the best stories

A/A*:   7–8 marks
B/C: 5–6 marks
D/E: 3–4 marks
F/G: 1–2 marks

10 Possible general comments:

jumbled cover, many ideas pressed together, suggests there are many articles compressed in the magazine. Title 'best' will attract attention, being so large

'Top story' presumably focused on stars – pictures likely to attract readers to look further; Lynda Bellingham has next most space; and reader might then, logically, look down to other positive story about the baby; final notice might be taken of more novelty-type stories at the top

Different interpretations are fine as long as supported with evidence and comment.

A/A*:   7–8 marks
B/C: 5–6 marks
D/E: 3–4 marks
F/G: 1–2 marks

---

pages 146–147

the target audiences

Ethletic: fair-trade/ethical emphasis; shoes on grass; 100% Vegan organic etc – appeal to those concerned for planet, fairness, etc.

Brantano: young adults (picture); women who love shoes/shopping (pictures + offer of trip stands out); lovers of romcoms ('PS I Love You')

how the Etheletic shoes are presented

big picture of shoe with Etheletic label to catch attention; is on grass to imply link to nature; two shoes casually crossed, like relaxed legs; neat lacing, looking smart; annotations pick out relevant qualities; heading implies they are light as well as ethical

the methods Brantano use to draw the consumer's attention

attractive couple from film; strong link with film poster; 'WIN'; offer in bold capitals; other prizes listed; shoes like a filmstrip, laid across the ad; firm evident at bottom

the essential differences in the advertisements

one focuses on shoes and ethics/other focuses on range of shoes, shopping trip and attractive couple; one focuses on Fairtrade, the other on the offer, etc: all illustrated by presentational features

A/A*:   10–12 marks
B/C: 7–9 marks
D/E: 4–6 marks
F/G: 1–3 marks

Extract from a Grade A* response

… So the advertisements are appealing to readers in totally different ways. The Ethletic shoes are presented simply: they are 'The Ethical Alternative' – nothing about them seems excessive, and they are pictured, naturally, on grass; whereas Brantano are selling high-heeled fashion, emphasised by the shoes, and focus on a movie, so the well-groomed stars are a main selling point for their products. Even the shoes are shown as part of a film-strip…

Relevant quotations, with explanations, might be used in any section:

	Taken	Now that's poetry
appropriate for audiences	Fans of action movies: 'muscular action thriller'; refers to Bourne; 'bone-crunching scraps'; 'varying degrees of brutality'; 'bloody one-man revenge mission'; 'fast-cut camera work'; 'relentless energy', etc. Explanations required	Lovers of poetry / Keats / poetic movies: 'verse captivating on screen'; 'artistic vision'; 'tough, replenishing, beautiful and true'; 'brilliant biography'; 'love affair'; 'gentle thoughtfulness'; 'speical soul'. Explanations required.
effects of words and phrases	Likely to examine the effect of many of phrases above. Also: 'straightforward shoot-em-up'; 'given a little heart'; 'spoilt but, y' know, adorable', etc.	Likely to focus on many of phrases above. Also: 'limp, airy or flouncy'; 'conjures the strange spirit'; 'he is given to laughter and boyish excesses', etc.
different styles	Comments on hard-hitting vocabulary, vivid and very descriptive (e.g. alliteration in 'deadbeat dad')	Comments on softer approach, focusing on words like 'vision', 'poetic'; alliteration in 'brilliant biography'; more 'gentleness'

A/A*:   13–16 marks
B/C: 9–12 marks
D/E: 5–8 marks
F/G: 1–4 marks

Extract from a Grade A* response

From the start, the language of these texts is very different. 'Taken' has 'muscular', 'thriller' and 'packs a punch', which are all very violent, whereas 'Now that's poetry' ends its initial sentence with 'poetical', and the by-line has already talked about 'making verse captivating'. Whilst 'Taken' has the emotive language of conflict (supported by the alliteration of thumping 'p's in 'packed a punch' so that we can already sense the fighting to come in the movie), the John Keats review begins by picking out more ethereal qualities like 'artistic vision'…

pages 150–152 Exam practice (Higher)

1 Appropriate details:

'award-winning escorted tour of your life'; 'expert tour managers'; 'quality hotels'; 'select excursions included'; 'head and shoulders above the rest'; 'over 30 years'; voted 'best tour operator'; 'topping consumer surveys'; 'best organisation, service, quality'; 'job is to make them perfect'; unique home departure service; '34 unbeatable itineraries'

A/A*:   7–8 marks
B/C: 5–6 marks
D/E: 3–4 marks
F/G: 1–2 marks

2 Possible presentational points:

Picture: links with text; gives impression of country and people; indigenous population happy; beauty of countryside

Headline: bold capitals, rhyme making things seem harmonious

Sub-heading: larger font to stand out; directs the reader to the picture; emotive approach – 'soaring', 'plunging', 'take your breath away'

Caption: sense of grandeur, reflected in picture; 'Highlight' – idea that there are particularly outstanding moments; also, the picture is from a high point

A/A*:   7–8 marks
B/C: 5–6 marks
D/E: 3–4 marks
F/G: 1–2 marks

3 Likely content:

liked it – 'This I cannot recommend highly enough'; amused – 'decorate the place'; mocks – 'such attractions as an altar made of rib cages' etc; fascinated – details such as the grim reaper; sarcastic – 'engagingly called…'; modern viewpoint – 'These guys must have been a barrel of laughs'; exaggeration – 'some guy coming along with a tape measure'; sees ridiculous side of it all – 'a half-mad monk with time on his hands'; cynical – 'nice little money-spinner'…

A/A*: 7–8 marks
B/C: 5–6 marks
D/E: 3–4 marks
F/G: 1–2 marks

Extract from a Grade A* response

Bryson is laughing about everything around him throughout the visit. He mocks the idea of 'decorating the place' with the bones of fellow monks and the idea of rib cages and so on being 'attractions'. When he talks about 'cheery sentiments', he means they are anything but that – just as the poem 'My Mother Killed Me' does not have an 'engaging' title. He is clearly bemused as to why all of this happened – living a life when there was always someone with a tape measure, ready to dispose of your bones when you died. It is not just that the place is 'too tacky for words', but that it is truly appalling in its very conception…

4 Possible language points:

The True Peru: rhyme in headline; 'soaring condors' – assonance gives sense of space; 'plunging gorges' – dramatic adjectives; 'take your breath away' – emotive metaphor / cliché; 'Literally' – short sentence to stop you; 'hamlet' sounds rustic; 'higher than…the roof of Europe' – metaphor indicates height; 'lunar' – vivid metaphor/adjective; 'I tilt my head back…' – sentence stretches and captures desperation for air, etc.

America: positive vocabulary throughout; adjectives of excellence; hyperbole – 'tour of your life'; clichés – 'head and shoulders above the rest; description of destination – 'delightful', 'stunning sights'; list of three – 'organisation, quality and service'; suggests credibility / professionalism – 'philosophy', 'investments'; superlative – 'perfect'; personalised – 'your front door', etc

Bill Bryson: sarcasm / irony throughout; colloquial style – 'some monk', 'barrel of laughs', 'some guy'; unexpected vocabulary – 'decorate'; rhetoric – 'Is that rich enough?'; long sentence about bones to show how the decorations stretch out; humour in detail – 'trimmed', 'fashioned', 'chandeliers'; ridiculous images – 'grim reaper in his hooded robe', etc.

A/A*: 14–16 marks
B/C: 10–13 marks
D/E: 6–9 marks
F/G: 1–5 marks

pages 153–155 Exam Practice (Foundation)

1 Any four from:

sight seeing tours, possibility of extending stay, all the sights of America's West Coast, plenty of free time, Grand Canyon, Las Vegas, Palm Springs, Hollywood, Pacific Coast, San Francisco

C/A*: 4 attractions
D/E: 3 attractions
F: 2 attractions
G: 1 attraction

2 Sights visited, Tour Manager, chance to extend stay, 'great value', 'plenty of time to relax and make own discoveries', flights from local airports, etc.

A/A*: 4 marks
B/C: 3 marks
D/E: 2 marks
F/G: 1 mark

3 Hospital: different from UK; unclean; syringes and flies; staff just spoke Turkish; place where you get singing and food after course of treatment

People: doctor knew what he was doing; orderly kind; efficient nurse; all workers appear kind

A/A*: 7–8 marks
B/C: 5–6 marks
D/E: 3–4 marks
F/G: 1–2 marks

Extract from a Grade A* response

Donald and his wife clearly had a difficult time on their holiday, and the writer gives a vivid description of what happened. He implies that their experience was even worse because of the state of the hospital they visited. He mentions the flies and the used syringes and blood on the walls: all of which you would not expect. However, this is offset somewhat by the kindness of the staff. If the orderly was stroking his wife's hair, that shows compassion…

4 Answers might include:

Clear: 'This is what happens…', 'After a minute…', 'Then…' etc – told like a story

Feelings stated simply: 'the people of Paris want me dead'

Interesting: 'turn you into gooey crepe' – vivid metaphor; 'So you wait' – short sentence sounds antagonistic; 'a quarter of a mile away' – exaggeration to stress size of road; humour – 'to look at the fin-de-siècle lamppost; children 'herded' like cattle.

A/A*: 10–12 marks
B/C: 7–9 marks
D/E: 4–6 marks
F/G: 1–3 marks

5

	Discover America's Golden West	Holiday Disaster
pictures	Main picture: tram, palm trees set scene, looks exotic; sunny, attractive Man looks happy; bridge behind to show what visitors will see	Prominent cartoon exaggerates problems in the hospital – syringes all over the floor, flies buzzing Man and wife looking anxious, with man making vain attempt to be reassuring, while doctor looks evil and as if he's really rather enjoying himself
other presentational features	Name of firm prominent; 'Discover…' bold and highlights sense of discovery; text boxes to simplify the information; plane to draw attention to plane information; phone number large at bottom and this text box has white on black to grab attention; cost of holiday highlighted, presumably to indicate it's cheap…	Bold text under the heading sets comic tone of article – Turkey is for Christmas, not holidays', with a play on the word 'Turkey' Skull and crossbones again emphasises the tone

A/A*: 10–12 marks
B/C: 7–9 marks
D/E: 4–6 marks
F/G: 1–3 marks

	Discover America's Golden West	Holiday Disaster
	Main picture: tram, palm trees set scene, looks exotic; sunny, attractive	Prominent cartoon exaggerates problems in the hospital – syringes all over the floor, flies buzzing

Producing non-fiction texts

No two people will write the same answer to the kind of tasks contained in this Exam Practice Workbook – or, indeed, in the exam itself. There is no such thing as a right or wrong answer when it comes to writing essays, but your examiner will expect you to demonstrate certain skills in your writing.

The following grid gives you an indication of the sort of grade your response is likely to achieve.

Grade	Skills required
A/A*	• content is detailed, well organised and convincing • totally suitable for the intended purpose and audience • likely to grab and hold the reader's interest • uses varied paragraphs which develop meaning • original and effective use of language • accurate spelling of an advanced but appropriate vocabulary • a wide range of accurate punctuation
B	• content is appropriate and well organised • appropriate for the intended purpose and audience • likely to hold the reader's interest • uses varied paragraphs • effective use of language • mostly accurate spelling of suitable vocabulary • a range of accurate punctuation
C	• content is appropriate for the task • clear understanding of the purpose and audience • interests the reader • uses well-structured paragraphs • uses language appropriately • mostly accurate spelling, with some more complex words • a range of punctuation
D	• content addresses the topic satisfactorily • some suitability for the purpose and audience • some interest for the reader • uses paragraphs, mostly of same length • language mostly used appropriately • generally accurate spelling • punctuation – mostly basic – used accurately
E	• content attempts to deal with the topic • attempts suitable style for purpose and audience • occasionally interesting • uses some paragraphs • language sometimes appropriate • uses some accurate spelling and punctuation
F/G	• content has some link with the topic • may not be a suitable style for purpose and audience • fails to interest the reader • might not use paragraphs • language might be inappropriate • some accurate spelling of simple words but often inaccurate punctuation

pages 162–163

1 and **2**

A/A*:	15–16 marks
B:	13–14 marks
C:	10–12 marks
D:	8—9 marks
E:	5–7 marks
F/G:	1-4 marks

page 165

Further practice:

A/A*:	6 marks
B:	5 marks
C:	4 marks
D:	3 marks
E:	2 marks
F/G:	1 mark

pages 166–167

1 Alternative versions are possible, e.g. the exclamation mark could be in a different place.

Why is it that some schools have some teachers that are far from perfect? Why is it that some students do not, as a consequence, reach the grades of which they should be capable? It simply is not fair. In my own case, the teachers in my school, most of whom have been here for many years, seem excellent. How lucky am I! What a relief it is to be here.

1 mark for each correct use:

A/A*:	8 marks
B:	7 marks
C:	6 marks
D:	5 marks
E:	4 marks
F/G:	1–3 marks

2 As soon as I walked into the classroom, Mrs Reynolds saw me.

"Just the young man I was looking for," she said. "I would like a word with you."

I immediately feared the worst.

"I don't think," I said, "that I have done anything wrong yet today."

"No. I just want some information," she said, smiling like a rattlesnake.

A/A*:	only one error (10 marks)
B:	2–3 errors (8–9 marks)
C:	4 errors (6–7 marks)
D:	5 errors (4–5 marks)
E:	6 errors (3 marks)
F/G:	more than 6 errors (1–2 marks)

3 Each of the schools in this area has been improved massively in the past few years: there are new buildings with state of the art computer facilities; two schools now have their own swimming pools; and in every school the libraries have been completely replaced.

A/A*:	correct (4 marks)
B/C:	1 error (3 marks)
D/E:	2 errors (1 mark)
F/G:	incorrect (0 marks)

5 The school's security measures weren't perfect, that's for sure. Some of the boys' lockers were ransacked and one girl's bag was stolen.

A/A*:	all correct (5 marks)
B:	1 error (4 marks)
C:	2 errors (3 marks)
D/F:	3 errors (2 marks)
G:	more than 3 errors (1 mark)

6

A/A*:	6 marks
B:	5 marks
C:	4 marks
D:	3 marks
E:	2 marks
F/G:	1 mark

pages 168–169

1 Extract will be more formal and sentences will be corrected.

A/A*:	6 marks
B:	5 marks
C:	4 marks
D:	3 marks
E:	2 marks
F/G:	1 mark

2 Two marks for each improved alternative.

3 Response will be in linked sentences, with a topic sentence, etc.

A/A*:	6 marks
B:	5 marks
C:	4 marks
D:	3 marks
E:	2 marks
F/G:	1 mark

4 Language will be formal and suitable for a public performance.

A/A*:	6 marks
B:	5 marks
C:	4 marks
D:	3 marks
E:	2 marks
F/G:	1 mark

Answers Producing non-fiction texts

pages 170–171

For all questions, using the marking grid on page 15:

A/A*: 6 marks
B: 5 marks
C: 4 marks
D: 3 marks
E: 2 marks
F/G: 1 mark

pages 172–173

4 and **5**

Language should be suitable for the audience and the similes and metaphors should not be clichés.

A/A*: 6 marks
B: 5 marks
C: 4 marks
D: 3 marks
E: 2 marks
F/G: 1 mark

Further practice:

A/A*: 10 marks
B: 9 marks
C: 7–8 marks
D: 5–6 marks
E: 3–4 marks
F/G: 1–2 marks

pages 174–175

2 and **3**

The language is likely to be less formal because of your audience, but should still be in correct English, to impress an examiner.

A/A*: 6 marks
B: 5 marks
C: 4 marks
D: 3 marks
E: 2 marks
F/G: 1 mark

Further practice:

A/A*: 15–16 marks
B: 13–14 marks
C: 10–12 marks
D: 8–9 marks
E: 5–7 marks
F/G: 1–4 marks

pages 176–177

1, 2, 3

A/A*: 6 marks
B: 5 marks
C: 4 marks

D: 3 marks
E: 2 marks
F/G: 1 mark

Further practice:

A/A*: 15–16 marks
B: 13–14 marks
C: 10–12 marks
D: 8–9 marks
E: 5–7 marks
F/G: 1–4 marks

pages 178–179

1, 2, 3, 4, 5

A/A*: 6 marks
B: 5 marks
C: 4 marks
D: 3 marks
E: 2 marks
F/G: 1 mark

pages 180–181

Both questions should be set out correctly and be appropriate for the audience, so their tone and style should be different.

A/A*: 15–16 marks
B: 13–14 marks
C: 10–12 marks
D: 8–9 marks
E: 5–7 marks
F/G: 1–4 marks

pages 182–183

1, 2, 3, 4, 5, 6

A/A*: 6 marks
B: 5 marks
C: 4 marks
D: 3 marks
E: 2 marks
F/G: 1 mark

pages 184–186

1 Points should be different and possibly in direct contrast.

A/A*: 8 points (4 marks)
B/C: 6–8 points (3 marks)
D/E: 4–5 points (2 marks)
F/G: 1–3 points (1 mark)

2, 3, 4, 5

A/A*: 6 marks
B: 5 marks
C: 4 marks
D: 3 marks

E: 2 marks
F/G: 1 mark

Practice essay title:

Use the marking grid on page 15.

pages 186–187

1

A/A*:   5 points, well explained in other columns
            (5 marks)
B: 5 points, with explanations in other
            columns (4 marks)
C: 5 points, with some explanations
            (3 marks)
D/E: 4–5 points, with attempted explanations
            (2 marks)
F/G: some points, with little explanation
            (1 mark)

2 The letter should be formal and set out properly.

A/A*:   8 marks
B: 6–7 marks
C: 4–5 marks
D: 3 marks
E: 2 marks
F/G: 1 mark

3, 4, 5

A/A*:   6 marks
B: 5 marks
C: 4 marks
D: 3 marks
E: 2 marks
F/G: 1 mark

Practice essay title:

Use the marking grid on page 15.

pages 188–189

2, 3

A/A*:   6 marks
B: 5 marks
C: 4 marks
D: 3 marks
E: 2 marks
F/G: 1 mark

4

A/A*:   11–12 marks
B: 9–10 marks
C: 7–8 marks
D: 5–6 marks
E: 3–4 marks
F/G: 1–2 marks

Practice essay title:

Use the marking grid on page 15.

pages 190–191

Second section of plan should contain 6 points,
with some detail in explanations.

A/A*:   6 points, with full explanation (6 marks)
B: 5 points, with detailed explanation
            (5 marks)
C: 4–5 points, with explanation (4 marks)
D: 3–4 points, with attempted explanation
            (3 marks)
E: 2–3 points, with some attempted
            explanations (2 marks)
F/G: attempts the task (1 mark)

2, 3, 4

A/A*:   6 marks
B: 5 marks
C: 4 marks
D: 3 marks
E: 2 marks
F/G: 1 mark

Practice essay title:

Use the marking grid on page 15.

pages 192–193

1, 2, 3, 4, 5, 6

A/A*:   6 marks
B: 5 marks
C: 4 marks
D: 3 marks
E: 2 marks
F/G: 1 mark

Practice essay title:

Use the marking grid on page 15.

pages 194–195

1

A/A*:   6 points, with detailed advice (6 marks)
B: 5 points, with detailed advice (5 marks)
C: 4 points, with clear advice (4 marks)
D: 3+ points, with advice (3 marks)
E: 2–3 points, with attempted advice (2 marks)
F/G: attempts the task (1 mark)

2, 3, 4, 5, 6

A/A*:   6 marks
B: 5 marks
C: 4 marks
D: 3 marks
E: 2 marks
F/G: 1 mark

Practice essay title:

Use the marking grid on page 15.

1 Other ways of punctuating this are acceptable.

I did not know where to turn: I had bills to pay, the car had broken down and my sister said, "It's no good. We will have to leave here. The rent is too high." What an awful day that was!

B/A*:	all correct (3 marks)
C/D:	1–3 errors (2 marks)
E/G:	more than 3 errors (1 mark)

2 Correct spellings:

unfortunately; temperature; sitting; unprecedented; decimate; fragile; communities; governments; lifestyles; know

A/A*:	10 correct (10 marks)
B:	9 correct (9 marks)
C:	8 correct (8 marks)
D:	6–7 correct (7 marks)
E:	4–5 correct (4 marks)
F:	3 correct (3 marks)
G:	1–2 correct (1 mark)

3

A/A*:	6 marks
B:	5 marks
C:	4 marks
D:	3 marks
E:	2 marks
F/G:	1 mark

4 Other alternatives are possible.

My next door neighbour is the most boring person I have ever met. For a start, he loves basketball and I hate it; but he spends hours hammering a ball against the wall of his house and we get the noise in ours. When he's not bouncing the ball around, he's talking about basketball or watching basketball or dreaming about basketball, I guess.

When he first moved in, I thought he could be a good friend and I tried to get along with him, but he didn't want to know. 'Yeah, we can go out,' he said. 'There's a basketball game on Sunday at the leisure centre: we could go there.' And that was that. I could just see him sitting there eating a burger or something and drinking coke as if it were a proper meal and then jumping up and spilling chips or fries (as that's probably what they are called at a basketball match) all over the place. I just don't get it at all. I didn't go and you wouldn't have either, would you?

His sister must lead a terrible life because she has to be around him like all day long. She seems nice, but what a sad life, eh? It's awful being next door, so it must be extremely unpleasant in the same house.

His parents never seem to come out at all. I don't know what they look like. They probably look like him: really tall, with a baseball cap on all the time and a basketball in their hand all the time, and there might be pictures of basketball players on all the walls and framed ones on top of the television, like a museum in a way.

I just don't understand. How boring can you be?

A/A*:	10 marks
B:	9 marks
C:	7–8 marks
D:	5–6 marks
E:	3–4 marks
F/G:	1–2 marks

Notes

Notes